D1239003

ALSO BY JAMES GRANT

Mr. Speaker!: The Life and Times of Thomas B. Reed,
the Man Who Broke the Filibuster

Mr. Market Miscalculates

John Adams: Party of One

The Trouble with Prosperity

Minding Mr. Market

Money of the Mind: Lending and Borrowing in America
from the Civil War to Michael Milken

Bernard M. Baruch: The Adventures of a Wall Street Legend

1921: The Crash That Cured Itself

THE
FORGOTTEN
DEPRESSION

★ **JAMES GRANT** ★

SIMON & SCHUSTER

NEW YORK LONDON TORONTO SYDNEY NEW DELHI

Simon & Schuster
1230 Avenue of the Americas
New York, NY 10020

Copyright © 2014 by James Grant

All rights reserved, including the right to reproduce this book or
portions thereof in any form whatsoever. For information address
Simon & Schuster Subsidiary Rights Department,
1230 Avenue of the Americas, New York, NY 10020.

First Simon & Schuster hardcover edition November 2014

SIMON & SCHUSTER and colophon are registered trademarks of
Simon & Schuster, Inc.

For information about special discounts for bulk purchases,
please contact Simon & Schuster Special Sales at 1-866-506-1949
or business@simonandschuster.com.

The Simon & Schuster Speakers Bureau can bring authors to your live event.
For more information or to book an event contact the Simon & Schuster Speakers Bureau
at 1-866-248-3049 or visit our website at www.simonspeakers.com.

Jacket design by Janet Perr

Manufactured in the United States of America

10   9   8   7   6   5   4   3   2   1

Library of Congress Cataloging-in-Publication Data

Grant, James, 1946–
    The forgotten depression : 1921, the crash that cured itself / James Grant.
        pages   cm
    1. Depression—1920.   2. Financial crises—United States—History—20th
century.   3. United States—Economic conditions—1918–1945.
4. United States—Economic policy—20th century.   I. Title.

HB37171920.G73   2014
330.973'0913—dc23   2014021387

ISBN 978-1-4516-8645-6
ISBN 978-1-4516-8648-7 (ebook)

In memory of A. Alex Porter, investor, scholar, bon vivant.

In the economy, an act, a habit, an institution, a law, gives birth not only to an effect, but to a series of effects. Of these effects, the first only is immediate; it manifests itself simultaneously with its cause—it is seen. The others unfold in succession—they are not seen: it is well for us if they are foreseen.

—Frederic Bastiat, "That Which Is Seen, That Which Is Unseen," 1850

CONTENTS

THE
FORGOTTEN
DEPRESSION

PREFACE

This slim volume describes a weighty and wonderful event. In 1920, the American economy entered what would presently be diagnosed as a depression. The successive administrations of Woodrow Wilson and Warren G. Harding met the downturn by seeming to ignore it—or by implementing policies that an average 21st century economist would judge disastrous. Confronted with plunging prices, incomes and employment, the government balanced the budget and, through the newly instituted Federal Reserve, raised interest rates. By the lights of Keynesian and monetarist doctrine alike, no more primitive or counterproductive policies could be imagined. Yet by late 1921, a powerful, job-filled recovery was under way. This is the story of America's last governmentally unmedicated depression.

The United States was not without a government in the early 1920s, of course. It taxed and regulated. It furnished courts, the rule of law, a dollar defined in law as a weight of gold and an army and navy. Federal officers examined the nationally chartered banks. Other public officials infused illiquid though solvent banks with cash. Contemporaries credited the latter functionaries—new hires of the Federal Reserve—with forestalling an otherwise certain money panic. What the government did not do was socialize the risk of financial failure or attempt to steer and guide the national economy by manipulating either the rate of federal spending or the value of the dollar. Compared to the federal establishment that would take form in the 1930s (or to that which had recently waged the war against Germany), it was a small and unintrusive government.

The hero of my narrative is the price mechanism, Adam Smith's invisible hand. In a market economy, prices coordinate human effort. They channel investment, saving and work. High prices encourage production but discourage consumption; low prices do the opposite. The depression of 1920–21 was marked by plunging prices, the malignity we call deflation. But prices and wages fell only so far. They stopped falling when they became low enough to entice consumers into shopping, investors into committing capital and employers into hiring. Through the agency of falling prices and wages, the American economy righted itself.

I write in the fifth year of a historically lackluster recovery from the so-called Great Recession of 2007–09. To address the crisis of failing banks and collapsing credit, the administrations of George W. Bush and Barack Obama borrowed and spent hundreds of billions of dollars. They threw a governmental lifeline to dozens of financial institutions, some of which would have otherwise drowned. The Federal Reserve pushed its money-market interest rate to zero and materialized trillions of new dollars (thereby further subsidizing the banks and government-sponsored enterprises whose errors of omission and commission had helped to precipitate the crisis in the first place). Yet for all these exertions, some 9.8 million Americans remain out of a job while millions more have given up hope of finding one.

Just about no one with a public voice nowadays would dare to propose the policies that the government implemented (or, more to the point, refused or neglected to implement) almost a century ago. But the fact is that, in the wake of those decisions, growth resumed and the 1920s proverbially roared. We can't know what might have been if Wilson and Harding had intervened as presidents of the late 20th and early 21st centuries are wont to do. Herbert Hoover, Harding's secretary of commerce, was seemingly champing at the bit to act; the slump was ending by the time he swung into action. When, as the 31st president, Hoover did intervene—notably, in an attempt to prevent a drop in wages—the results were unsatisfactory.

Recessions and depressions don't announce their own arrival. Economists rather piece together the chronology after the fact. The recognized arbiter of the cyclical calendar, the National Bureau of Economic Research, dates the start of the downturn of 1920–21 in January 1920 and its conclusion in July

1921; which is to say that things stopped getting better in January 1920, and they stopped getting worse in July 1921. The elapsed time was 18 months.

On the one hand, a year and a half is a very long time to any who suffered unemployment, bankruptcy or destitution. On the other, it is a great deal shorter than the 43 months of the Great Depression of 1929–33. I propose that constructive federal inaction contributed to the relatively satisfactory outcome. To the financiers and capitalists weaned on the idea of laissez-faire, federal passivity did not destroy confidence but rather enhanced it.

"Confidence" is a concept as vital as it is amorphous. What imparts a feeling of trust to one generation may frighten another. What seemed to brace up the generation of Americans who confronted the 1920–21 slump was a collective belief in the underlying soundness of American finance. In a world that in many ways had seemed to have lost its moorings, the dollar was still as good as gold. A bipartisan determination to pay down the federal debt and to protect the purchasing power of the U.S. dollar thus likely contributed to a belief that the bad times couldn't and wouldn't last.

"If a government wishes to alleviate, rather than aggravate, a depression, its only valid course is laissez-faire—to leave the economy alone," wrote Murray Rothbard in his history of the 1930s, *America's Great Depression*. "Only if there is no interference, direct or threatened, with prices, wage rates and business liquidation, will the necessary adjustment proceed with smooth dispatch."[1] Whatever might be said about that proposition in general, the American experience in 1920–21 and 1929–33 does not disprove it.

The Great Depression was the historical touchstone of the advocates of a muscular federal response to our own Great Recession. It was to close the door on any possible repetition of the experience of the early 1930s that the Federal Reserve, under the leadership of Chairman Ben S. Bernanke, embarked on a radical program of money printing, interest-rate suppression and financial market manipulation, policies still in place more than five years after economic healing officially began. In a speech at Jackson Hole, Wyoming, in August 2012, Mr. Bernanke candidly described these experiments as "learning by doing."

There was no such improvisation in the monetary and fiscal councils of 1920–21, unless the refusal of the still unseasoned Federal Reserve to budge from its policy of high interest rates even in the teeth of plunging prices can be viewed as experimental. In any case, to the best of my knowledge, no American policy-maker invoked the extraordinary events of 1920–21 as a potentially relevant precedent during the crisis of 2008; the collapse of 1929–33 rather monopolized the market in historical analogy. One can anticipate the arguments in defense of this choice. Thus, in 1920–21, the economy was much smaller than it is today. The political environment was wholly different than ours and the statistics produced to measure the expansion and contraction of economic activity were, at best, crude. Besides, there was no federal safety net and no easily accessible credit, either of the personal or mortgage variety. All this is true, yet each objection might be applied with nearly equal force to the Great Depression itself.

There is something else to consider: Following the 1929 Crash, President Hoover set in motion an unprecedented program of federal activism to head off the threatened business downturn. While these interventions—the "First New Deal," some called them—were an undisputed failure, the non-intervention of Wilson and Harding constitutes an uncelebrated success.

If the events of 1920–21 are anything but irrelevant, they are—to the advocates of government intervention in business-cycle downturns—inconvenient. If sick economies need governmentally administered medicine, how did an economy force-fed with what most practitioners today would regard as a kind of policy arsenic ever right itself?

In his review of *Austerity: The History of a Dangerous Idea,* Mark Blyth's 2013 attack on the notion of a government *not* pulling out the stops to combat a downturn, Lawrence Summers, the former secretary of the Treasury, quoted his own dictum: "As I have often said, the central irony of financial crisis is that while it is caused by too much confidence, too much lending and too much spending, it can only be resolved with more confidence, more lending and more spending." The 1920–21 experience refutes Summers's Paradox, as it was certainly not resolved with lending and spending.*

---

*Certitude about the need for federal activism in the face of economic dislocation finds its ultimate expression in the pronouncement of another Harvard professor, Kenneth Rogoff. The Obama administration had no choice but to enact the American Recovery and Reinvestment Act of 2009, said Professor Rogoff, an accomplished chess player as well as the author of the 2009 best-seller *This Time Is Different.*

Just how severe it was is a question yet unsettled, and perhaps destined never finally to be settled. Official data as well as contemporary comment paint a grim picture. Thus, the nation's output in 1920–21 suffered a decline of 23.9 percent in nominal terms, 8.7 percent in inflation- (or deflation-) adjusted terms. From cyclical peak to trough, producer prices fell by 40.8 percent, industrial production by 31.6 percent, stock prices by 46.6 percent and corporate profits by 92 percent.[2] Maximum unemployment ranged between two million and six million persons—those were the range of estimates at the national conference on unemployment called by President Harding in September 1921—out of a nonagricultural labor force of 31.5 million. At the high end of six million, this would imply a rate of joblessness of 19 percent. Bankruptcies claimed myriad nonfarm businesses, including Truman & Jacobson, a Kansas City haberdashery coowned by the future 33rd president of the United States.*

The adage that "the past is a foreign country" is nowhere more apt than in economic history. In the case at hand, anachronism is inherent in the very language of economics. Readers of this book speak and think about "aggregate demand" and "aggregate supply." Having imbibed at least the rudiments of macroeconomics, they casually talk about the national income. In the early 1920s, such ideas were yet unformed. You can comb through the professional economics journals of the day, as I have done, without finding a single article espousing the notion of macroeconomic management.

Whatever the defects of 21st century American economic statistics, the data available to Wilson and Harding were worse. Modern national income accounting did not come into existence until the 1930s and 1940s. The services portion of the American economy was not systematically measured until the 1990s.

The 1920–21 affair was the 14th business-cycle contraction since the panic year of 1812. Commercial and financial disturbances of one kind or another

---

The so-called stimulus act was, indeed, an "only move," he was quoted as saying by the *New York Times* in 2012. In chess, an only move is one without which a player would certainly and immediately lose.
*"There were between five and six millions of our workers without employment. Industries were closed or closing. Economic authorities predicted industrial panic. We were on the highway to the economic chaos which at present prevails in Europe." So wrote President Harding's secretary of labor, James J. Davis, in his 1923 annual report. Even making allowances for the fact that some of the goings-on to which the passage referred took place in a Democratic administration, the secretary's choice of words is striking. [p. 90]

occurred in 1818, 1825, 1837, 1847, 1857, 1873, 1884, 1890, 1893, 1903, 1907, 1910 and 1913. Not since the early 19th century had prices fallen so far or so fast as they did in 1920–21. "In this period of 120 years," according to a contemporary inquest, "the debacle of 1920–21 was without parallel."[3]

Christina Romer, a distinguished economic historian who served as chair of President Obama's Council of Economic Advisers, has contended that the ordeal of 1920–21 was not so severe as it was subsequently portrayed statistically. In so many lay words, she characterized the slump as a not especially troublesome recession. In further support of my contention that the depression of 1920–21 was just as intense as contemporary reports made it out to be, I submit an item of noneconometric evidence. Herewith a sample of the bitterly sardonic lyrics to the 1921 hit song "Ain't We Got Fun?"

> *Every morning, every evening*
> *Ain't we got fun?*
> *Not much money, oh, but honey*
> *Ain't we got fun?*
>
> *The rent's unpaid, dear*
> *And we haven't a bus*
> *But smiles were made, dear*
> *For people like us*
>
> *In the winter, in the summer*
> *Don't we have fun?*
> *Times are bum and getting bummer*
> *Still we have fun*
>
> *There's nothing surer,*
> *The rich get rich and the poor get children*
> *In the meantime, in between time,*
> *Ain't we got fun?*
>
> *Landlord's mad and getting madder*
> *Ain't we got fun?*
> *Times are so bad and getting badder*

Still we have fun
There's nothing surer
The rich get rich and the poor get laid off
In the meantime, in between time
Ain't we got fun?

"Depression" is a term of no hard and fast statistical definition. It is a term that many contemporaries—the Harvard Economics Society and the Federal Reserve Bank of New York, among others—used to describe the depth of the downturn, and it's the term I have chosen to use in this history. I will posit, too, that they don't write songs about recessions.

Especially foreign to the time-traveling contemporary reader may seem the banking and monetary arrangements of the Wilson and Harding era. In 1920 there was no federal deposit insurance and no doctrine that some banks were too big to fail. If a bank became impaired or insolvent, chances were that its stockholders (never the taxpayers) would receive a call to stump up funds with which to reimburse the depositors. It was, after all, the stockholders' bank, in sickness as in health. This standing reminder of the potential cost of mismanagement by no means forestalled failure. But as much as any law or convention it delineated the boundaries between public and private interest. Such was the record of safety and soundness in banking during the first two decades of the 20th century, the Panic of 1907 notwithstanding, that the senior federal bank regulator could express the hope that bank failures in America were a thing of the past. This was in the summer of 1920, six months after the economy had begun its slide into depression.

The dollar in those days was still defined as a weight of gold, as it had been since Alexander Hamilton's time at the Treasury: An ounce was the equivalent of $20.67 and could be exchanged for that sum at the option of the holder. And because anyone could make the exchange, the Federal Reserve was inherently constrained. It could do only so much to salve a wounded economy, even if it believed that monetary medication was within its congressional remit, which it certainly did not. Any proposal to anticipate the 21st century policy of printing money with which to stimulate business activity ("quantitative easing") would have been laughed out of court.

Politicians were no more inclined than economists to throw the weight of the government behind policies to keep the national economy on an even keel. This was not necessarily because the political class was philosophically averse to regulation or taxation. Woodrow Wilson ran for president in 1912 promising to bring Wall Street and big business to heel. In 1917, following America's declaration of war on Germany, the administration blazed new trails in government economic intervention and control. But even if the president had wished to graft his experiments in wartime socialism on to the postwar American economy, he would probably not have gotten far. At first, he was preoccupied with his battle to win Senate approval of the peace treaty and the League of Nations. Later, after his September 1919 stroke, he became incapacitated, as did his administration. By no means did Wilson espouse the Jeffersonian doctrine that that government is best which governs least. It was by accident that the Progressive Democrat presided over America's final laissez-faire depression.

The story of a depression that healed itself is necessarily short on political craftsmanship. Histories of the response of the administration of Franklin D. Roosevelt—and, before him, of Herbert Hoover—to the Great Depression brim with chronicles of action. Here is a history of instructive inaction.

Then and Now: A Statistical Snapshot of Two Eras
in $ millions except per capita figures or where otherwise indicated.

	1920	per capita	% of GNP	2010	per capita	% of GNP
Population (millions)	106.5	-	-	310.04	-	-
Union labor as % of work force	12.1%	-	-	11.4%	-	-
Average life expectancy (years)	56.4	-	-	78.7	-	-
Average annual wage ($)	$1,342	-	-	$39,959	-	-
NYSE volume (shares millions)	227			601,146		
GDP/GNP	91,500	859	-	14,958,300	48,198	-
Federal Gov't spending	6,358	60	7	3,457,079	11,139	23
Federal debt held by the public	25,952	244	28	9,018,882	29,060	60
Total public and private debt	135,700	1,275	148	51,395,500	165,603	344
Total assets of the Federal Reserve	6,254	59	7	2,427,844	7,823	16

Composition of the Economy

	1920*	2010†
Total	100	100
Agriculture	10.5	1.1
Mining	2.5	1.7
Munfacturing	21.9	11.2
Construction	4.4	3.6
Transportation	9.8	4.9
Trade	13.6	11.6
Services	11.6	31.5
Government	9.6	13.6
Finance and misc.	16.1	20.8

*average between 1919 and 1928 based on National Bureau of Economic Research estimates of national income.
†GDP value added by industry, Bureau of Econmonic Analysis estimates.

THE GREAT INFLATION

The coda to the murderous Great War of 1914–18 was an influenza pandemic even more lethal than the war itself. But the wounded world of 1919 could count one saving grace, at least. The oft-predicted postwar depression had failed to materialize. Quite the contrary: Business was booming.

Here was a most pleasant anomaly. History taught that peace would bring depression. Such had been the experience of America after both the War of 1812 and the Civil War. The Great War was a world war. No doubt, many reasoned, a worldwide economic adjustment would prove even more disruptive than the slumps that had followed more isolated conflicts of the past.

No template for government action to resist depressions was yet in place. Long-established economic doctrine rather favored laissez-faire. As the natural seasons turned, so did the economic ones: summer and winter, boom and bust. Individuals might prepare for the inevitable lurches to the down side—a workman might save, a farmer might market his crops in anticipation of lower prices, a banker might call in loans to brace for a depositors' run. But from the government, not much was expected but to balance its budget, maintain a sound currency and allow business to take its natural, improving course. "[T]hough the people support the government, the government should not support the people," declared President Grover Cleveland in vetoing a $10,000 appropriation to pay for the distribution of seed grain to drought-stricken Texas farmers in 1887.[1]

It was the letter of the Cleveland doctrine rather than the spirit that still prevailed in some policy-making circles. Many voices now pressed the government to intervene. "Progressive," the speakers styled themselves, though the progress to which they aspired concerned not the management of the business cycle but redressing the supposed injustice in the distribution of income. By 1892, the Populist Party was demanding inflation of the currency, a graduated income tax, strict limitations on corporate ownership of land and the nationalization of the railroads and telephone and telegraph companies.[2] By 1908, Eugene Debs was demanding a republic in which the working class governed the plutocracy, rather than the other way around. By 1910, Theodore Roosevelt, no avowed socialist, was demanding that "human welfare" be raised above "property."[3]

"From the same prolific womb of governmental injustice we breed the two great classes—tramps and millionaires," the Populists had alleged. Certainly, electrical illumination, the internal combustion engine and related marvels lightened the burden of labor and thereby liberated many from drudgery and want. But, equally, according to the composite Progressive indictment, the rich had never been richer, nor the gap between rich and poor provokingly wider.[4]

In the 1912 presidential election, Debs drew 6 percent of the popular vote on the Socialist ticket, the best showing by any left-wing candidate in any presidential contest before or since.[5] He finished fourth.

William Howard Taft, the 300-odd-pound Republican incumbent, campaigning on the doctrine that "[a] National Government cannot create good times" (but could, through ill-advised policy, institute bad times), won a mere two states, Utah and Vermont.[6] He came in third.

Theodore Roosevelt, who had bolted from the GOP to preach that government could, in fact, effect the very improvements that Taft resisted, pledged to "use the whole power of government" to resist "an unregulated and purely individualistic industrialism."[7] He placed second.

Candidate Wilson vowed to tame the "trusts," rein in the big Wall Street banks, lower tariffs and—to compensate for lost revenue from reduced import duties—tax the rich. President Wilson, having beaten the divided GOP, proved as good as his word. By the close of his first year in office, the former president of Princeton University had presented the nation with an income tax and a central bank (in name, a kind of decentralized central bank). The federal government would never again lack the means of financing itself.

In 1916, at the end of his first term, Wilson sought a second. He was deserving on financial grounds alone, the Democratic Party platform asserted: "Our archaic banking and currency system, prolific of panic and disaster under Republican administrations—long the refuge of the money trust— has been supplanted by the Federal Reserve Act, a true democracy of credit under government control, already proved a bulwark in a world crisis, mobilizing our resources, placing abundant credit at the disposal of legitimate industry and making a currency panic impossible." Then, too, the Democrats commended themselves for "the splendid diplomatic victories of our great president, who has preserved the vital interests of our government and its citizens and kept us out of war."

New vistas of federal activism opened on April 6, 1917, when the president led the nation into war. As Washington drafted men, so it conscripted incomes. In House debate in 1913 over the proposed income tax, a seemingly wild-eyed Progressive had called for a schedule of rates culminating in 68 percent on incomes above $1 million. "The amendment was, of course, beaten," reported the *New York Times*, the paper seeming to roll its eyes at the very notion of so confiscatory a marginal rate of taxation.[8] By 1918, the Treasury was taking 77 percent of incomes above $1 million.[9] The Wilson administration took control of merchant shipping, the railroads and the telegraph and telephone companies. It rationed raw materials and set ceilings on prices and wages. It intervened in labor disputes. It allocated, requisitioned and commandeered private property. It liberalized the banking rules and thereby encouraged the expansion of credit: After June 1917, a New York bank could lend 38.8 percent more against every dollar of reserve it was required to hold than before the change was enacted.[10] Woodrow Wilson delivered the activist government that America's populists and socialists had long demanded.[11]

So when Frank Morrison, secretary of the American Federation of

Labor, warned in January 1919 that the government was the only instrument of postwar economic salvation—and that, barring federal intervention, there could be "bread lines in every industrial center before May 1"—his message had none of the shock value it would have had before the war.[12] More conventionally familiar was the fatalistic voice of the Babson economic forecasting service, which predicted "a period of trouble and depression." There was no getting around it, said the founder, Roger W. Babson: "We can prepare for reaction and prevent it from being disastrous, but to stop it is impossible."

Right as rain did the bears initially appear to be. Within four weeks of the November 11, 1918, Armistice, the War Department had cancelled $2.5 billion of its then outstanding $6 billion in manufacturing contracts;[13] for perspective, $2.5 billion represented 3.3 percent of the 1918 gross national product.[14] In January 1919 commodity prices tumbled. Steel mills, which had hardly been able to keep up with war-induced demand, now operated at 60 percent to 65 percent of capacity. Order books dwindled, that of the United States Steel Corporation by 42 percent between the Armistice and May 1919. Not since the Panic of 1907 had the giant steel maker seen the likes of it.[15]

But the Morrisons and Babsons had failed to reckon with the long-thwarted American consumer. Purchases patriotically deferred during the year and a half of U.S. belligerency were now exuberantly rung up. War or not, Americans had continued to drive their Fords and Chevrolets and Buicks (gasoline sales never wavered during the ostensibly luxury-free duration of the conflict). Now, with the peace, the people demanded silk shirts, new cars and a little fun.

European consumers, too, were buying American, their spending power enhanced by loans funneled through their governments from the U.S. Treasury. In the five years prior to the outbreak of war in Europe in 1914, American exports had averaged $2.1 billion a year. They accelerated during the war and soared again with the peace. In 1919, they reached nearly $8 billion.[16]

Doomsayers could hardly believe their eyes. Surely, they reasoned, a postwar boom was a contradiction in terms. What was needed—and what was, on form, inevitable—was a bust. As with physical objects, so with prices: What goes up would have to come down. Consumer prices had risen by 11 percent in 1916, by 17 percent in 1917 and by 18.6 percent in 1918. They were on their way to rising by 13.8 percent in 1919.[17]

Flyaway prices were symptoms of wartime financial disorder. Immense public borrowing, and the easy money to accommodate it, may or may not have been a necessary evil, but the Armistice now rendered it unnecessary. When governments stopped printing money for the very purpose of destroying life and property—when production and orthodox banking made their welcome reappearance—come this happy day, the experts promised, prices would certainly tumble.

But prices resumed their rise as the experts reconsidered their forecasts. In early May, the *Commercial and Financial Chronicle* was prepared to admit to its Wall Street readership that "merchants are less timid about buying." Before very long, the merchants were buying boldly. By the fall of 1919, plants were operating at full capacity, raw materials were unobtainable except at exorbitant prices and delivery dates were being pushed out by as much as a year.[18] Come Christmas, the *Chronicle*'s columns were reporting that "consumption plainly outruns production; in parts of the country what might be called a Saturnalia of buying prevails; the retail holiday business is said to be the largest on record."[19]

If Saturnalia it was, the inflationary boom of 1919 was a bitter and unhappy one. Wages couldn't seem to keep pace with prices, nor prices with costs. A pair of sensible shoes had cost $3 before the war. Now they sold for $10 or $12. Bankers scornfully spoke of the shrunken "fifty-cent dollar."[20] Pensioners, judges, professors—anyone on a fixed income—suffered a crippling loss in living standards. Class rose up against class and interest group against interest group.

Especially did the great inflation set labor against management, city dwellers against farmers, creditors against debtors and the Federal Reserve against a growing legion of monetary critics. The "high cost of living"—or the more headline-suitable acronym "H.C.L."—became the national hot button. And hovering in the background of these economic conflicts was the outbreak of revolution in Europe and the triumph of Communism in Russia. Was America next in line for a workers' revolt? "We are going to socialize the basic industries of the United States," vowed John Fitzpatrick, veteran president of the Chicago Federation of Labor, on September 18, 1919.[21]

Labor took out its anger on management, which not infrequently responded with allegations that the unions were stalking horses for the violent left. In 1919, one in five American workers was involved in a strike; it was an unprecedented figure at the time, and it has never been approached since.[22] The United Mine Workers, the nation's biggest union, struck the coal mines, and a quarter million steelworkers walked out on U.S. Steel. There was a police strike in Boston. There were strikes by machinists, iron workers, upholsterers, butchers, paper makers, boot and shoe workers, raincoat makers, oilfield hands, longshoremen, puddlers, metal polishers, carmen, waiters, garment workers, die sinkers, grain handlers, livestock handlers, silk weavers, petticoat workers, silk operatives, drop-forge men, painters, glaziers, braziers, tool makers, cigar makers, subway workers, actors, carpenters and pressmen.[23] In September 1919, President Wilson, setting off on his ill-fated cross-country trip to take his case for the League of Nations directly to the people, stopped in Columbus to deliver his first speech. The crowd was disappointingly small—it seemed that the Columbus trolleymen had struck.[24]

Many were the local and particular grievances that pushed workers and managements to break off negotiations and mount (or suffer) a strike. One common thread was the workers' loss of real income to sky-high prices. Another was radical politics.

The Bolshevik triumph in Russia in November 1917 electrified the American left. Here was the sign they had so long awaited. A general strike—the first in American history—shuttered Seattle for five days in January 1919. Yes, the Reds and anarchists and members of the Industrial Workers of the World—better known as Wobblies—were bound to admit, the reactionaries had cut short the people's uprising. But what an inspiring revolt it had been.[25]

Still inspired, the would-be vanguard of the socialist revolution marked May Day with the mailing of 30 letter bombs to members of the American Establishment. Lacking adequate postage, most of the bombs went undelivered. Reinspired, or refinanced, the revolutionaries tried again.[26] Among their targets was Wilson's energetic and ambitious attorney general, A. Mitchell Palmer.

Late on the night of June 2, an assailant dropped a bomb near the front door of Palmer's Washington, D.C., home. The device blew the would-be executioner to bits—he seemed to have tripped before he reached his target—but left Mr. and Mrs. Palmer physically unharmed. "Class war is on and cannot cease but with a complete victory for the international proletariat" was an excerpt from the dozens of copies of the anarchist pamphlet "Plain Words" that the bomber had not had the chance to distribute.[27]

Such acts of domestic violence did nothing to sweeten the relations between management and labor. Angry and fearful men glowered on either side of the bargaining table. "It might be that before we got through we would bring some one before a firing squad," Warren S. Stone, grand chief of the Brotherhood of Locomotive Engineers, had testified before a House committee in August in consideration of a bill to nationalize the nation's railroads.[28]

In November, 400,000 unionized bituminous coal miners walked off the job in defiance of a federal court injunction. During the war the union, led by John L. Lewis, had submitted to such wages as the operators vouchsafed to pay. Now the miners demanded a 40 percent increase (their opening demand was 60 percent, along with the nationalization of the mines); since 1914, as the Department of Labor did the sums, the cost of living in the mining districts of Brazil, Indiana, and Pana, Illinois, had jumped by almost 80 percent. The typical mining family earmarked 37 percent of its budget for food, the cost of which was soaring.

General Motors Corporation, founded in 1908 and already an American blue chip, registered sales of $270 million in 1918 and $510 million in 1919;[29] it earned $15 million in 1918 and $60 million in 1919; it had 49,118 employees in 1918 and 85,980 in 1919.[30] There was no doubting the boom in Detroit.

GM marked the first full year of peace with a burst of energy—prices, after all, were on the fly. It got into the tractor business, diversified into refrigerators, founded the General Motors Acceptance Corporation and purchased a controlling interest in the Fisher Body Corporation. And it was in 1919 that the GM executive committee approved construction of an imperial new headquarters. The Durant Building, named for the founder, Billy Durant, would have 15 stories, 4 wings, 1,700 offices and 30 acres of floor space. As the world's biggest office building at the time, it would cost a suitably imposing $20 million.

Anyone could see that the automotive field was still in its infancy. In July 1919 a motorized convoy of army vehicles set off from Washington, D.C., to San Francisco to demonstrate the need for more and better American highways. The troops—led by, among others, Captain Dwight D. Eisenhower—arrived in September. On good highways, the procession averaged almost 10 miles an hour.[31]

Taking the boom at face value, the GM front office accepted that raw materials were genuinely in short supply and that—contrary to experience, economic theory and even common sense—prices would rise more or less indefinitely. In such a state of mind, top management took to rubber-stamping the requests for investment funds that poured in from the heads of the company's various operating divisions. At one sitting of the executive committee, the GM chieftains approved $10,339,554 in unbudgeted spending. "The meeting was not unusual," relates Alfred P. Sloan Jr., who attended it. "Overruns on capital investment had become the rule."[32]

Just back from the war, Harry Truman, a former army artillery captain, resolved to do three things. He would quit farming, marry Bess Wallace and open a men's furnishings store in Kansas City, Missouri. And each of these things he proceeded to do, the store in partnership with his wartime buddy Eddie Jacobson.

Truman & Jacobson opened for business late in November 1919, at the northeast corner of Twelfth and Baltimore Streets. The location was prime—opposite the city's biggest and newest hotel, the Muehlebach—and the capitalization seemingly ample. Truman contributed some $15,000 in equity, much of which he had realized from the sale of livestock and machinery at the Truman family farm in Grandview. Jacobson chipped in between $900 and $1,000. Bank loans financed the inventory.

As prices were rising and Federal Reserve credit was available to member banks at concessionary rates of interest, bankers were eager to lend. Nor did consumers need to be cajoled into borrowing or buying. Soaring prices meant that money was better spent than saved. Besides, wartime scrimping was over and done with: People demanded the best and were prepared to pay for it. The partners handed out blotters to which were affixed a snappy line attributed to Dr. A. Gloom Chaser: "It takes 65 muscles of the face to make a frown and 12 to make a smile—why work overtime?" And the pitch: "Buy your men's furnishings from us at new prices. You will smile at the great reductions. We will smile at the increased business. Then none of us will be overworked."

Truman and Jacobson set the name of their enterprise in colored tiles in the Twelfth Street entryway. The partners were there early and late, opening at 8 AM and closing at 9 PM, six days a week. They sold shirts, hats, leather gloves, belts, underwear, socks, collar pins, ties and detachable collars. It was a dull customer who couldn't guess where the principals had spent the year 1918. On prominent display was a four-foot loving cup engraved to "Captain Harry" from the boys of Company D, 129th Field Artillery.

This was the prosperous Kansas City of the "Twelfth Street Rag," and the boys dropped in to shop. Cash registers were ringing, including the one at Truman & Jacobson's, which would have rung more profitably if their first clerk hadn't turned out to be a thief. "Twelfth Street was in its heyday and our war buddies and the Twelfth Street boys and girls were our customers," Eddie Jacobson reminisced. "Silk underwear for men, and silk shirts, were the rage. We sold shirts at $16." Adjusted by changes in the Consumer Price Index, a $16 shirt in 1919 would translate into a $202 shirt at this writing. Well and truly, austerity was over.[33]

Inflation fooled almost everyone, including—1,100 miles to the east—the once famously conservative National City Bank, forerunner of today's Citigroup. Safety had been City's stock in trade: It catered to "timid" people, a bemused federal examiner reported in 1891, "who feel that their money is a little safer in this bank than it would be in government bonds." This was at the very beginning of the James Stillman era. A master at the bankerly art of saying "no," Stillman could also prudently say "yes." By 1905, City was the nation's largest bank, with assets of more than $300 million, 27 percent more than the runner-up, National Bank of Commerce. It was hugely profitable besides.

It was not infallible. On the eve of the Bolshevik Revolution, it set about building Russian branches, gathering Russian deposits and investing in czarist bonds. "[O]f all the foreign countries," declared Stillman's protégé, Frank Vanderlip, in 1916, "there is none that offers a more promising outlook than Russia." Vanderlip, the second in command, lost his job when the victorious Communists dealt the bank its first lesson in sovereign political risk. Absent Vanderlip (Stillman had died in 1918),[34] the bank sailed rudderless into the 1919 boom.

Soaring prices beguiled borrowers and lenders alike. To finance rising inventories, customers clamored for credit, and City profitably loaned. The Federal Reserve Bank of New York would lend to City at 4.75 percent, whereas City could lend to its customers at 5.6 percent. In the second half of 1919, City's book of business loans expanded by 30 percent.

Cuba seemed an especially promising theater of operations to the bank that made its offices at 55 Wall Street. The price of raw sugar, Cuba's top export, had vaulted to 22 cents a pound in the spring of 1920 from four cents a pound in the fall of 1918. American housewives, the Wilson administration and the National City Bank were now of one mind: Sugar prices were going to heaven.

City plunged into Cuba as Vanderlip had tried to commit to Russia. It built 22 branches in 1919 and loaned heavily to finance construction of sugar mills, railroads and other infrastructure that would presently assure much larger sugar production—and, ultimately, much lower sugar prices. (The enthusiasm was contagious: Chase National and Guaranty Trust, City's New York neighbors, also loaned in Cuba). By June 1920, exposure to Cuba and its one-crop economy came to total $79 million, or 80 percent of City's capital. "Management's bet on this single commodity had been imprudent to the point of folly," to quote City's own corporate history.[35]

If this giant of Wall Street could be duped by the inflationary distortion of values, no less confused were the nation's farmers. Never before had they sweated so little to earn so much. They had planted fence post to fence post during the war, and they retrenched not at all in the peace. Acreage planted to wheat in 1919 reached a record that stood until World War II. Tractor sales soared in tandem with crop prices. "Power farming" became the motto of a new personage on the American rural scene, the mechanized agricultural businessman.

In 1919, farm income from production reached a new high of $16.9 billion, no less than 152 percent above the prewar average of $6.7 billion. This record, too, would stand until the 1940s.[36] Having money to spend, farmers bought breeding stock as well as tractors. In May 1919, "Rag Apple the Great," a purebred Holstein-Friesian bull, fetched a heretofore unimaginable sale price of $125,000.[37]

The land on which the likes of Rag Apple regally grazed was by now in its own bull market. As crop prices were zooming, farmers and bankers reasoned, so should the capitalized value of the land on which the seeds were planted. In 1919, black Iowa corn ground fetched prices some 40 percent higher than the prewar average. In 1920, the premium was 70 percent.

Optimistic farmers borrowed to expand. "Most land purchases were made with at least a first mortgage," recorded an agricultural historian of the period, "and sometimes even third mortgages, which looked far into the future for liquidation." As levitating prices for land and crops and breeding stock were signs of the times, so, too, was the climb in agricultural mortgage debt. "People ask me," said the president of the Iowa State Board of Agriculture in December 1919, "if I think this land will stay at that price [$200 to $500 per acre] and I say it certainly will. It may not go any higher for some time, but I do not think it will go back."[38]

★ **2** ★

COIN OF THE REALM

Woodrow Wilson's secretary of labor, William B. Wilson (no relation to the president), insisted that irksomely high prices would soon be falling.[1] At the end of a war, they always had. But prices were not falling in 1919, and the people—not to mention their Republican representatives in Congress—demanded action against the fearful depreciation in the purchasing power of the good-as-gold American dollar.

In the summer of 1919, President Wilson's mind was elsewhere: on the unfinished business of peace making in Europe, on the unratified Versailles treaty and on the willful GOP senators who would thwart his determination to bring America into the League of Nations. But when at last he saw the high cost of living for the make-or-break political issue it was, the president summoned his attorney general. As Palmer emerged from a meeting with his chief on August 5, he vowed to the waiting White House press corps: "The Department of Justice will use all its agents throughout the nation to hunt down the hoarders and profiteers in food."[2]

A more fruitful search for the causes of the great inflation would have begun and ended in Washington, D.C., and in the capital cities of the other former belligerents. It was governments that had caused the runup in prices, or—a more analytically clarifying image—the rundown in the value of the money they so copiously printed. The warring nations had fought their fight on the cuff. They spent more than they raised in taxes, and they borrowed the difference. And to one degree or another, they printed the money they couldn't otherwise secure by taxing the people or tapping the people's savings. By means of the printing press, needy states created the means to buy without creating a corresponding supply of things *to* buy. More money in pursuit of the same volume of goods points to higher prices. More money in pursuit of a reduced supply of goods—the business of war making having preempted civilian production—implies even higher prices. Cockeyed finance was the cause of the great postwar inflation. Rising prices were the symptom.

The president wouldn't admit it. Greed was the problem, to hear him and Palmer tell the story. In the tawdry hope of making a profit, grocers withheld eggs, meat, butter and sugar from the market. They would sell by and by at higher prices—and at a fattened profit. In so doing, the administration contended, they were breaking the law. Wartime controls had criminalized certain kinds of inventory building. "Hoarding" was the stigmatizing word for this otherwise conventional business practice. And as America had as yet signed no treaty of peace to bring the war to an official close, the emergency regulations were still in effect.

In campaigning for the presidency in 1912, Wilson had laid responsibility for a much milder inflation at the feet of allegedly gouging businessmen: "The high cost of living is arranged by private understanding," he charged.[3] Now, in August 1919, he repeated the allegation. Why, demanded the president, in the face of a 10 percent rise in the supply of fresh eggs over the previous 12 months, had the wholesale price of those eggs climbed by one third, to 40 cents a dozen? In the fullness of time, he averred, the government should be empowered to license corporations engaged in interstate commerce to prevent "unconscionable" profits in production and marketing. But that was work for some enlightened future day. In the here and now, the wartime Food Control Act was still in force. Its antihoarding provisions should be broadened to encompass all of life's necessities. As a kind of demonstration project, the president asked Congress to lower the boom on hoarders and profiteers in the District of Columbia, where congressional "legislative authority is without limit."

Had he made a better diagnosis of the cause of inflation, Wilson would have turned for relief to his Treasury Department, which did the government's borrowing, and the Federal Reserve, which provided the Treasury with artificially low interest rates at which to borrow. Instead, the president tapped the Department of Justice. To shame the merchants who would charge more than a governmentally sanctioned "fair" price, Attorney General Palmer reactivated a wartime corps of federal food-price administrators. And to shake loose the groceries that the enemies of the people were secreting, he organized federal raiding parties. On August 16, Palmer's operatives announced the seizure of millions of eggs in Detroit and Nashville and 200,000 pounds of sugar in Canton, Ohio. Raids on the larders of suspected profiteers continued for weeks thereafter, the impounded merchandise encompassing, among other delicacies, dry salt pork, salmon and pigs' ears. The government was prepared to return these items to their owners once the chastened profiteers agreed to sell them at a "reasonable" price and under the watchful eye of a federal officer.

Palmer's biographer, Stanley Coben, related that the attorney general was well aware that the inflation of 1919 and early 1920 was the world's problem, not only America's. Between 1919 and 1920, wholesale prices climbed by 21.1 percent in Australia, 20.4 percent in Britain, 42.9 percent in France and 9.7 percent in Japan.[4] Yet, Palmer contended, "I am one of those who believe that a large part of the high cost of living is due to the fact that a number of unconscionable men in the ranks of the dealers have taken advantage of these other conditions. . . . If we can make a few conspicuous examples of gougers and give the widest sort of publicity to the fact that such gougers have been and will be punished, in the future there will be little inclination to profiteer in this country."[5]

"Before the war" was a phrase that, in 1919, evoked the irrecoverable arcadia of peace, health and prosperity. But there was contention, too, not least in monetary affairs. In America, a generation-long period of falling prices, 1873–96, had provoked a political movement for cheaper, more plentiful money. Give us silver, they cried, William Jennings Bryan, the Nebraska orator, crying longest and loudest. Running for president in 1896 on the Democratic ticket, Bryan finished second to the gold-standard Republican,

William McKinley, and there the monetary question was politically resolved. With passage of the Gold Standard Act of 1900, which instituted gold alone as the official American monetary metal (instead of either gold or silver), the electoral result was memorialized in the federal statute books.

The facts were on McKinley's side. Prices subsided in the final quarter of the 19th century but not because of a shortage of money or credit. There was, indeed, no shortage. Between 1860 and 1891, wholesale prices fell by 58 percent, while currency in circulation rose by 344 percent—and check clearings in New York City climbed by 471 percent. While the stock of money rose, the rate at which that money moved from hand to hand rose faster.[6]

The source of the decline in prices in the final 35 years of the 19th century was rather a superabundance of enterprise and invention. Technological progress slashed production costs. And as costs fell, so did prices—and so did wages, although not so fast as prices. Between 1865 and 1900 average real wages of nonfarm employees rose by 75 percent.[7]

Then prices turned on their heels. They rose, at retail, between 1896 and 1914 at an average rate of 2 percent or more a year. Through long experience, 21st century consumers have become inured to the upcreep in living costs (or the downcreep in the purchasing power of their paychecks). There was no such expectation in the early years of the 20th century. For shoppers of a certain age, rising prices took some getting used to.

It was inflation without an evident cause—at least, no cause that a 21st century economist would likely think of without prompting. The federal budget was not always in surplus, but the deficit years were the exception (after 1865, they encompassed 1894–99, 1904–05, 1908–10, 1913–15 and 1917–19). Neither was there any heavy-handed cranking of the presses by the American monetary authorities. Indeed, there were no such authorities (except, as in the panic year of 1907, when the Treasury assumed some central banking responsibilities) until the Federal Reserve opened its doors in 1914.

Gold was the coin of the realm in those prewar years. People would pull a $20 gold coin from their pocket and plunk it down on the shopkeeper's counter. So struck, the coin rang; hence, "sound" money. Or, more likely, a shopper would produce a paper bill from his or her wallet, paper being more portable than coin. There were national bank notes, silver certificates, Treasury certificates and—once the Fed was up and running—Federal Reserve notes, not to mention checks drawn on a bank account. Paper dollars they were to the touch, but each was ultimately exchangeable, at the option of the holder, into gold. Gold coins themselves accounted for 16 percent of the 1913 supply of circulating American money.

Under the gold standard, money derived its value not from the imprint of the government, but from the intrinsic value of the metal. In law, the dollar was defined as a weight of gold, 23.22 grains pure. Inasmuch as there are 480 grains in an ounce, the number of dollars in an ounce was expressed as 480 divided by 23.22, or $20.67. Throughout the world—the "civilized" world, as the richer peoples were pleased to be identified—gold was money par excellence. No country's gold was better than another's. No national currency was privileged over another.

Money went where it was treated well. If America's interest rates were more attractive than Europe's, French gold would be put on a ship to New York. There the metal would be converted into dollars and invested in bonds or commercial paper. The influx of money would tend to press American interest rates down to European levels. As the incentive to ship gold disappeared, the flow of metal to New York would stop.

Alternatively, if American interest rates fell below world levels, overseas dollar holders would exchange those pieces of American paper for gold and take coins and bars and ingots home. The exodus would tend to raise American rates until the outbound movement of gold stopped.

An influx of gold tended to be inflationary; it expanded the supply of money. An outflow of gold tended to be deflationary; it contracted the supply of money. Tendencies they were. An influx of supply met by a lift in demand might have no inflationary impact. So, too, with an exodus of supply. The quantity of money alone automatically determined nothing.

At an extreme, gains and losses of gold would, even without overt political management, reverse themselves. Gold would stop entering a country when that country's prices became uncompetitively high. Alternatively, gold would stop fleeing a country when that country's prices became enticingly low.

"Imbalances" in trade and payments could thus not persist for long. By consuming more than it produced, a country would eventually run short of gold. The resulting strains on its money and credit "would have worked for a lower price level and a growing export trade," as a contemporary economist described the synchronous mechanics of the gold standard.[8] The system met with near universal approval among the advanced economies: "Only a trifling number of countries were forced off the gold standard, once adopted, and devaluations of gold currencies were highly exceptional," to quote the 20th century monetary historian Arthur I. Bloomfield.[9]

In the setting of interest rates and the moving of money, central bankers played a supporting role. They employed few economists and took little part in "macroeconomic management." To attract or repel gold, they adjusted the interest rate they controlled, or, in the case of France, the size and suitability of coins they were prepared to pay out in exchange for bank notes. Their main job was to exchange gold for currency, and vice versa, at the lawful rate. In times of crisis, they loaned to solvent banks at high interest rates against good collateral. With rare exceptions, "bailouts" were unknown. In London, the failures of Overend Gurney in 1866 and of Baring Brothers in 1890 elicited a helping hand from the Bank of England, but not from the taxpayers (though a quasi public institution, the Bank was investor-owned). The day of the celebrity central banker was still in the future.

Four years after the 1918 Armistice, John Maynard Keynes looked back longingly on the monetary arrangements in place before the shooting started. "If the gold standard could only be reintroduced . . . ," he wrote in the *Manchester Guardian*, "we all believe that the reform would promote trade and production like nothing else, but also stimulate international credit and transfers of capital to places where they are most useful. One of the greatest elements of uncertainty would be repressed."[10]

The gold standard was no more perfect than any other human contrivance, clearly. But was it not the least imperfect monetary system ever to function in human society? Irving Fisher, brilliant professor of political economy at Yale University, was not prepared to concede the point. He had not one doubt that the wit of man—his, for instance—could devise something better.

Fisher was a man of few doubts and boundless energy. He advocated for public health (with all the authority of the tuberculosis survivor that he was), prohibition, common stocks, eugenics, longevity through vegetarian-ism, Indian meditation—and government economic management. An en-lightened central bank could neutralize booms and busts alike by controlling the stock of money, or so he proposed.

Fisher rejected the Bryanite campaign for lots of silver dollars. But he did not reject the notion that the quantity of money was of the utmost im-portance in determining prices and wages. Neither did he share his contem-poraries' fatalism with respect to the cycles of credit and business.

Stability was the ticket, he said. The price level should neither rise nor fall but should remain the same. Justice to debtors and creditors demanded it. And enlightened central bankers might achieve it. The age of laissez-faire was over, declared Fisher in 1906.[11]

This was not just the theorizing of any college professor. Economists of the stature of Alfred Marshall in Britain and Leon Walras in France pro-claimed Fisher a genius. So did, much later, the American economist Paul Samuelson. Certainly, a glance at his burning eyes suggested a ferocious intelligence.

Fisher could accept the truism that the value of the dollar was stable in terms of gold. It had to be; it was defined as a weight of gold. But that mathematical identity did not deliver anything like real stability. In terms of gold, the prices of commodities were obviously unstable. They had spent most of the final quarter of the 19th century declining. And they had spent what little there was of the 20th century increasing. Falling prices were a gift to creditors; rising prices returned the favor to debtors.

How much better it would be, Fisher proposed, if the gold weight of the dollar could undergo periodic adjustments to reflect changes in the purchas-ing power of gold at the cash register. Retire gold coins from circulation, he urged; they were only tokens anyway. Let the economic technocrats perform the calculations that would assure continuous adjustment and, therefore, constant purchasing power. "We now have a gold dollar of constant weight and varying purchasing power," Fisher wrote; "we need a dollar of constant purchasing power and varying weight." No need to trust the impersonal movement of gold to balance and rebalance national economies. Economists could do the job better.[12]

Fisher got a respectful hearing on his ideas at the 25th annual meeting of the American Economics Association in 1913, and he looked forward to proselytizing his colleagues again at an anticipated international conference on the high cost of living in 1914. With the outbreak of war, the conference was cancelled, and the cost of living zoomed in ways that the participants in the 1913 academic roundtable likely did not imagine.

Fisher's preoccupation with the mild inflation of the early 1900s (and, before that, with the mild deflation of the late 1800s) seemed to blind him to the quite remarkable long-term stability in the purchasing power of gold. An ounce would buy in 1930 approximately the same basket of commodities as it had bought in 1650, according to research published long after Fisher's death.[13] With his tongue evidently stuck halfway into his cheek, Fisher was wont to say that a carpet standard—or an egg standard—could be made to work as well as a gold standard.

But not even Fisher could imagine a monetary system not essentially gold-based. Gold was nature's own monetary material: scarce, homogeneous, ductile, durable, indestructible and beautiful to behold. Looking at it, anyone could see it was money. As for the gold standard, it knit together the incomes and cost structures of the participating gold-standard nations. As it flourished, so did trade and so did the frictionless movement of capital across national boundaries.

"I am sure," the economist acknowledged to his fellow economists in 1913 concerning his plan for monetary improvement, "I am under no illusions as to the possibility of the early adoption of any plan to standardize the dollar. This may require centuries, but I hope that the present generation of economists may, at any rate, lay the foundations by threshing the subject out."[14] Actually, for the complete overhaul of the world's monetary and banking institutions, Fisher would have to wait not centuries but only a few years. The war disposed of the international gold standard as cleanly as it did czarist Russia.

But before the deluge, how neatly things had worked. "Perfect" was the word chosen by the English financial journalist Hartley Withers to describe the functioning of finance in the City of London under the gold standard and the private stewardship of credit. No major British bank had failed since the

City of Glasgow Bank in 1878, and none was likely to fail any time soon, he predicted. "Good banking," Withers declared in 1909, "is produced not by good laws but by good bankers."[15] The system virtually managed itself.

America had plenty of laws, Withers went on, including seemingly airtight regulations concerning the minimum level of cash that a nationally chartered depository institution must set aside against a potential run. Yet depositors ran nonetheless—breathlessly, in the Panic of 1907. Perhaps America lacked good bankers.

Good, bad or indifferent, a banker was a dealer in promises. He accepted deposits (which he promised to redeem), and with those deposits he loaned or bought securities (which the obligor had committed to redeem). On the banker's balance sheet, the deposits were—and are—liabilities. The loans and securities are assets.

A liquid asset is one that can be turned into cash in an instant—or, better, that will turn itself into cash. A commercial loan—say, a 90-day credit backed by finished goods in transit—is essentially liquid. A mortgage—say, a five-year loan against a farm or house or warehouse—is essentially illiquid. A prime commercial loan is indeed "self-liquidating," because the collateral is marketable. In all probability, someone would step up to pay for the goods, thereby providing the cash with which to extinguish the loan. A mortgage provides no such probable source of cash. Someone might very well—eventually—make a bid for the warehouse. But there can be no supposition that that bid would be forthcoming as the loan fell due.

And why would a banker prize liquidity? Because the depositors might ask for their money back. Entrusted with funds, the banker appropriates them for his own use. He invests them or lends them to someone. So a banker was—and is—a kind of juggler. To satisfy the depositors, he must remain liquid (especially so before the 1933 enactment of federal deposit insurance). But to earn a profit, he must do something with the depositors' money besides stacking it in a vault. Americans knew the rudiments of banking as well as their British cousins, yet still—every 10 years or so—the United States financial system dissolved in panic.

Maybe the fault lay in the sheer number and variety of American banks. There were state-chartered banks, nationally chartered ones, savings banks and trust companies: 22,491 in all as of April 28, 1909.[16] Different kinds of depository institutions received different kinds of oversight. Nationally chartered banks were monitored by the federal government and state-chartered banks by the states. National banks issued their own dollar bills, backed dollar for dollar by U.S. Treasury bonds (the tax laws made it unprofitable for state banks to do the same). The notes of one nationally chartered bank looked much like another's, but each bore the stamp of the issuing institution. A New Yorker might carry ordinary green dollars branded "First National Bank" or "National City Bank" or "National Bank of Commerce." Critics carped at the "inelasticity" of these arrangements. The volume of currency was tied to the volume of Treasury obligations available to stand behind it. And as Congress tended to balance the budget, the Treasury issued precious few bonds. Let the demand for currency increase—as it did, for instance, at fall harvest time or during a financial panic—and that demand met a rigidly fixed supply.

Then, too, the reformers' indictment of American finance continued, banks and banking assets were concentrated in the big cities, especially New York. Campaigning in 1912, Wilson alleged that a "money trust" ruled Wall Street, and at the top of this monopoly reigned just a dozen willful men. Representative Carter Glass, a Virginia Democrat who made the overhaul of American banks and currency his special project, concurred. Dollars laid aside in reserve against panic or stringency were all too likely to be gallivanting around Wall Street instead of slumbering safely in a vault or doing the honest work of financing the nation's trade or agriculture.

"Under existing law," the Virginian thundered against his critics in New York in October 1913, "we have permitted the banks to pyramid credit upon credit, and to call these credits reserves. It is a misnomer. They are not reserves, and when financial troubles come and country banks call for their money with which to pay their creditors, they find it is invested in stock-gambling operations. There is suspension of payment and the whole system breaks down under the strain, causing widespread confusion and almost inconceivable damage. The avowed purpose of this bill is to cure this evil, to withdraw the reserve funds of the country from the congested money centers and to make them readily available for business uses in the various sections of the country in which they belong."[17]

"This bill" was the Federal Reserve Act. It was "an act," so the preamble said, "to provide for the establishment of Federal Reserve banks, to furnish an elastic currency, to afford means of rediscounting commercial paper, to establish a more effective supervision of banking in the United States, and for other purposes." The founders, good Democrats, wanted their creation to know its political place. It would exercise none of the centralized power that had caused Andrew Jackson and, before him, Thomas Jefferson to denounce their respective central banks (each named the Bank of the United States) as menaces to the Constitution. The Federal Reserve would therefore be, above all things, decentralized. Its interest-rate-setting authority would be dispersed among 12 regional Reserve banks, not imposed by the Federal Reserve Board in Washington.

On December 23, 1913, President Wilson affixed his name to an act of modest—by 21st century standards, almost diffident—scope. He used a gold pen, for the reformers were adamant that the dollar would remain as good as gold. Though it came into the world on the eve of the war that shattered Withers's perfect financial world, the Federal Reserve bore the intellectual stamp of the classical gold standard.

Notable was what the new creation would have nothing to do with. Missing from the Reserve banks' original remit was an obligation to stabilize the price level, promote full employment, iron out the business cycle, buy up Treasury bonds or pull an oar for economic growth.

Neither was the Federal Reserve expected to create credit. Gold was money, credit the promise to pay money. The principal source of credit was a business deal. "I'll pay you in 90 days," one transacting party would say to the other. The two recorded their intentions on a legal document, a commercial bill. Against this bill, a bank might lend. "To discount" was (and is) the term of art for such an extension of credit. That is, the bank would advance fewer than 100 cents on the dollar. The discount from face value expressed the rate of interest charged.

Commercial banks discounted bills for their customers. In the same way, the Federal Reserve banks would "re-discount" bills for *their* customers, their customers being the nationally chartered banks, which had no choice but to join the Federal Reserve system. The Federal Reserve (nobody called it the "Fed" just yet) would lend to banks that wanted to turn their sound, self-liquidating loans into cash.

The legislative architects of the Federal Reserve therefore bristled when opponents impugned their contemplated new currency, the Federal Reserve note, as "fiat." It was anything but, they retorted. It was as good as gold because it was convertible into gold. It was, indeed, better than gold, because—besides precious metal—it would be ballasted by first-class banking assets and by the credit of the nationally chartered commercial banks: two pairs of suspenders besides that golden belt.

Far from dictating to the market, the Federal Reserve would take the market's lead. It would operate passively through the technique of rediscounting, rather than actively by buying and selling securities in order to expand or contract the volume of money coursing through the channels of trade ("open-market operations," as this method, widely used today, is known). The Federal Reserve would accommodate the needs of the community, not determine what those needs ought to be.

The bill had much to please the bankers. It relaxed the old prohibitions against real estate lending. It reduced the percentage of deposits that a bank must put aside in reserve. Twenty-five cents out of every dollar had had to lie fallow under the Civil War–era National Bank Act, as that law related to big banks like City; now they could get by with 18 cents on the dollar. Altogether, City liked the looks of monetary reform, which—in another welcome innovation—allowed it to open foreign branches. The Wilson administration had set out to clip the wings of the Wall Street behemoths but wound up, instead, letting them soar even higher.[18]

Passage of the Federal Reserve Act was a political certainty when, on December 13, 1913, Elihu Root, Republican of New York, rose up in the Senate to denounce it. To the Democrats' claims that the nation was going to be the lucky recipient of an "elastic" currency, Root retorted that it would rather get an "expansive" one—all growth and no contraction. And as the stock of redundant dollar bills grew, events would take their time-honored inflationary course. "With the exhaustless reservoir of the Government of the United States furnishing easy money," he said, "the sales increase, the businesses enlarge, more new enterprises are started, the spirit of optimism pervades the community. Bankers are not free from it. They are human. The members of the Federal Reserve Board will not be free of it. They are human. Regional bankers will not be free of it. They are human. All the world moves along on a growing tide of optimism. Everyone is making money. Everyone is growing rich"—until the boom gives way to bust.

"That, sir, is no dream," Root went on. "That is the history of every movement of inflation since the world's business began, and it is the history of many a period in our own country. That is what happened to greater or lesser degree before the panic of 1837, of 1857, of 1873, of 1893 and of 1907. The precise formula by which the students of economic movements have evolved to describe reasons for the crash following the universal process is that when credit exceeds the legitimate demands of the country the currency becomes suspected and gold leaves the country."

Complementing news coverage of the signing of the Federal Reserve Act in the *New York Times* of December 24, 1913, was a message of congratulations from the United Cigar Stores Company. The new legislation was a Christmas gift to the nation. It would, indeed, take its place in the American documentary pantheon alongside the Declaration of Independence. America was free of panics at last.[19]

MONEY AT WAR

For technical assistance on his speech assailing the Federal Reserve Act, Root turned to the senior vice president of Bankers Trust Company. The banker-consultant Benjamin Strong had deep misgivings about the proposed federal monetary institution.

Some of his Wall Street brethren resented any government intrusion in money matters. What Strong wanted was a real central bank, not a decentralized makeshift. Then, too, said Strong, the act vested too much power in political appointees, too little in the bankers who would, after all, own the stock in the 12 Reserve banks and manage them (they actually knew a little something about banking). Finally, and most worryingly, the act provided that Federal Reserve notes would be made obligations of the U.S. government as well as of the Reserve banks.

Here was a nuanced concern. A "note" is a debt obligation, an IOU. A Federal Reserve note was more than a piece of paper. It was a standing promise to pay gold at the option of the holder. Strong was well aware of the intentions of the authors of the act: that the notes would be convertible into gold and backed not only by that precious metal but also by sound banking assets (e.g., self-liquidating commercial bills). Why, then, was it necessary to superimpose the credit of the government? "This is a provisional return to the heresies of Greenbackism and fiat money," Strong contended some weeks before Wilson's signature on the objectionable measure made his protests moot—and not quite a year before the hypercritical banker accepted the position of governor of the Federal Reserve Bank of New York, the most important post in the new system. (To clarify: "President" is the title of the head of a 21st century regional Federal Reserve bank; then it was "governor," the same title, confusingly, accorded the chairman of the Federal Reserve Board in Washington. Thus, both Strong and W.P.G. Harding—not to be confused with the president of the United States—were each addressed as "Governor.")

Strong was more than a vice president of Bankers Trust. Having married the president's daughter (it was his second marriage) and having for some time discharged the president's duties, the vice president was chief executive in all but name; the title itself he acquired in 1914. In his early 40s, Strong had come to look a little like J.P. Morgan, with whose financial interests he was closely associated. Strong's nose, like Morgan's, was the principal topographical feature of his face, and Strong's eyes, like Morgan's, were bold and piercing. "After studying that face," wrote Strong's biographer, Lester V. Chandler, "one can easily believe the stories of a grim Strong sweeping into waste baskets important papers of Bankers Trust officials who twice ignored his instructions to clear their desk tops before going home."[1]

The clean-desk man was born in Fishkill, New York, in 1872. His first American forebear named Strong was a Puritan father of 18 who arrived in Massachusetts Bay in 1630. A great-grandfather of Strong's served at the U.S. Treasury as Alexander Hamilton's first clerk and helped to institute the Seamen's Bank for Savings. Presbyterianism and philanthropy were common fruits of the spreading family tree. What was lacking in the Fishkill Strongs was ready money. When the time came for young Benjamin to attend college (he had set his mind on Princeton), he had to find work instead; the job he found was on Wall Street.

The cut of his jib appealing to successive employers, Strong was not a clerk for long. In 1904, he was made secretary of the newly organized Bankers Trust; Henry P. Davison, the bank's founder and a neighbor of Strong's in Englewood, New Jersey, hired him. The next year, Strong's first wife committed suicide, leaving him with four young children, two daughters and two sons; presently, the elder daughter died. The surviving children went to live with the Davisons, "and Strong plunged himself even more deeply into his work," as Chandler related.[2]

Come the Panic of 1907, Davison was tapped to manage the effort to save the banks that, though they might have been illiquid, were not insolvent. Davison, in turn, deputized Strong to perform the analysis to separate the illiquid sheep from the bankrupt goats. For Strong and the eminently sound Bankers Trust, it was a very good panic.

Yet, concurred the men who had served as a kind of de facto lender of last resort in 1907, the time had come to render American finance panic-resistant. This determination yielded the Aldrich-Vreeland Act of 1908, which authorized the Treasury, in an emergency, to issue currency collateralized by assets other than U.S. government securities. Here was a panic-melioration device rather than a panic-prevention device. Better, the leading lights of New York finance reasoned, would be a central bank fashioned along the lines of the Bank of England or the German Reichsbank. Strong was among the attendees of a secret meeting of top financiers at Jekyll Island, Georgia, in November 1910, to plan the political and financial steps required to create just such an institution.

But when such an institution—a central bank in substance if not in name—emerged from the legislative sausage-making machinery at Christmastime 1913, Strong held firm to his main objection. If the Federal Reserve's notes were as good as gold, or even better, what call was there for the Treasury to back them? Paul Warburg, another attendee at the Jekyll Island conclave and an appointee to the Federal Reserve Board, had been pushing Strong to accept the governorship of the Federal Reserve Bank of New York, should the offer come his way. Still Strong demurred: "I am unalterably opposed to the United States Government lending its credit to the notes to be issued by the Federal Reserve Banks," he wrote Warburg in August 1914. "It may someday spell disaster to the credit of our Government."[3]

Strong's opposition melted under the persuasion of Warburg and Davison, who invited him to the country for a week and pressed him hard.[4] So the erstwhile president of Bankers Trust said goodbye to his numerous private interests (including a trusteeship in his ancestor's institution, the Seamen's Bank for Savings) to become the first governor of the Federal Reserve Bank of New York. The date was October 5, 1914. The war in Europe was two months old.

The war came out of the blue. To judge by the action of the world's stock markets, not even the money men saw it coming. "Up to the final moment of the launching of the ultimate between the European governments," attested H.G.S. Noble, president of the New York Stock Exchange, "no one thought it possible that all our boasted bonds of civilization were to burst overnight and plunge us back into medieval barbarism."[5] As the impossible proceeded to unfold, the belligerents abandoned the gold standard, declared debt moratoria and closed stock exchanges. Money was a war materiel, like steel and military-age males, and the warring nations commandeered it. The least imperfect monetary system known to man was among the first casualties.

America, distant and neutral, was out of the line of fire. But America's stocks and bonds were not exclusively the property of American citizens. In July 1914, Europeans held $7 billion of American securities, whereas American citizens owned just $1 billion of the Europeans'.[6] The city of New York, which in 1910 had floated an issue of bonds across the Atlantic, itself owed $80 million to European creditors. What would happen if the gold-hungry Europeans descended on New York to exchange their dollar-denominated claims for bullion? Wall Street bankers lay awake at night wondering.[7]

One by one, starting on July 28, the world's stock exchanges were shuttered—Montreal, Madrid, Vienna, Budapest, Antwerp, Berlin, Rome, Paris, St. Petersburg—until, on July 31, the London Stock Exchange itself suspended trading indefinitely for the first time in its long history. Better not to know the war-deflated value of British securities than to allow the market to broadcast that dispiriting information, the authorities judged. And better to permit no one to trade than to allow foreign nationals, possibly including agents of the Central Powers, to dump London-listed stocks and shares.[8]

But at the corner of Broad and Wall Streets, the governing authorities resolved to stay open. Financial force majeure had closed the New York

Stock Exchange only twice before in its 122-year history—for 10 days during the Panic of 1873 and for a single day in the wake of the 1901 Northern Pacific Corner.[9] It gave some confidence to market watchers that American stocks were reasonably valued. Pessimism, in fact, was the ruling sentiment before the storm broke, though seemingly not because of any inkling of the imminence of a European war. The buyers and sellers had rather reached a joint decision that the policies of the Wilson administration were bad medicine.[10]

A 6.9 percent plunge in prices on July 30 slightly wilted the defiance of the elders of the exchange. The early morning of Friday, July 31, brought news that the London Stock Exchange had closed, that financial settlements on the Continent had been suspended indefinitely and that the Bank of England had doubled its discount rate, to 8 percent. Concerning the shuttering of the London exchange, the *New York Times* headline—"Appeals of 100 Firms, Facing Ruin, Force the Governors to Take Action"—could not have helped but speak in a most personal way to the partners of New York Stock Exchange member firms. Many of these gentlemen made their way to Noble's offices on the sixth floor of the New York Stock Exchange, shortly before the scheduled 10 AM start of trading. There they found an impromptu meeting of the Governing Committee in progress. The one and only item on the agenda: Should, or should not, the opening bell be gonged?

Most of the governors were senior partners in member firms of the Stock Exchange. It appeared that not a few of their banking and brokerage houses would fail if the market crashed, as it likely would. By reason of their position as partners, the governors were personally responsible for the debts of the firms they led. To them, therefore, business failure meant possible personal ruin. There would likely be bank failures, too. A run on the commercial banks could precipitate a run on the savings banks, repositories of workingmen's money.

It wasn't just the Europeans who wanted to get out. American investors, too, were telling their brokers that price was no object: Just sell. If trading resumed, stock prices would collapse, surely through the lows of 1907, and so would the value of the loans collateralized by stocks. In panics past, British and Continental funds had arrived in time to cut short the American crisis. European bargain hunters sent gold, extended loans and bought securities. But the foreign opportunists, this time, were in no position to assist. Evidently, indeed, there were no buyers anywhere, except for those forehanded people who were betting on a decline or who had cash at the ready to avail themselves of panic-induced bargains.[11] Nothing so ghastly had happened in the living memory of anyone working on Wall Street.

Elsewhere in lower Manhattan, the city's top bankers were simultaneously deliberating. Perhaps, the bankers suggested, the brokers could wait to decide until they, the leaders of the city's leading financial institutions, had formulated their recommendation? A telephone line was opened to connect the two meeting places.

But only one of the great men offered a sign—do not close, he advised. The huddling governors could wait no longer. To trade or not to trade? At last they cast their ballots: Not quite unanimously, they voted to close. Receiving the verdict, the secretary of the exchange, George W. Ely, clambered on top of a desk in the midst of the milling floor brokers. He shouted out the news to a "wild outburst of cheering," as the *New York Times* reported. "Men who had feared that the next hour would bring disaster to their firms ran about embracing one another."

Immediately following the decision, President Noble paid a call on the banker who had tendered the 11th hour advice to remain open. Too bad about the shutdown, this financial personage mused to Noble. Had the governors chosen instead to grin and bear it, New York would have been well on its way to becoming the financial capital of the world.*[12]

As the New York Stock Exchange went dark, so did much of the American economy. Exports stopped—civilian ship owners wanted no part of the belligerents' struggle for control of the North Atlantic sea lanes. Grain prices slumped, consumers stopped buying, industrial activity slowed to a crawl. The collapse in demand left the United States Steel Corporation operating at a scant 30 percent of its productive capacity.[13]

By the looks of things, unemployment was reaching crisis proportions,

---

*William L. Silber, in his excellent history *When Washington Shut Down Wall Street: The Great Financial Crisis of 1914 and the Origins of America's Monetary Supremacy*, contended that the secretary of the Treasury, William G. McAdoo, personally ordered the closing of the exchange. The author's source for this claim is McAdoo's 1931 autobiography, *Crowded Years*. I find no contemporary evidence to corroborate McAdoo's memory. Noble and the Governing Committee hardly lacked for reasons to make the decision themselves.

but this was only by appearances;* there were as yet no hard facts. That deficiency the U.S. Bureau of Labor Statistics, under the direction of the pioneering statistical economist Royal Meeker, began to address in partnership with the Metropolitan Life Insurance Company. Results of a February 1915 census of every family residing within 104 New York City blocks found that 16.2 percent of wage earners were unemployed. A March–April survey in 16 eastern and midwestern cities turned up an aggregate rate of joblessness of 11.5 percent (understated, no doubt, related the BLS, because 16.6 percent of the canvassed wage earners worked only part time). "Unemployment in America was discovered in America in 1914," said Meeker.[14]

Currencies lost their moorings. The value of the pound sterling had been fixed at $4.8665 since time out of mind: It was as certain a value as there was in the Edwardian world. But the war unfixed it, and now the pound commanded $6 and even $7. If gravity itself had ceased to operate, Wall Street would not have been more thunderstruck. A $7 pound was, in its way, an impossibility as monstrous as the war itself; the previous high in sterling (or low for the dollar) was $4.91, set in 1907.[15]

Currencies were anchored not by opinions but by laws. In statute, the pound was 113 grains of pure gold to the dollar's 23.22 grains. The former divided by the latter gave the exchange rate: $4.8665. And if, through some market perturbation, the dollar/sterling exchange rate deviated from this bedrock value, shipments of gold would move to restore it to parity.[16]

But in the early days of the war, no sensible person would risk his gold on the contested North Atlantic. Besides, the gold standard was suspended for the duration in Britain and on the Continent, which meant that the value of the pound was no longer a law but an opinion. So the dollar weakened under selling from Britons and Europeans who wanted to turn their American investments into cash.

The Federal Reserve existed in law but not yet in function. Eight months after President Wilson signed the bill to spare the nation another financial

---

*"In recent days," the New York City police commissioner, Arthur Woods, told members of the Conference on Hospital Social Service in November 1915, "we have arrested here in New York numbers of men who said they have been driven to theft because their families had nothing to eat, and the appearance of these unfortunates indicated that they were telling the truth." [*New York Times*, November 25, 1914]

panic, the decentralized central bank was still in the process of organizing itself.

Especially impatient for the opening of its doors was the ambitious secretary of the Treasury, William Gibbs McAdoo. In private life, McAdoo had led the company that built the tunnels connecting New Jersey and New York. He coined his company's slogan—"the public be pleased," a Progressive era inversion of William Vanderbilt's "the public be damned"—and did not protest when grateful commuters took to calling these holes in the ground the "McAdoo Tubes." A Democrat and transplanted southerner, McAdoo married Eleanor Randolph Wilson, the daughter of another Democrat and transplanted southerner, who now happened to occupy the Oval Office.

It was no easy matter to translate the Federal Reserve Act into a functioning Federal Reserve System.[17] Indeed, many urged that the effort be suspended until after the European hostilities had had a chance to blow over. Bankers, among the putative beneficiaries of the act, were far from unanimous in welcoming the institution it called into being. It worried the critics that they would be expected to ship a meaningful portion of their gold for safekeeping to their local Reserve bank rather than holding it, as they had long been accustomed to doing, in their own vaults.

This was in the North. There was no such foot dragging in the South, where the plunging price of cotton had set off a desperate hunt for credit. Burdened with rising inventories of a depreciating commodity, the farmers and businessmen of Texas were united in the cause of opening the Federal Reserve Bank of Dallas as soon as possible. They wanted credit with which to finance the warehousing of their inventories until the market recovered. McAdoo heard their cries—he was "confident," he said, "that the prompt opening of the Reserve banks will be very helpful to the cotton situation"— and so the Federal's progenitors pushed ahead.[18]

On November 16, 1914, the Federal Reserve Bank of New York opened for business in temporary quarters at 62 Cedar Street in lower Manhattan. Most of the staff of seven officers and 85 clerks was on loan from Wall Street.[19] To Chemical National Bank went the honor of initiating the first rediscount transaction. The choice harkened back to a different world. Chemical—whose nickname "Old Bullion" derived from its reputation for invincible safety in times of trouble—had withstood the panics that Senator

Root had enumerated in his speech decrying the new monetary legislation. Without recourse to a central bank, Chemical had paid out gold from its own vaults to the depositors who worried—unnecessarily, it invariably turned out—about its liquidity.

In Europe, rumors of war had set off a scramble for gold. Thirty thousand Frenchmen formed a queue a mile long outside the Bank of France on July 29 to exchange paper francs for gold while there was still gold to pay out.[20] The people knew what their government was loath to admit: Whatever else would come out of the war, the franc would be a loser.

Americans were old hands at panicking. With the war in front of them and the crisis of 1907 not so far behind, would they run for their money again? In the last week of July and the first week of August, New Yorkers withdrew $73 million in gold from the city's banks. It didn't matter that the people who carried away the coins in satchels seemed not at all breathless. Even this "orderly" exit, as the papers styled it, was financially constricting. Credit was built on the foundation of gold; every dollar in gold supported $4 or more in loans. As a bank lost its gold, it similarly lost its capacity to lend.[21] And as the banks were squeezed, so were their customers: Money-market interest rates pushed up to 8 percent.[22]

"As the situation presented itself to most people on August 1," recorded the contemporary financial commentator Alexander Dana Noyes, "the American markets were confronted with a complete collapse of credit in the outside world, with financial and commercial panic at home (which had apparently been obscured only by the closing of the stock exchanges), with blockades of international commerce and with a 'run' by Europe on the gold supply of every other country which did not protect its own position (as the European belligerents had done at once) by an outright embargo on gold exports."[23]

America, too, could "protect" itself by falling in with the belligerents. But it would not—exactly. It would not put its gold under governmental lock and key, as Belgium, France, Germany and Great Britain had done. Still less would it move to a paper-currency basis, as a few unreconstructed populists urged. "General disaster would follow," snapped James B. Forgan, president of the First National Bank of Chicago.[24]

But neither would the United States roll out the welcome mat for any who wished to exchange dollars for gold at the lawful rate. The closing of the New York Stock Exchange was one avenue of monetary defense. An evident conspiracy of New York City bankers was another. Early in August, a man walked into his bank in lower Manhattan, presented his personal check for $2,500 and asked the teller to pay out the funds in gold (his substantial account more than covered the check). The teller excused himself to speak to the president of the bank, who returned to confront the customer.

"It is none of your business," replied the depositor to the banker's question of what he intended to do with 121 ounces of bullion. To which the banker shot back, "We do not want the account of anyone who is selfish enough to desire to withdraw and hoard gold." And the banker warned: "You will find it difficult to get any bank to take your account if you refer them to me or to this bank as your last depository." To which the *Wall Street Journal*'s account of the incident added, "The depositor tells this story himself and verifies all the bank president prognosticated in the matter of finding another depository." [25]

America's European creditors might be seen, collectively, as a very large, very nervous depositor. Gold in the vaults of major American banks represented less than twice the foreign obligations that would presently fall due. A drawn-out war, opined the redoubtable Irving Fisher, would collapse American exports, drain American gold and ring down a depression on the 48 states. The depression would last as long as the shooting did.

In the normal course of business, not much gold moved across the Atlantic to settle up international accounts.* [26] To discharge their debts to Europe,

---

*That any was on the water struck some as nonsensical. In 1909, Major Thomas B. Kirby, longtime money editor of the *Wall Street Journal*, had had a modest proposal. "[T]he only way we can ever settle the problem of the shipment of gold to Europe, foreign exchange ... and details, would be to have an International Congress of the World's Powers agree to load the world's hoard of gold on worn-out ships. Against this gold the International Congress should issue negotiable certificates of the various powers representing the amount of gold each owned on these vessels.

"Then," Kirby went on, "on a given day all of these gold-laden vessels should set sail for the middle of the Atlantic Ocean. When the vessels met, their holds should be loaded with dynamite, a time-fuse set and the crews withdrawn. The explosion would send the gold to the bottom and settle for all time this nonsensical performance of carting the stuff back and forth across the ocean." [*Wall Street Journal*, August 15, 1914]

Americans would sell merchandise or stocks and bonds, not ship bullion. Or New York banks would borrow from London banks; they would borrow in the spring when American imports were heaviest and American exports were lightest, and repay in the autumn when the trade situation was reversed.[27] But the war scrambled these well-worn commercial customs. American gold would now do nicely—every warring nation wanted more.

Britain especially needed it—and the German navy keenly wanted Britain not to have it. A Federal Reserve–organized committee on which Benjamin Strong took a position of leadership set about collecting the gold held in innumerable American banks. A part or all of this treasure would be pledged to pay British claims. Sensibly, it would be shipped not to London but to the Canadian capital, Ottawa. The committee's credible promise of $100 million in American gold to a secure portion of the British Empire more than satisfied London's gold craving.[28]

The answer to America's own craving was the monetary stopgap of 1908. Under the Aldrich-Vreeland Act, a national bank could apply for emergency currency secured not by U.S. government bonds but by state, local and municipal securities (banks applying as members of specially formed associations had a wider variety of collateral from which to choose). No bank had ever availed itself of the privilege. By applying for such accommodation in normal times, an applicant would be confessing to illiquidity, if not insolvency.

The outbreak of the first Continental European war since 1815 was, of course, highly abnormal. Frightened Americans wanted gold, or—a better, more portable alternative—currency as good as gold. To render the currency responsive to extraordinary surges in demand was the founding purpose of the Federal Reserve.

But because the Federal Reserve was still in the process of collecting staff and office furniture, it was to Aldrich-Vreeland that the government and the bankers turned. They did so without stigma, after the secretary of the Treasury and officials of the Federal Reserve Board sat down with New York's leading bankers at the Vanderbilt Hotel on the evening of August 2 to plan for the distribution of the emergency scrip. To general relief, notes to the value of $380 million were presently issued. The public accepted them gladly (at a glance, they looked no different than national bank notes) and thought nothing worse of the banks that distributed them.

Though banks had the means to lend, McAdoo complained, all too many were refusing to do so or were lending at exorbitant rates of interest. To prod them to greater openhandedness, the secretary circulated a list of 247 alleged "hoarding" banks. Nationally chartered institutions—not the big banks but the small fry—were sitting on cash equivalent to 25 percent or more of their deposits. The most notorious of the lot, the First National Bank of Kemp, Texas, was husbanding cash equivalent to 74 percent of its deposits. These provokingly timorous institutions would get no federal deposits—nor currency, either—from the government until they saw fit to open their vaults to the legitimate credit demands of their clientele. "If the large amount of loanable funds that are kept from employment as indicated by these figures," said McAdoo, wielding his list, "was invested in commercial or agricultural paper or loaned in proper security the present situation would be greatly improved."[29]

A great improvement was already in the works. Not only—thanks to good fortune, the cessation of Stock Exchange trading and a strong injection of emergency currency—was there no panic. And not only did the United States distinguish itself among the advanced nations of the world by choosing to hew to the letter, if not entirely to the spirit, of the gold standard. But also, to top it all off, the bottom did not drop out of the American economy, as it seemed all too ready to do in those August days. By December, there were emergent signs of a boom.

Nobody need have worried over the flight of American gold to London in August 1914. In December, the prevailing direction of monetary traffic across the Atlantic switched from eastbound to westbound.[30] From that time until America joined the fight in the spring of 1917, the United States imported $1.1 billion more gold than it exported. "A thousand million," whistled the newspapermen, not yet accustomed to ten-digit figures.

The Federal Reserve Act delivered another monetary pick-me-up. No more, as mentioned, did the biggest banks have to put aside 25 cents in every dollar of deposits; only 18 cents on the dollar was now required. As a larger part of every deposited dollar was available to be loaned or invested rather than stacked up in the vault, money was easier to obtain than it would otherwise have been. It was easier to get a loan, easier to float an issue of stocks or bonds.[31]

Not all at once did the nonfinancial portion of the American economy mimic Wall Street's heartfelt sigh of relief. The most imprecisely measured national unemployment rate in 1915 topped 8 percent.[32] At the quoted price of seven cents a pound, cotton was a dead loss; it cost more than that to grow. Steel mills were working at half their rated capacity. Americans knew full well that wars delivered economic advantages to neutral states. But, as Noyes observed, "in no previous war had a neutral state been confronted with what appeared to be the financial insolvency of the entire outside world."[33]

It quickly developed that the belligerents were not actually broke. They were, however, preoccupied, and they turned to the United States for the food, clothing and munitions with which to make war on each other. Before 1914, American exports had never topped $2.6 billion in a year. In the 12 months to June 1915, they reached $2.8 billion, and in the next 12 months, $4.3 billion.

Never before had the United States enjoyed a prosperity so large and comprehensive. To fill the European demand for barbed wire, firearms, shell casings, explosives, shoes, uniform cloth, wheat and medical supplies, factories hummed and ports bustled. Bethlehem Steel had $46.5 million in orders on its books at the close of 1914, $175.4 million 12 months later.[34] As late as the middle of 1915, the Wilson administration was laying plans to mobilize government unemployment relief.[35] Europe solved the problem.

And these manifold blessings seemingly came without strings. In 1915, interest rates were low and steady. Consumer prices rose by an estimated 1 percent, yet stock prices soared. A share of Bethlehem Steel started the year at $46.13 and ended it at $459.50.[36] Over the course of those 12 golden months, the Dow Jones Industrial Average climbed by 81.7 percent. The gross national product, after adjusting for the purchasing power of the dollar, climbed by what the statisticians decided was 7.9 percent.[37]

For Benjamin Strong, Walter Bagehot, the Victorian author of *Lombard Street*, a treatise on the workings of the London money market, was the ultimate authority on central banking. And the Bank of England was his beau ideal of a central bank.

Concerning the 12 Federal Reserve banks, Strong wished that there were 11 fewer of them.[38] One would do—the Federal Reserve Bank of New York—if that one institution could only emulate the success of Great Britain's central bank, the famous Old Lady of Threadneedle Street.

With a flick of its discount rate, the Bank of England assured that any who wanted to exchange pound notes for gold (or gold for pound notes) would never be turned away. Universal confidence in the integrity of the pound owed not to the size of the Bank's gold reserve (which, in relation to potential claims on that reserve, was small) but rather to the depth of the London money market and the artistry of the Bank's interest-rate policy. If gold were wanted in London, the Bank would raise its rate. What gave potency to these adjustments was Britain's standing as money market to the world. Foreigners loaned and borrowed in London; a sterling bill drawn on one of the mighty London banks was money—good the world over.

Strong saw no reason why New York could not rival London as a financial center—why it could not attract large foreign deposits and finance immense volumes of international trade. To speed the day, he advocated for development of an American market in the kinds of negotiable banking instruments in which London excelled. "Bankers acceptances," tradable drafts on a bank that agrees to pay a certain sum at a certain time, were a particular favorite of Strong's. Let a market in BAs achieve critical mass, and American trade and finance would wonderfully prosper.[39]

There was, however, an important precondition: The typical American banker must be persuaded or cajoled into pooling his reserves in time of crisis rather than clutching them fearfully to his breast. "Frankly," said Strong, "our bankers are more or less an unorganized mob."[40]

In 1916, Strong was diagnosed with tuberculosis. In the same year, his second wife, the former Katherine P. Converse, left him, taking their two young daughters; the couple would divorce in 1920.[41] Edmund C. Converse, Strong's father-in-law and former boss at Bankers Trust, was to leave an estate valued at $20 million on his death in 1921; clearly, Mrs. Strong had no financial reason to remain in an unhappy marriage.[42]

In February 1916, Ben Strong sailed to Europe for a two-month inspection of central banking operations in France and Britain and a tutorial in the modern methods of war finance. It was always on the mind of the governor of the Federal Reserve Bank of New York to join hands with the central bankers of Europe. On March 18, the visiting American dined with Montagu Norman, soon-to-be governor of the Bank of England, in whom Strong found a monetary soulmate. Within minutes of this, their first conversation, Strong noted Norman's worry about the flood of Britain's wartime borrowings and the new paper pound in which these claims were denominated. "[H]e expressed very much the same feelings that I have felt," Strong jotted—"that the ease with which this great mass of Government short loans and currency note issues has been absorbed in circulation would lead to a lot of political quackery and financial heresies, especially with regard to fiat currency or silver issues." [43]

"Price stability," that chestnut of modern central-bank doctrine, was no part of the original remit of the Federal Reserve (the urgings of Irving Fisher notwithstanding). Under the gold standard, prices were reasonably stable in the short to medium run, uncannily stable over the long run. Wiser heads than Fisher doubted that any central bank should even try to tamp down (or, for that matter, raise up) the average level of prices.

With Britain, France and Germany off the gold standard, frightened money found a safe haven in the neutral nation whose currency was still as good as gold. The golden influx swelled the American "monetary base," the foundation on which credit is erected.

In 1915, the base registered growth of 11.2 percent. It grew by 15.2 percent in 1916 and by 20.6 percent in 1917, extraordinary and inflation-propagating rates. [44] The high cost of living over which Fisher had agonized in 1913—consumer prices that year had risen by all of an estimated 2 percent—now went sky high.

The Federal Reserve Act was drafted in a world of peace and limited government. It was implemented in a world of war and statism. It was as if a central bank designed to function on Earth were somehow relocated to Mars. Fixed exchange rates and free gold movements were the hallmarks of prewar monetary arrangements; the Federal Reserve had to adapt on the fly to untethered exchange rates and immobilized stocks of gold.

As vice president of Bankers Trust, Strong had fretted that Federal Reserve notes would be made obligations of the U.S. Treasury. As the Bank of

England's dinner guest, he had shaken his head over the unorthodox turn of Britain's currency and public finances. Yet as governor of the Federal Reserve Bank of New York, he was about to facilitate a 24-fold increase in the American public debt and a questionable union of the central bank with the Wilson administration. At a stroke, Strong became the Treasury Department's monetary yes-man. The perfection that Hartley Withers had perceived in the Edwardian organization of banking and monetary affairs was gone with the wind.

Before the war, it went without saying that no central bank should go buying up the debt of its own government. Such a thing violated the canons of common sense as well as the unspoken rules of the gold standard.*

Besides, before the war there was not much government debt to buy. The calibration of public spending, borrowing and taxing to stabilize the business cycle—"fiscal policy," it has come to be known—was yet uninvented. In the United States, the Treasury had no blanket authority to borrow; Congress reserved to itself the approval of individual security issues or of designated types of securities. Not until 1917, with passage of the Second Liberty Bond Act, did the lawmakers cede to the executive branch the flexibility to borrow in any fashion it chose up to a specified limit, the limit every 21st century newspaper reader knows as the "debt ceiling."[45]

With America's declaration of war, on April 2, 1917, a bipartisan aversion to public debt yielded to a patriotic determination to win the war. There would be no financial constraint on victory, however frighteningly immense the cost might prove to be. In 1916, the government had taken in $783 million and spent $734 million. By 1919, it was taking in $5.1 billion and spending $18.5 billion.[46] Taxes provided just 28 percent of those 1919 outlays. The rest was borrowed.

---

*Or the rarely spoken rules: In 1922, John U. Calkins, later governor of the Federal Reserve Bank of San Francisco, spelled out the taboo against central-bank purchases of government debt at a Federal Reserve governors conference.

"Probably," Calkins asserted, "the most important effect of the Federal Reserve Act was to set up the machinery necessary to provide elastic currency; elastic in that it would be based on self-liquidating credit instruments arising out of the production and distribution of commodities. An obligation of the United States does not represent a transaction of this character . . . to the extent such obligations back the currency such currency is fiat currency." [Meltzer, *History of the Federal Reserve*, 70]

Before America joined the fight, Strong had fretted about the relevance of the Federal Reserve. It could not seem to find a "normal and natural place in the banking structure of the country," he said—and it probably wouldn't, he added, "until it has met the test of a real crisis."[47]

The real crisis, when it came in April 1917, found him nursing his tuberculosis in Colorado. By June, he was back at his post in New York. In the same month, President Wilson signed legislation to bring about the concentration of American gold in Federal Reserve vaults and to expand the number of banks holding Federal Reserve membership. Already, the war was smiling on America's central bank.

The Bank of England had been founded to finance a war (that was in 1694), and Strong rather liked the prospects of the Federal Reserve becoming "banker to the Government." It would raise the system's prestige, especially that of the New York branch, it being understood that Strong and New York would discharge the principal offices of war finance.[48]

While breathing deep the medicinal mountain air, Strong had been studying fiscal policy. Taxation should be the government's primary source of funds, he concluded. Loans should mainly consist of short-term bridges to future tax income. Long-dated bonds should be placed with savers, not excluding the humblest wage earners, who, by investing, would learn the advantages of receiving interest income, instead of paying it. (Not a few of the novice bond holders would incorrectly assume that it was they who owed interest to the government, not vice versa.)[49] To mobilize prospective investors, the nation should mount "an educational campaign of huge proportions," Strong urged.[50] The Federal Reserve, standing on principle, must not itself purchase government debt or directly lend the Treasury newly minted paper dollars, lest inflation run even hotter.

Many were the temptations to do the wrong thing. From some of the most seasoned bankers on Wall Street came the unsolicited advice to funnel dollars directly into the Treasury in the shape of loans or securities purchases. And when the ignoramuses continued to press him, Strong finally challenged them. Maybe, he said, he would do it just so you bankers can find out for yourselves what a $500 million cash infusion would do to the already alarming rate of inflation—$500 million, that is, of fiat currency, no better than the Continentals of the Revolutionary War.[51]

Fiat? Was the dollar still not convertible into gold, which continued to be defined as 23.22 grains of pure gold? It was, indeed, so defined; as to exercising the right to conversion, the authorities discouraged it. And they all but prohibited gold from leaving the country.[52] So the monetary standard to which the United States adhered, alone among the major combatants, was the gold standard chiefly in letter. In spirit and practice it was something more like an expression of intent that, come the peace, the good old dollar would be sound again. Still, it was an expression that not every European belligerent could plausibly make.

The key, Strong told the American Bankers Association in a September 1917 address, was not to allow the exigencies of war to permit a permanent, inflationary expansion of bank credit. The function of the Reserve banks "is to make these temporary loans during periods of strain, whether occasioned by war and government financing, by domestic difficulties, or by any other cause," said Strong. "The exercise of self-control in these matters means that the Reserve banks will see to it that the expansion which they afford to our banking system is that temporary expansion which is represented by a portfolio containing self-liquidating bills and loans which mature within a reasonably short time and which Congress has wisely fixed at 90 days and no longer."[53]

This was on the eve of the Second Liberty Loan, by which the Treasury aimed to raise $3.8 billion. The target would have seemed unreachable, even unimaginable, except for the success of the First Liberty Loan; by June, the government had succeeded in borrowing $1.99 billion. Up until that signal event, the record holder for federal financing was the $200 million raised in 1898 to defeat the Spaniards.[54]

There were Second and Third Liberty Loans, in the respective sums of $4.2 billion and $6.99 billion, both in 1918, as well as a $4.99 billion Victory Loan in 1919. Altogether, the sales brought in $21.5 billion, a figure unlikely to impress a 21st century student of the American public debt but one that elicited gasps from a nation whose debt, at the close of the 1916 fiscal year, had totaled a mere $1.2 billion.[55]

In not every particular did Strong realize his ideal program of war finance. Tax revenues contributed less than 30 percent of the cost of the war. And banks took up a much larger share of the government's issuance than Strong deemed prudent. True, the Federal Reserve did not—except for the relatively modest sum of $330 million—infuse funds directly into the Treasury. But it made a significant, if roundabout, contribution to the roaring inflation of the war era by lending against the collateral of Treasury securities at artificially low interest rates.

"Borrow to buy" was the investment proposition that Strong extended to the American people. A wage earner could borrow the cost of a bond at a bank. He or she could repay the loan at the rate of $1 or $2 a week.[56] The interest rate on the loan was identical to the yield on the bond, which ranged from 3.5 percent to 4.5 percent. For the lending bank, there was money to be made in borrowing from the Federal Reserve. If the bond yielded 3.5 percent, for instance—and the bank's loan against that bond was priced at an identical 3.5 percent—the bank could borrow from a Reserve bank at a cost of as little as 3 percent. If the bond yielded 4.5 percent—and the bank's loan against the bond was priced at the identical 4.5 percent—the bank could borrow from a Reserve bank at as little as 4 percent.[57] Or a bank might choose a more direct route to reap the government-furnished guaranteed profit. It might—as many did—buy Liberty Loans for itself. A Reserve bank would lend against this collateral just the same as it loaned against the collateral of a loan to a bond-buying wage earner.

The nation's bankers did not refuse this valuable gift. The ideal of the self-liquidating loan was all well and good for peacetime. But the war was serving up an intriguing new set of incentives and subsidies. Favoring Liberty Loans over workaday commercial credits, the Reserve banks posted lower lending rates against Treasury obligations than they did against business loans. The bankers proceeded to borrow from the Federal Reserve against little besides the collateral of government securities. Between mid-1917 and mid-1919, commercial bank loans and investments grew to $36.6 billion from $28.3 billion. Between early 1917 and mid-1919, a telltale measure of Federal Reserve accommodation (known as Reserve Bank credit) jumped by tenfold, to more than $2.5 billion.[58]

Up rose the edifice of credit. Disapprove though it might, the Federal Reserve took its marching orders from Congress and the secretary of the Treasury. It was they who determined how much money the government needed and the rate of interest that the government was prepared to pay. The Federal Reserve, an institution not quite five years old on Armistice

Day, could hardly have argued even if it had been inclined to, which it was not.

The ensuing inflation would poison American politics, embitter the relations between American labor and capital, distort the structure of American production, test the Federal Reserve (and find it wanting) and set the stage for a worldwide deflationary depression.

$\star$ **4** $\star$

LAISSEZ-FAIRE
BY ACCIDENT

The war still raged in January 1918 when Woodrow Wilson laid down his Fourteen Points. From the first ("Open covenants of peace, openly arrived at") to the last ("A general association of nations must be formed"), the president described a vision of perpetual peace and perfect and disinterested justice. European diplomats, who approached peace making in a more transactional vein, rolled their eyes.

Preoccupied by war and peace, Wilson left the brainstorming on domestic policy matters to his secretary, Joe Tumulty. "We must no longer attempt to regulate," Tumulty urged his chief in a memo titled "The Revolt of the Underdog." "We must control, own and operate . . . the basic needs of our life." As it was, the government was doing a great deal of controlling and operating. Invoking its emergency war powers, the administration had taken control of the railroads in December 1917 and the telephone and telegraph companies in July 1918. And as it fixed the price of coal, it might as well have owned the coal fields, too. Tumulty regarded these measures as a laboratory in public policy. "[A]fter 1918," he proposed, "we can go to the country, standing for the permanency of those instruments whose use in the War has been demonstrated to be practicable."[1]

"Practicable" by which lights? Wilson's war economy was neither capitalist nor socialist but a dysfunctional amalgam. Inflation had distorted the information embedded in prices and wages even before America had joined the fight. With war came a host of rules and edicts and controls to confound the price mechanism still further. In the case of the railroads, the administration instructed freight forwarders to whisk essential war-related materiel to its destination. But the forwarders' definition of "essential" proved so broad that nothing much changed, except that the towering, stationary piles of boxes were now stamped with the word "priority." Then, too, though the railroads had surrendered effective ownership of their track and rolling stock, each had retained its proprietary and competitive feelings toward its erstwhile private-sector rivals. All in all, there wasn't much to show for the communitarian experiment in government-directed railroading.[2]

The Wilsonians had had their knives out for big business in peacetime, and they liked it no better in wartime. They made no exception even for E. I. du Pont de Nemours and Company, the nation's principal maker of gunpowder. The war was food and drink for the Delaware chemical giant. In 1916, explosives sales to the Allied Powers had pushed DuPont to a profit of $82 million, a sum more than three times greater than the company's gross revenue as recently as 1914. To skim some of these extraordinary earnings for the benefit of the Treasury, the administration enacted a munitions tax, against which DuPont vehemently protested.

Following the American declaration of war, the government went shopping for gunpowder. The army's chief of ordnance, Major General William Crozier, not unreasonably approached DuPont, and the company and the army sat down to negotiate. The resulting contract, which would have been the biggest the government ever signed, went unsigned. Withholding his signature was Newton D. Baker, Wilson's secretary of war, who, while serving in Cleveland's city government before the war, had championed the municipal ownership of streetcar lines and utilities. The United States, he was heard to say, would "win this war without DuPont."

Luckily for the war effort, the nation didn't have to. A costly, ideologically animated and slow-moving attempt to create a government-owned and -managed powder works failed to deliver an ounce of explosives until the day of the Armistice. Belatedly, DuPont and Baker did effect a rapprochement, and the resulting production facility at Muscle Shoals, Tennessee, turned out 35 million pounds of powder. Apropos of the relationship between man and state, Robert Brookings, the chief price controller of the War Industries Board, had spoken for at least some of the Wilsonians with these words: "I would rather pay a dollar a pound for powder for the United States in a state of war if there was no profit in it than pay the DuPont Company 50 cents a pound if they had 10 cents profit in it."[3]

In January 1918, America's economy was stymied and half frozen. Coal was in short supply in the coldest winter in half a century. The reason for the scarcity lay neither with the miners nor with the mine operators—nor, really, with the newly commandeered railroads. The underlying difficulty was rather a price set too low to ration demand or to call forth adequate supply. And who was this errant czar of the coal price? Why, none other than Woodrow Wilson.

Three dollars a ton was a good and fair price for bituminous coal, a high-level conference of coal producers and federal officials had decided in the summer of 1917. The president brushed aside that consensus opinion; the maximum price of soft coal would rather be $2 a ton, he ruled.[4] Miners and operators each protested, the operators contending that the price Wilson imposed would shut off 22 percent of American production by forcing the closure of marginal mines.[5] The president refused to budge.

It didn't help that winter produced a spell of arctic cold sufficient to freeze Boston harbor; the ice on which the Bostonians skated on New Year's Eve was six inches thick. The below-zero temperatures reduced the efficiency of freight engines by a quarter, even as it locked up waterborne transportation in ice. In the decade leading up to 1917–1918, Americans had consumed an average of 10,705 trillion Btus of bituminous coal per annum; in those two economically charged (and, in the case of 1918, freezing) wartime years, they consumed an average of 14,212 trillion Btus per annum.

It would have taken a United States fuel administrator of superhuman prescience to match the success of the market in organizing the production and distribution of coal. The president's point man in fuel, Harry A. Garfield, the president of Williams College, was not that freak of nature. The son of assassinated President James A. Garfield (he had watched his father get shot), he failed at his impossible job.

Garfield seemed not to suspect how great were the odds against him. Under interrogation by hostile U.S. senators on January 16, 1918, he affirmed his belief in the necessity of government rationing. It was to stretch the nation's inadequate supply of coal, Garfield said, that he ordered non-essential eastern factories to close for five consecutive days—and on each Monday, and four other days besides, up to and including March 23.

Senator James Alexander Reed, Democrat of Missouri, asked Garfield how the forced suspension of production by three million workers for 15 days in the middle of the epic cold snap would help win the war. "We have been told that food will win the war," the senator reminded him; "we have been told that coal will win the war, and we have been told very frequently that money and bonds will win the war." It was all very well to say that one must sacrifice and that mere dollars were not the point of the war effort, but wealth itself was a weapon. Why toss it away?

Garfield parried that the shutdowns would allow him to divert precious coal to the bunkers of coal-burning ships then idled for lack of fuel, as well as to the furnaces of freezing American homeowners. But in the time-honored way of price controls, one regulation created the need for others. The more Garfield promulgated, the greater the number of clarifying rules and exceptions to those rules he found it necessary to issue. In Boston, James J. Storrow, the fuel administrator for New England, telegraphed Garfield in early January to beseech him to redirect 5,100 tons of coal to Boston from Hampton Roads, Virginia, where it had been landed for the account of the Great Northern Paper Company, a manufacturer of newsprint.[6] In shivering New York City, all the coal that anyone could want was piled up across the Hudson River in New Jersey. What no one could seem to figure out was how to move it lawfully across the water. "Railroad men," the *New York Times* reported, "commenting on the statement that it was the duty of the carriers to put the coal into New York docks, said that of the hundreds of railroad tariffs promulgated by the Interstate Commerce Commission not one provided a tariff for coal from the mines to New York City. The tariffs all provided charges for transportation of coal from the mines to tidewater."[7]

The cold would eventually break—one could depend on that, at least—but there was no such confidence in the leadership of the president, nor in his ability to administer the formerly free-market economy by executive fiat.

Ten months after the American declaration of war, American-made planes and machine guns had still not made their appearance in France. The administration's much-vaunted ship-building program was drastically behind schedule. The cost of living was zooming higher. And now, on top of "Meatless Mondays" (an institution of the food administrator, Herbert Hoover), came a succession of "Heatless Mondays" courtesy of Harry Garfield.

"[T]he military establishment of America has fallen down," Senator George E. Chamberlain, Democrat of Oregon and chairman of the Senate Committee on Military Affairs, told a glittering lunchtime throng at the Astor Hotel in New York on January 19, 1918. And the reason it fell, declared the senator, was "because of inefficiency in every bureau and department of the Government of the United States." To set things right, Chamberlain urged that a new, three-man "war cabinet" take over from the administration's discredited planners. The luncheon guests rose to their feet and applauded the senator for a full minute; Theodore Roosevelt and Winston Churchill were among them.[8]

The military establishment of America righted itself in time to contribute to the stirring Allied successes in the early autumn of 1918. As to the American financial establishment, it made its own contributions to the war effort. And at the head of this massed money power was Benjamin Strong in his dual capacities as governor of the Federal Reserve Bank of New York and chairman of the Liberty Loan Committee. It was Strong to whom the White House turned to make a speech at the Metropolitan Opera House in New York on September 27, 1918, on the occasion of the opening of the sale of the Fourth Liberty Loan. Following Strong on the dais would be President Wilson himself.

For Strong, the assignment was more than a personal triumph. It marked the arrival of the Federal Reserve on the national stage. An institution that could not seem to find a place in American finance now bathed in the limelight.

The Met seated 3,500, but the personnel of the "Liberty Loan Army," Strong's bond-selling shock troops, numbered 30,000. The evening's festivities were intended to celebrate them. With room for 50 notables on the stage and standing room for another 1,450, attendance would approach

5,000. New York's affluent patriots had begged for tickets—said they would pay any price—only to be told that none were for sale.

Strong led off the evening with a pledge that, over the next three weeks, the people of the Second Federal Reserve District—his district—would raise no less than $1.8 billion of a planned $6 billion. "Dollars for democracy," the central banker called them. It would be easy enough to *compel* subscriptions, he said. "But by that method we would lose the moral and spiritual forces which are behind the loan, behind the war and behind our men. We must not only sell bonds—we must sell the war to all the people of the United States."*

Wilson won the loudest cheers of the night by just walking into the hall. (He had been cheered all afternoon as he drove around Manhattan in an open car; acknowledging the people, he had smiled and doffed his top hat.) But Strong, too, stirred the crowd. He read aloud a message that the White House had received concerning the first day of a new American offensive. This was the push into the Meuse-Argonne, an engagement that would last for six weeks and claim more than 26,000 American lives, the deadliest toll of any battle in American history. Neither knowing nor anticipating these terrible facts, Strong rather said:

"Cables from France today indicate a continuous advance of the American forces over a front of 20 miles, from the Argonne Forest to the Valley of the Meuse, north of Verdun, passing beyond the Hindenburg Line on the entire front and gaining back 100 square miles of French territory. The movement was sharp and quick. Our casualties were light."

A month and a half later, on November 11, the guns fell silent. The war was won. As to the peace, President Wilson resolved to secure it himself.

As he himself admitted, Wilson had a "single-track mind." When dealing with problems, he tackled them one at a time. Come the Armistice, his singular focus was on peace. He waited only a week to announce his intention personally to achieve a settlement to conform to the letter and spirit of the Fourteen Points. And hardly had the Republican side of the Senate regained

---

*Strong later testified that he himself had sold almost everything he had and invested the proceeds in Liberty bonds. [*Wall Street Journal*, August 10, 1921]

its composure over the news of this most extraordinary demarche than the American peace commission set sail for Europe aboard the SS *George Washington.*

Had the president noticed the results of the 1918 congressional elections, in which the Republicans picked up 38 additional seats in the House, to give them a majority of 238 to 193; and 12 more seats in the Senate, to make a Republican majority of 2?[9] It seemed he had not. It would fall to the Senate to vote up or down any treaty that the president managed to negotiate. Yet the president had chosen to invite not one prominent Republican, senator or other, to join the peace commission. In the opinion of the Republican chairman of the Senate Foreign Relations Committee, Henry Cabot Lodge of Massachusetts, Wilson's newfangled idealism cloaked a most conventional partisanship.

Never before had a sitting president left the country, let alone taken leave for the purpose of negotiating with foreign powers. There was, of course, no flitting back and forth from Europe in those days, no shuttle diplomacy. A speedy voyage took eight or ten days. Tumulty, left behind in Washington to look after domestic affairs, corresponded with his chief by post and cable.

Wilson landed in France on December 13 and remained for more than two months; he returned to the United States on February 23, 1919. Intending to put into New York, the SS *George Washington*, bearing the president's party, instead repaired to Boston on account of a dockworkers' strike at the port of New York—an ominous reminder of the fractured state of American labor relations. Wilson was then back in Paris on March 13, and remained there through the spring.

"Issue of high cost of living most acute . . . ," Tumulty cabled him on May 10. "You cannot understand how acute situation is brought about by rising prices of every necessity of life."[10] On June 4, the day after the bomb exploded on Attorney General Palmer's doorstep, Tumulty addressed a heartfelt letter to his boss on the urgent need for a radical redistribution of the national income between capital and labor.

"[A]sk Congress to avow its faith in the principles found in the Peace Treaty with reference to the fundamental rights of labor," Tumulty advised. "I think this plan will do more than anything else to save the situation which now threatens us." What, practically speaking, would such a strategy entail? Among other things, a federal minimum wage, a federally mandated eight-hour day "affecting all business and industry," old-age pensions, federal health insurance, federal housing, "control of fundamental raw materials," federally subsidized mortgages, the federal regulation of securities issues and a federal employment agency.[11] The proposed Tumulty agenda was a kind of pre-vision of the next several generations' worth of social, economic and regulatory legislation. Missing from the program was that attention to the overall economy that dominates 21st century public policy debate; federal management of the business cycle was an idea yet uncrystallized.

On June 16, Tumulty advised his chief: "There have been many dangerous symptoms of economic unrest, but we have succeeded, at least, in lessening them and keeping them in check."[12] Wilson returned, once and for all, to America on July 8. Next day, the headlines about his landfall—New Yorkers celebrated it with a tickertape parade[13]—knocked the high cost of living off the front page.

Wilson and Tumulty, each a political animal, shared the erroneous conviction that inflation was a political problem. It could not be addressed until the conclusion of a satisfactory peace, Tumulty said.[14] From this misconception sprang the non sequitur that what blocked the path to stable prices was neither the Treasury nor the Federal Reserve but the Senate Foreign Relations Committee.

Economic life was, and deserved to be, politicized, Wilson believed. A measure of socialism was certain, he remarked to friends one evening at the White House in the summer of 1919. "I am perfectly sure that the state has got to control everything that everybody needs and uses," the president said. From which fact it followed that his successor must "be a man who reflects long and deeply on these complicated relationships of our time."[15]

This was the "Red summer" of murderous race riots, including, between July 19 and July 22, pitched battles between blacks and whites fought in Washington, D.C.[16] Not so far in the background was the soaring cost of living, up in July in the 48 states by an average of 15.2 percent. Wilson's mind was elsewhere. "Shall we or any other free people hesitate to accept this great duty?" the president demanded in his July 10 address to the Senate, urging ratification of the peace treaty. "Dare we reject it and break the heart of the world?"

• • •

The fight for the treaty and the League was the fight of his life, and the president was determined to bring his case to the people. Naturally, he would travel by train—if, that is, he could secure one. The railroads had been hobbled for months by wildcat strikes. And now the shopmen threatened a nationwide walkout for September 2. As the railroads were still under federal control, the president was, in effect, the national railroad chief executive. Meeting with union leaders late in August, he mollified them with a 5.9 percent raise and some commiserating talk about their "common enemy . . . the profiteer." The unions had demanded more, but Wilson assured them that the rate of inflation had "certainly reached its peak." Deploring Wilson's concessions to "the autocratic brotherhoods," the *Wall Street Journal* editorially called for the 19th century president who had expounded the doctrine that, while the people should support the government, the government shouldn't support the people. "Oh for one hour of Cleveland!" the editors sighed.[17]

The strike was off, and the tracks were clear. Wilson would depart from Union Station, Washington, on September 3 at 6.40 PM, on a journey of 9,981 miles and 27 days. He would be accompanied by the First Lady, Edith Bolling Wilson; Tumulty; and the president's personal physician, Cary Grayson. The train's seven cars would carry assorted White House staff, including one servant each for the president and First Lady, eight Secret Service men, two dozen reporters and a double train crew.

"This is a business trip, pure and simple," Wilson had reproached those who, like Grayson and his wife, begged him to allow some time for rest. He would be making ten or more speeches a day from the rear platform of the train. There would be 26 major stops. Rest was out of the question.[18]

On the evening of the 22nd day of the journey, on the edge of Wichita, Kansas, Wilson suffered a raging headache. He couldn't sleep—in no position could he compose himself. The agony persisted when he sat up in a chair. Propped up by pillows, he slept for a while, then roused himself to shave and dress for his next speech. But when he emerged from the bathroom, Grayson and Mrs. Wilson noticed that his face had fallen. And as he mumbled his words, saliva dribbled from the left side of his mouth. "Gentlemen," Tumulty presently addressed the newspapermen. "We are not going to Wichita. The president is very ill. It will be necessary for us to start back for Washington as soon as the railroad arrangements are completed, and we will go through with no stops other than those that are imperative."[19]

Wilson had had a stroke. Visible enough was the damage to the left side of his body. Invisible was the intellectual impairment that Grayson was sure he detected, but of which he breathed not a word to anyone outside of the White House inner circle.

The president's special train pulled back into Union Station on Sunday morning, September 28. A thousand or so people watched a man with a lopsided smile walk under his own power to a waiting open car. Though the Sunday streets were almost deserted, the president "reached up and took off his hat and bowed as if he were returning the greetings of a vast throng," related Gene Smith, in *When the Cheering Stopped*. "Enough people saw what he had done to send flying through Washington the information that the President is physically all right but salutes empty sidewalks. He has lost his mind."[20]

At the White House, Wilson's head continued to pound. He couldn't sleep or work or read. He saw no visitors. During moments of surcease, he would go to dinner with members of his family, sign some minor bills, read the Bible aloud or shoot some billiards. Then one morning—it was October 2—he awakened to find that he had lost all feeling in his left hand. His wife helped him to the bathroom. While she left him long enough to summon Grayson, Wilson took a fall. She returned to find him unconscious on the floor. "The President is a very sick man," said Grayson's bulletin to the press. "His condition is less favorable today and he has remained in bed throughout the day." He was, in fact, paralyzed.[21]

Rumor rushed in to fill the vacuum of fact. "From the beginning of his illness to the present moment," the Democratic *New York World* editorialized, "not a word has come from the sick-chamber that can be regarded as frankly enlightening. Mystery begets mystification."[22]

On October 3, the first trading day after release of the incomplete news of the president's illness, prices on the New York Stock Exchange quickly recovered from opening losses. "Not only are big owners of stock induced to retain their holdings by considerations arising out of the income tax," the *Wall Street Journal* said," but they realize that the war has brought about vast improvement in the financial status of the majority of the larger industrial corporations of the United States."[23]

At about this time, former President William Howard Taft, returning from a visit to Washington, bumped into William McAdoo on the train.

According to McAdoo, the president was in "a state of collapse," though his mind was "clear." His doctors had ordered him to not engage in public affairs.[24]

Vice President Thomas R. Marshall, an Indiana politician chiefly remembered for the aperçu "What this country needs is a really good five-cent cigar," knew no more than the average newspaper reader about what had happened to Wilson. The secretary of agriculture, David F. Houston, knew the truth because Tumulty had confided in him. But Houston would not break his confidence with Tumulty to enlighten even the next in line for the presidency.[25] Anyway, Marshall preferred his own job to Wilson's: "No responsibilities," he noted.[26]

On October 6, the cabinet met at the behest of Secretary of State Robert Lansing. "The business of the government must go on," the secretary of state said. But how? Grayson was summoned. Exactly what is the president's condition? Lansing demanded. In his reply, the doctor came closest to the truth when he said "the scales might tip either way and they might tip the wrong way." Grayson added that Wilson had directed him to ask by whose authority the meeting had been called.[27]

So the government that during the war had seemed to be everywhere and anywhere now grew slack and inert. Mrs. Wilson stood ferocious guard over her husband. Nobody saw him, no paper passed in front of his eyes, except by her leave. No more First Lady, the joke went, Mrs. Wilson had ascended to "Acting First Man."[28]

Lansing wrote the Thanksgiving Day proclamation, and Tumulty, after soliciting suggestions from the cabinet, drafted the president's annual message to Congress. Most official correspondence was left to pile up, unanswered, though Mrs. Wilson attended to some of it in her own way:

> Over the wide left margins of an elegantly typed letter, down to the bottom space under the typing, up the right margin and then across the top, weaving in and out of the title of the writer and his seal of office, there were each day penciled notes by a woman who had a total of just two years of formal schooling and whose round and enormous script resembled that of a twelve-year-old.[29]

Though President Wilson was anything but himself, he retained his single-track mind. The peace treaty consumed what little attention he still could summon. Left to sort themselves out were, among other difficulties, a threatened coal strike, racial violence, the Red scare, inflation and—in November 1919—a rise in interest rates sufficiently steep and surprising to jolt the formerly imperturbable stock market. The treaty—the League—was the all-absorbing focus of the capital city.[30] To Wilson, it was the all-absorbing question not only of politics but also of morality. "Better a thousand times to go down fighting than to dip your colors to dishonorable compromise," he said.[31]

A sick man under his wife's protection, the president settled in for a war of attrition with the Senate. It seemed "as though our Government has gone out of business," recorded the journalist Ray Stannard Baker late in December 1919.[32] "The deadlock is so complete that one would almost be justified in saying that the United States had no Government," the new British ambassador to the United States, Sir Auckland Geddes, advised Prime Minister Lloyd George in June 1920.[33]

Circumstances had set the stage for the last governmentally untreated business depression in America.

★ 5 ★

A DEPRESSION IN FACT

In 1920, Americans spoke of "prosperity" and "depression," of "inflation" and "deflation," but not yet of an "economy."* Still less did they identify an organic enterprise for the government to manage and stimulate. In the 1920 Republican Party platform, the only comment on "national economy" referred to the stewardship of the federal finances.

It was possible, still, to see that the bottom was dropping out of business. According to *Historical Statistics of the United States*, gross national product, before adjustment for changes in prices, plunged to $69.6 billion in 1921 from $91.5 billion in 1920, a loss of 24 percent. Even after making allowances for falling prices, the decline in national output amounted to 9 percent. For perspective, the Great Recession of 2007–09 delivered a drop

---

*The word "macroeconomics" was coined by the Norwegian Nobel laureate Ragnar Frisch in the 1930s, though the Austrian economist Eugen Bohm-Bawerk anticipated Frisch by writing, in 1891: "One cannot eschew studying the microcosm if one wants to understand properly the macrocosm of a developed country." [Mark Skousen, *The Making of Modern Economics: The Lives and Ideas of the Great Thinkers* (Armonk, N.Y.: M. E. Sharpe, 2001), 353]

in nominal gross domestic product of 2.4 percent, a price-adjusted fall of 4.3 percent. From 1920 to 1921, the Federal Reserve's index of industrial production fell by 31.6 percent; in 2007–09, it declined by 16.9 percent.

Christina D. Romer, a leading economist of the present day, has contended that defective government data vastly overstate the ostensible 9 percent decline in real GNP. Yes, commodity prices collapsed, Romer acknowledged, but their very plunge was a tonic for commodity consumers. Manufacturers' profit margins fattened as the cost of raw materials fell. In effect, Romer would downgrade the apparent 1920–21 economic hurricane to a kind of middling tropical storm.*

Twenty-first century measurements of national output are fiendishly complex and, in part for that reason, inexact. One therefore treads lightly on the statistical ground of 1920–21. The U.S. Department of Labor, which traces its bureaucratic roots to 1888, had made no attempt to measure unemployment prior to the 1914 slump. A canvass in 1921 found that 4,270,000 Americans were jobless. Out of a nonfarm labor force of 27,989,000, this would have put a crude measure of the unemployment rate at 15.3 percent (without reference to those who, discouraged, may have abandoned the search for work, or who worked less than they wanted to or needed to). The data are, at best, indicative. Indicative of the national mood was the May 1921 enactment of a bill to restrict immigration to 3 percent of the nationals of each country who were present in the 48 states in 1910. Legislative sponsors couched the Quota Act as a safeguard of the body politic against foreign radicalism. The executive council of the American Federation of Labor opposed the measure because, in a time of high unemployment, it did not go far enough to protect the interests of American job seekers.[1]

More easily documentable than the rise in unemployment is the fall in prices. Over the course of 12 months, wholesale prices plunged by 36.8 percent, consumer prices by 10.8 percent and farm prices by 41.3 percent (for speed of decline, not even the Great Depression would match the break of

---

*Romer, a former chairman of the Council of Economic Advisers, presented her research, titled "World War I and the Postwar Depression," in a 1988 essay in the *Journal of Monetary Economics*. The case she made for discarding one set of GNP estimates for another is highly technical. But a lay reader may be struck by the fact that neither the GNP data she rejected, nor the ones she preferred, were compiled in the moment. Rather, each set was constructed some 30 to 40 years after the events it was intended to document.

1920–21). The Dow Jones Industrial Average, then comprising 20 stocks rather than today's 30, crested in November 1919 at 119.62 and bottomed in August 1921 at 63.9, for a peak-to-trough decline of 46.6 percent. Bond prices fell, too, dealing large losses to patriotic buyers of the government's Liberty and Victory issues. Especially hard hit were those who had taken up the Federal Reserve on its invitation to invest with borrowed money. While the value of the asset in which they had invested bore a sharp markdown in price, the debt they had shouldered to buy it remained fixed at 100 cents on the dollar. By May 1920, the Liberty 4¼s of 1947 changed hands for as little as 82 cents on the dollar to yield 5.5 percent. Not since the Civil War had the quoted value of the government's obligations reflected so jaundiced a view of the nation's credit.

There is no such precision in calculating the decline in national income. In contending that the 1920–21 downturn was little more than a bump in the road, Romer invoked data compiled by the econometrician John Kendrick in 1961. She judged these figures to be a large improvement over the official Commerce Department estimates that Kendrick also helped to prepare and that were published in 1959 and revised but once, in 1965, and then only superficially.[2] These data, certainly inadequate by 21st century standards, are perpetuated in the standard reference volumes of *Historical Statistics of the United States.*

It is useful here to recall the contention of the 20th century economist Oskar Morgenstern that the best of the estimates of national output are educated guesses. The educated guesses derived from 40-year-old statistics of uncertain accuracy would seem especially problematic. (Not until 1990—seven decades after the events in question—did government econometricians actually begin to measure the service portion of the American economy.) Quoting Simon Kuznets, the dean of national income accounting, Morgenstern observed: "Since the data in national income studies are 'partly a by-product of administrative activity, partly a result of direct observation of complex phenomena without controls designed to reduce the variations observed, the best we can do is to express an opinion in quantitative form.'"[3]

What, then, can one say about the slump of 1920–21, and on the strength of which evidence can one say it? One can observe that the depression had a visible cause—namely, the preceding inflation. Inflation distorts not only prices and values but also the very architecture of an inflating economy. The inflation of 1915–19 changed the way people invested, consumed and planned. Rising prices invited speculation. Low interest rates and easy money emboldened the speculators. Easily accessible credit distorted the visible odds on success and failure alike. Businesses that otherwise might have gone under enjoyed a new lease (or many new leases) on life, thanks to their optimistic lenders. In the 1915–19 runup to the depression, the number of bankrupt businesses, and the liabilities of those bankrupts, dropped to half of what they had been before the war.[4]

Because 1919 had failed to deliver the widely anticipated postwar depression, industrialists, bankers and farmers made plans for a still hotter boom. Certainly, many industrialists invested, some bankers loaned and most farmers planted as if more inflation were in the offing. When those expectations collided with the facts of tight credit, punitively high interest rates and falling prices, the industrialists, bankers and farmers recoiled. Recorded the business-cycle historian Wesley Clair Mitchell, writing in the late 1920s: "Every price decline made the financial position of overexpanded enterprises worse, reinforced the fears of insolvency and the pressure for liquidating indebtedness, thus increased the pressure to realize upon stocks of goods, and so forced prices still lower."[5]

By the contemporary reckoning of the English economist T.E. Gregory, the world in 1921 was "nearer collapse than it has been at any time since the downfall of the Roman Empire."[6] Certainly, in America, there was no mistaking the postwar zeitgeist with the Era of Good Feelings. Preceding the race riots and Red scare of 1919–20 was the worldwide influenza pandemic of 1918–19; it killed 40 million people, including 675,000 Americans.* With the advent of Prohibition in January 1920, a major industry was outlawed (yes, said the evangelist Billy Sunday, but "Hell will be forever for rent.").[7] On September 16, 1920, a terrorist explosion on Wall Street killed 38 and wounded 300.[8] Later, in September, a grand jury started hearing evidence into the Chicago White Sox's alleged fixing of the 1919 World Series.

Joblessness in 1921 was a problem of sufficient national gravity to spur the newly elected Warren G. Harding to convene the President's

---

*The population of the United States stood at 103 million; American battlefield deaths in World War I totaled 117,465.

Conference on Unemployment. Herbert Hoover, the hyperenergetic secretary of commerce (and, the quip went, the assistant secretary of everything else), took the lead in this undertaking. An outgrowth of the conference was a sprawling survey that was published in 1929 under the title *Recent Economic Changes in the United States.**

Hoover et al.'s more than 1,000 pages of facts, description and analysis make a good case that 1920–21 was something much worse than a recession. Thus, for instance, between those two years, auto production fell by 23 percent, the number of companies reporting net income in excess of $100,000 fell by 45 percent and hourly manufacturing wages fell by 22 percent. According to *Recent Economic Changes*, average disposable farm income (derived only from farming, as opposed to sideline occupations) between 1919–20 and 1920–21 fell by 56.7 percent, no small thing when the agricultural economy contributed between 17 percent and 18 percent of national income.[9] Commercial failures tripled between 1919 and 1921, from 6,451 to 19,652, while the aggregate liabilities of the bankrupts climbed by more than fivefold, from $113 million to $627 million.[10] "The physical volume of product turned out by American manufacturing industry has increased steadily since 1899," Hoover et al. asserted. "There has been but one year of marked drop, namely, 1921."

A 1920 recession turned into a 1921 depression, according to Mitchell, whose judgment, as a historian, business-cycle theorist and contemporary observer, is probably as reliable as anyone's. This was no mere American dislocation but a global depression ensnaring nearly all the former Allied Powers (the defeated Central Powers suffered a slump of their own in 1919). "Though the boom of 1919, the crisis of 1920 and the depression of 1921 followed the patterns of earlier cycles," wrote Mitchell, "we have seen how much this cycle was influenced by economic conditions resulting from the war and its sudden ending. . . . If American business men were betrayed by postwar demands into unwise courses, so were all business men in all countries similarly situated."[11]

So depression it was: What would the government do about it? It would

---

*An evident homage to a volume of the same title by David A. Wells, published in 1889. In making sense of the hurtling transformation of America's economy in the late 19th century, Wells, a newspaperman, inventor and statistician, anticipated Joseph Schumpeter's notion of "creative destruction." The Hoover-organized study took a Wellsian approach to the dizzyingly inventive decade of the 1920s.

implement settled doctrine, as governments usually do. In 1920–21, this meant balancing the federal budget, raising interest rates to protect the Federal Reserve's gold position and allowing prices and wages to find a new, lower level. Critically, what it would *not* do was what the Hoover administration so energetically attempted to do a decade later: There would be no federally led drive to maintain nominal wage rates and no governmentally orchestrated work sharing. For this reason, not least, no one would wind up affixing the label "great" on the depression of 1920–21.

In New York City on the evening of December 19, 1919, Charles M. Schwab, founder of Bethlehem Steel Corporation, looked out over the vastness of the Waldorf Astoria's ballroom to address the well-dressed diners of the Pennsylvania Society. Labor and capital must come together to reap the rewards of a certain and beckoning prosperity, the industrialist said. But, he cautioned, "There are breakers ahead; there are rapids through which we must pass."

"What breakers?" the auto magnates of Detroit might have demanded of Schwab in return. America's auto industry—almost the nation's biggest and certainly its most vibrant line of business—saw only green lights.* Production was on its way to doubling in 1920, after having almost doubled in 1919.[12] Ford would build one million cars and trucks, GM almost 900,000.[13]

Billy Durant, the flamboyant visionary who headed GM, did go on record in October 1919 to warn against the practice of investing funds the company intended to earn but did not actually possess.[14] Nor was the man after whom the projected Durant Building named happy about spending many millions of dollars on an edifice to house a growing and costly GM bureaucracy.[15]

But the optimists—and Durant was usually among the most bullish of the lot—carried the day. After all, an overheated boom seemed a happy kind of problem. Fuel, materials and railcars were in short supply. Satisfied workers, too, were scarce, to judge by the strikes in steel and coal.[16] And credit

---

*Fully imbibing the boomtime optimism of his parishioners, the Reverend Dr. Thomas G. Sykes resigned from the affluent Grosse Pointe Church in suburban Detroit on February 17, 1920, to enter the real estate business. "I do not care to end my days in a home for ministers," said Dr. Sykes, whose vestry had paid him $4,000 a year with free rent and utilities. [*New York Times*, February 18, 1920]

was becoming costly, if not yet scarce, as the Federal Reserve started to raise interest rates. But of opportunity, there was a world's worth. Motorized transport was scarcely out of short pants. Out of every thousand residents, California recorded only 160 passenger car registrations; Florida had 66 and New York 51. In the same three states, not even a quarter of the roads were surfaced.[17]

In automobiles, therefore, the sky was the limit. It only remained for Detroit to solve such temporal problems as the chronic shortage of sheet steel. In 1919, the steel industry obliged with the construction of a single cold mill. In 1920, it built 87 and had 48 more under construction.[18] Pittsburgh saw what Detroit saw.

General Motors was all forward motion. In vain did the corporation's inventory-allotment committee lecture the GM division heads about the need for cautious buying. As prices would certainly be higher tomorrow than they were today, the operating chiefs reasoned, it was prudent to buy today. In the circumstances, it was prudent to pay most any price.[19]

The car-buying public demurred. By springtime 1920, consumers had stopped buying. The dip in demand coincided with a rise in interest rates and a bulge in GM's inventories to $185 million in June, from $137 million in January.[20]

Demand continued to weaken until, in July and August, it nearly vanished. On September 21, 1920, Henry Ford announced a price cut on the Model T to $440, from $575 (optional was a $70 electric starter).[21] General Motors at first refused to match the Ford reductions, then bowed to necessity. By late October, inventories of parts and materials reached $210 million, some $60 million over budget.

In flush times, General Motors was self-financing; now it turned to its banks. Before the macroeconomic brakes started to screech in early summer, GM had sold an average of 52,000 vehicles a month; in November, it sold 13,000; in January 1921, just 6,150. Great piles of parts and sheet metal were not only redundant but also, in view of the collapse in industrial-metals prices, overvalued; $84.9 million worth of inventory was written off as a dead loss.

Durant himself carried a double load of care, not only for the company he founded and led, but also for its sinking stock price. In the opening months of 1920, a share of GM was quoted in the mid-30s; by early July, it traded at 25. Durant, a major GM investor, bought more as the price weakened. Critically, he did not own his shares outright but borrowed to buy them; in Wall Street parlance, he was "margined." Margin debt enhances the intensity of the speculative experience. Putting down as little as 10 cents on the dollar, as one could in those days, a speculator would double his money on a 10 percent rise in the price of the margined shares. Alternatively, he would lose everything on a 10 percent decline. In case of a decline, the broker would call for more collateral—a "margin call." If the call went unanswered, the client's shares would be dumped for whatever price they might fetch.

An intuitive and impulsive business manager (although one who could amaze and confound his subordinates by his mastery of operational detail), Durant was a daring and not altogether focused speculator. It came to light in November 1920 that he had no real idea how many GM shares he owned—too many, certainly, in view of their falling price—or how much money he owed his brokers. His brokers, at least, had an idea: It was their belief that he owed as much as $38 million.[22]

The facts, as they finally emerged, shocked and frightened even such steady hands as the partners of J.P. Morgan & Co. They judged that the size of Durant's exposure posed a risk not only to Durant and GM but also to the nation's financial system. To the rescue, therefore, rode the Morgan bank, as well as E.I. du Pont de Nemours and Company, the latter a substantial investor in GM. Over the course of four days, including an unrestful Sunday, the sleep-deprived rescue team managed to raise some $60 million, enough to allow Durant a dignified, though anything but remunerative, exit from his position. After cleaning up his debts, the entrepreneur confessed that he was dead broke.[23] As of December 1, 1920, he was out of a job, too.[24]

"The automobile market had nearly vanished and with it our income," recounted Alfred Sloan of the state of the company at the close of 1920. "Most of our plants and those of the industry were shut down or assembling a small number of cars out of semifinished materials in the plants. We were loaded with high-priced inventory and commitments at the old inflated price level. We were short of cash. We had a confused product line. There was a lack of control and of any means of control in operations and finance, and a lack of adequate information about anything. In short, there was just about as much crisis, inside and outside, as you could wish for if you liked that sort of thing."*

American farmers, assuredly, had even less zest for crisis than did the management of General Motors, but the depression treated them even worse than it did the company that Durant built. A little like GM, agriculture enjoyed the boom, though it was enjoyment without the modern conveniences. Only a small fraction of farmers were able to respond "yes" when the 1920 federal census takers inquired if their homes had indoor plumbing, a radio or electricity. Better was the farmer's position in relative terms. The lingering wartime inflation pushed up prices of the things he sold. The total value of the 1919 harvest reached $15.9 billion, up from $14.2 billion in 1918, $13.5 billion in 1917—and an average of $5.9 billion a year in the five years ended in 1914. True, the shrunken dollars of 1919 bought less than did prewar money, and costs went up along with income. But farmers in 1919 had at least kept pace with the improving circumstances of their city cousins.[25]

The farm economy still played a critical part in the now largely industrial United States. Some 10.6 million people, or 28 percent of the American workforce, were engaged in agriculture. Almost half the American population still lived in open country or in villages of fewer than 2,500 people.[26] Everyone either farmed or knew someone who did. And though country people were deficient in spending power, they still had the vote.

In the first full year of peace, the overseas demand for American food and fiber seemed inexhaustible. To feed and clothe war-ravaged Europe, farmers planted 49,261,000 acres, the highest figure in American history, 15.6 million more than the average in the five years till 1914.[27] Improved growing methods made heretofore untilled land ripe for the plow. Yields per acre, which long had been rising, would continue to rise, anyone could see. New machinery and insecticides, better crop-rotation methods, improved

---

*Improved management methods saw General Motors through the Great Depression in relatively sound condition. "With the big depression—from 1930 to 1934—there was contraction at General Motors," Sloan related. "But this time, unlike 1920–21, and despite its greater severity, the contraction was orderly." [Sloan, *My Years at GM*, 199]

plant strains and more canny use of fertilizers held out the promise of sustained prosperity.[28]

Such was the cheerful prospect as the 1919 bumper harvest was carried in. The spring of 1920—backward, cold, wet—seemed for a time to break the charmed cycle. But the skies brightened, and farmers got into their fields. Prevailing high prices induced planting from fencepost to fencepost.

Costs kept pace with inflating prices and presently outran them. After they had literally or figuratively seen Paris, many returning doughboys opted not to return to the farm. Those who did could command $5 a day for their services, 140 percent above the 1914 average.[29] Land prices were soaring—Iowa corn fields commanded $225 an acre in 1920, up from less than $100 an acre in 1910—and interest rates were elevated; to raise an operating loan for the 1920 growing season, a farmer could pay as much as 8 percent.[30] Mortgage debt was another burdensome expense, though one that bullish farmers had loaded on themselves. Secured debt on owner-operated farms had more than doubled, to $4 billion from $1.7 billion, between 1910 and 1920. Real estate taxes were twice as high as the prewar average,[31] though they were as nothing compared to the ruinous surge in railroad freight rates. Effective August 26, 1920, just in time for the fall harvest season, railroads lifted their rates by 25 percent to 40 percent. It was a long-overdue adjustment to peacetime economics from wartime controls, as the railroads saw the situation. The farmers called it theft.

Rising costs, though never welcome to those who pay them, did not seem insupportable in the spring of 1920. Prices were high enough to allow a farmer to absorb them. Then, too, Herbert Hoover was warning about food shortages, and the sophisticated New York press was speculating about $5 per bushel of wheat, up from the then-quoted price of $2.25 a bushel: In the *New York World*, some guesswork about still higher crop prices was run out under the headline "The Farm Crisis and the Fear of Food Shortage."[32] Prices had, in fact, by that time already begun to wobble, in the city as well as in the country. The Federal Reserve had begun to tighten credit, and Japan had suffered its deflationary panic. But the wobbling was more evident in hindsight than it was in the moment. In June, *Wallace's Farmer*, a widely read agricultural journal, shrugged off "vague rumors of a panic in the near future."

"[P]ersonally," the *Wallace's* editors ventured, "we do not believe it is possible for a panic of the old-fashioned type to develop at the present time, [because] not only do we have the federal reserve bank which is designed to prevent such an occurrence, but there is also a continued demand for many kinds of goods."[33]

The highest prices that most farmers saw in 1920 were the ones they read about as they planted. In the second half of the year, the average price of 10 leading crops fell by 57 percent. By May 1921, that average was but a third of what it had been 12 months before. By November 1921, it had sunk below the level of 1913.[34] Not only had prices collapsed; ruinously, costs remained upright.

The intensity of a farmer's suffering depended on what he raised, how much he had borrowed and where he lived. By these criteria, an even moderately encumbered corn farmer in northwest Iowa was among the top losers. As likely as not, he had borrowed to buy cropland at the fanciest prices on record. He had perhaps stretched to buy a new tractor. He had planted in the cold 1921 springtime, expecting to receive something like the price that was then quoted in Chicago around May 1—namely, 61 cents a bushel. In the event, he did not even receive the 50 cents a bushel at which, by December, buyers and sellers on the Chicago Board of Trade were transacting but, rather, got just 56 percent of that inadequate sum.

As recently as 1919, producers had received 80 percent of the proceeds on the sale of a carload of corn that might have been shipped from Sioux City to Chicago; elevator charges and commissions absorbed 12 percent and freight costs the remaining 8 percent. By the final weeks of 1921, elevator charges and commissions ate up 10 percent, while the railroads—following the late August rate shock—grabbed fully 34 percent. So the man from Iowa who had dreamed of receiving 80 percent of 61 cents a bushel, or 49 cents, instead got 56 percent of 50 cents a bushel, or 28 cents a bushel. It was likely not much more than his cost of production. "Widely quoted," related the agricultural historian James H. Shideler, "was the story of a Kansas farmer who shipped a carload of alfalfa to the Kansas City market and, when asked what he got for it, said: 'I got to grow it.'"[35]

· · ·

But gentle humor was not the farmers' characteristic response to "The Crime of 1920" or "The Great Conspiracy."[36] Trying to do something for themselves against a cruel and faceless market, Kansas farmers called a wheat strike. They vowed to reduce their planting in 1921 by 30 percent and withhold such wheat from the market as they might have had to sell. As the average cost of production of a bushel was $2.77, the mobilized wheat producers demanded a price of $3 a bushel. "Show that you have the moral courage to go to jail, if necessary," the president of the National Farmers Union, Charles Barrett, harangued his audience at the November 1920 NFU convention.[37] The editorial page of the *New York World* to the contrary notwithstanding, a bushel of wheat in 1921 fetched not $5 but $1.

At that, the wheat men were paragons of passive resistance compared to the cotton planters and the tobacco growers. For their pains in delivering the bumper crop of 1920, the cotton producers watched the price of their crop fall to 10.3 cents a pound in June 1921, from 41.4 cents a pound in April 1920. Demoralization and financial ruin were all the more bitter in comparison to the recently ruling boomtime optimism. The planters marched on Washington and held their cotton off the sagging market. Some who refused to join their fellow sufferers faced violent reprisals against their cotton or themselves. In January 1921, in Walton, Kentucky, tobacco growers swarmed on to an auction floor in protest against the distressed sale of 30,000 pounds of white burley. So swarming, they stomped the leaves into unmarketable shreds.[38]

In the late spring of 1921, the newly installed Harding administration created a Joint Commission of Agricultural Inquiry to look into the causes of the crisis. After a quick-paced succession of hearings, the commissioners produced a report that made reference to a "great depression, such as that from which we are now emerging."[39] To the farmers, it seemed *very* great.

It might have seemed great, too, to Harry Truman and Eddie Jacobson, whose Kansas City haberdashery came a cropper in the 1921 deflationary collapse. As prices plunged and business stopped cold, the par value of the partners' debts came easily to exceed the value of the shirts, ties, hats, gloves and fixtures they counted as assets. Hanging heavy over their heads was

$30,000 in liabilities they had accumulated to finance their rapidly depreciating inventory.

In April 1922 the partners threw in the towel. Everything had to go: Arrow shirts for $1.30, any belt in the store for 69 cents, French-folded silk ties for 39 cents. Or the public could carry away the fixtures: "Shelving for sale—light fixtures for sale. Show cases for sale—hat case for sale."

Of the many creditors the partners faced, the bankers proved toughest, and the Security State Bank, holder of a note in the sum of $6,800, most obdurate. The bank pushed and pushed, but the erstwhile haberdashers had neither the assets nor the income to pay what they owed. Jacobson declared personal bankruptcy in 1925, listing debts of $10,676.50—chiefly his share of the value of the note—and assets of $507. Of the latter sum, just $28 was in cash.

Truman was in a better position than his partner to resist the importuning creditors. In 1922, he was elected eastern judge on the Jackson County (Missouri) Court. As the wages of a public official could not be garnished, Judge Truman's salary was safe, though his bank accounts enjoyed no such protection. In 1930, a lawyer with an attachment order plucked a Truman account in the sum of $110.87.

Truman's debt shadowed him for years. Though he had paid down more than $1,000—this was in 1923—interest kept accruing on the balance. By 1929, he was on the hook for $8,944.78. But deflation treated his antagonist no more gently than it had him. "As it happened," related Robert H. Ferrell, a Truman biographer, "the Security State note passed into the hands of a successor bank, the Continental National Bank, which failed in 1933; when Continental National's assets went up at a sheriff's sale in 1935, Truman obtained the note for $1,000."[40]

CITY BANK ON THE CARPET

On June 26, 1920, John Skelton Williams, comptroller of the currency—that is, chief examiner and regulator of America's nationally chartered banks—prepared to address the annual meeting of the Maine Bankers Association in Bangor. According to modern business-cycle dating methods, the country was six months into a depression. Yet Williams, an emotive and pugnacious Virginian, could not have seemed less careworn.

He began his speech with a family story. His father's elder brother was an officer in the Confederate Army. Badly wounded, he was captured by Union forces in 1865. Luckily, his captors were not only brave soldiers but also "kindly and chivalric gentlemen." And they were from Maine. "Remember always, my son," Williams quoted his uncle as saying, "if you meet anywhere a member of the Eleventh Maine Regiment, to treat him as you would your brother."

So the southern comptroller and his northern audience formed an instantaneous bond. "Your state," Williams reminded the Yankee bankers, "has the remarkable record of no failure of a National Bank since the system was established fifty-seven years ago. That absolutely clean score is a higher and better eulogy of the character and quality of the men who conduct your Banks and of their predecessors than any words of mine could express.

"If," Williams added, "we were blessed with like conditions elsewhere, the Division of Insolvent Banks in the Comptroller's Bureau would have nothing to do and we would be rid of one office at least."

It was not so far-fetched a vision, after all, the comptroller went on to say. In the prior 22 months, not one of the more than 8,000 banks under his jurisdiction had become insolvent, a span encompassing 10 months of war and 12 months of adjustment to the peace and a great deal of virulent inflation besides. It was a record 30 times or 3,000 percent better than the average for the 40 years up until 1913.

"I am optimist enough to hope that men now here will live to see the time when a bank failure anywhere in the United States will be a thing unthought of," Williams declared. "We are told it used to be so in China after the establishment of the system of chopping off with an ax the heads of all officers of a failed bank; but a much better way of prevention is to make sure that the officers have their heads and keep their heads about them and their eyes open."[1]

Williams was far from the only optimist in American banking. Belief that prices would keep rising was prevalent enough to support a good many loans that, from the vantage point of 1921, would have been better left unmade. Even as Williams spoke, the financial breakers to which Charles Schwab had alluded at the close of 1919 were audibly beginning to crash.

Interest rates had been rising for six months. On November 3, 1919, the Federal Reserve Bank of New York raised the rate at which it loaned to member banks against the collateral of commercial paper; 4 percent was the old rate, 4.75 percent the new one. The New York money market instantly tightened. By November 11, the cost of an overnight loan was quoted as high as 30 percent. Easy money had financed the boom. Now dear money began to smother it. In November, the Dow Jones Industrial Average lost 12.8 percent of its value.

There was another turn of the screw on January 23, 1920—up went the New York Federal Reserve bank's rate to 6 percent—but this time the stock market barely shuddered. "There is an atmosphere of cheerfulness and an unmistakable sense of relief in banking circles at the action of the Federal Reserve Board in putting up discount rates," said the *Wall Street Journal* in raising an editorial glass to the firmer tone of monetary policy.[2] General Electric reported that the second half of 1919 had delivered "the greatest influx of orders and accompanying jump in production the company has ever known."[3]

Inflation was proving to be a tough customer; in the first five months of 1920, wholesale prices climbed by 17.5 percent. Interest rates remained elevated, but the bulls explained them away: The demand for funds reflected the wealth of investment opportunity, they said.[4]

On April 18, the failure of a single Tokyo bank sent the prices of rice, cotton and silk into a tailspin and forced the closing of Japanese commodities exchanges. Next day, prices buckled on the New York Stock Exchange, shares of General Motors dropping by 8 percent. Japan, like America, had profited from the Great War. In the space of less than two years, silk prices had soared by 400 percent.[5] Inflation, and the expectation of perpetually more inflation, captured the Japanese imagination. New businesses were conceived, publicized and financed. Up and up went share prices. When the gait of American silk purchases suddenly slowed early in 1920, the heavily mortgaged edifice of Japanese speculation came crashing down.

Americans may not have wanted "deflation," but they did yearn for lower prices. The persistently high cost of living provoked city-dwelling consumers to don country overalls, symbols of plain, noninflationary living. Fed-up shoppers formed overalls clubs and old-clothes clubs. In New York City, 30 publicity-conscious consumers banded together to announce the creation of an "army which is to kill the prodigious cost of living,"[6]

Deflationary events beat the anti-inflation warriors to the punch. By the third week of April, prices were being marked down alike in Brooklyn department stores and on the New York Stock Exchange. On May 3, the Philadelphia retailer John Wanamaker advertised an across-the-board, 20-percent-off sale. Competitors fell in behind Wanamaker, and the deflationary ball was visibly set rolling.[7] As if someone had flipped a switch, sellers' markets became buyers' markets.

Falling prices made liabilities of carefully husbanded inventories. Under the influence of inflation, businessmen had placed multiple orders, so that one such purchase, at least, might be filled on time. Now they set about cancelling all but the one they really needed (and perhaps even that one). There was no known inoculation against "cancellitis," a new communicable American business disease.*

If the officers of the National City Bank could have heard Comptroller Williams declaim on the unshakable solvency of American banking, they might have blushed. Their bank, at least, was not so unquestionably rock solid. In the opinion of Sherrill Smith, the federal examiner who inspected City's books in February 1920, the former timid bank for timid people had seemingly undergone a corporate personality change.

"This Bank in the past has had an enviable record for keeping excessive reserves and until lately has not been a large borrower, certainly not for any considerable period," Smith recorded, "but now its borrowings are unusually large and indications are that this will be the case for some time to come." The balance sheet at the time of the examination, which concluded on March 24, 1920, showed $368.7 million in demand deposits; here was the basic, customary and unobjectionable source of funding. But the snapshot also revealed $181.7 million in borrowings from other banks and $61.1 million from the Federal Reserve. The once dowdy City was stretching to expand.

Ambition was writ large in the bank's overseas operations. For the institution as a whole, the sum of capital, surplus and retained earnings was only $26 million more than the combined $53 million of liabilities in City's foreign branches. Smith confessed he was worried. It was the owners' interest in the bank—the capital, surplus and retained earnings—that shielded the depositors against loss in a crisis.

"The bank is, I believe," Smith commented,

doing its utmost to keep pace with the growth of business here and throughout the many branches but one cannot but decide that this is becoming increasingly difficult. It is also becoming evident that the establishment of foreign branches, which are banks of deposit and discount, means

---

*Under the headline "Blames Depression on Lack of Religion," the *New York Times* of November 29, 1920, quoted Oliver M. Fisher, president of the Boston Boot and Shoe Club, attributing the rampant cancellation of orders to the immorality of the times.

the continual investment of large, and increasing, sums in the business life of those countries. [I]n the aggregate the amount can easily become a fixed investment and often, even if it can be withdrawn, it may only be with-drawable by taking considerable loss through the change in exchange rates and this loss can easily wipe out or greatly reduce the earnings from such branches as was recently found to be the case at Havana.[8]

For instruction in the perils of foreign banking, the examiner continued, look no further than City's misadventures in Russia. They showed, Smith advised Washington, "how conditions beyond human power to control may wipe out an investment and result in the loss of millions." Perhaps, as City contended, the worst was behind it and management had written off all but the dregs of potential Russian losses, though Smith had his doubts. Too, as the examiner concluded his comments, the bank had taken to running up large exposures in foreign exchange. It really had no choice, management had told him; it was the cost of maintaining the bank's high standing in the rarefied realm of international finance. "This may be true," Smith remarked, "but it also makes the Bank subject to the risk of large losses, as well as prof-its, and is thought unwise for a bank of deposit."

A bank of deposit was duty-bound to safeguard the public's funds, and this fundamental obligation City was failing to discharge. Especially was it derelict in Cuba.

Sugar was what the island nation produced and what the world could seemingly not get enough of. From four cents a pound at the time of the Armistice, the price zoomed to eight cents a pound in 1919 and to 22 cents a pound in the spring of 1920. It had been profitable to grow sugarcane at four cents a pound. At eight cents, let alone 22 cents, new investment in sugar mills, railroads and related infrastructure promised stupendous returns. The investors only needed credit, and this City Bank proceeded to supply. Twenty-two new City branches opened in Cuba in 1919.[9]

As bankers will in a boom, the men from City failed to dot every *i* or cross every *t* during the Cuban growth spurt. Especially did they give short shrift to credit analysis; rising prices seemed to render that tedious chore unnecessary. City loaned to finance the working capital of sugar mills and to the businesses that supplied them, and it loaned to build new sugar-making capacity and to finance mounting sugar inventories. The American chocola-tier Milton S. Hershey and his Hershey Corporation owed City more than $5 million, though he, at least, was a serious businessman investing in "tre-mendously valuable properties," as a visiting federal bank examiner, Frank L. Norris, judged the situation.[10] More representative of City's dealings in Cuba were loans to the unbusinesslike kind of businessman.[11] By the close of 1921, the bank's overall exposure to the Cuban sugar trade amounted to $79 million, or 80 percent of City's capital.

Sugar did not fetch 22 cents a pound for long. By late 1920, when Norris made his tour of City's Cuban branches, the price was back to where it had started its speculative surge. Plainly, Norris reported to headquarters, some-one was going to bear a considerable loss, "and from present indications it won't be the owners of the sugar."

And to his higher-ups, Norris addressed this rhetorical question: "Should a bank owing a sacred duty to its depositors gamble on a future crop of cane which is so dependent for its yield upon . . . the weather and the grasping avarice of overextended speculators, who lease but do not own their own Plantations?"

A Democrat, John Williams served as the nation's top bank examiner at the president's discretion. And as the voters elected a new, Republican president, so, effectively, did they fire Williams. His last day of work, like Woodrow Wilson's, would be Inauguration Day, March 2, 1921. Williams had occu-pied the comptroller's office since 1914. It had been a tempestuous seven years, for he had a zest for action and a sharp and antagonizing tongue. He was the bankers' nemesis, a rigid and indomitable enforcer of the rules and the dreaded author of long and argumentative letters. It was said of Wil-liams that he could "strut sitting down."[12]

"It was not so much what Mr. Williams did when he was Comptroller that subjected him to so much criticism and made his administration so unpopular," a predecessor of Williams's in the comptroller's office wrote, "as it was the manner in which he did it." Certainly, there were bankers at the National City Bank who could vouch for that appraisal.

Williams had briefly studied law of the University of Virginia. In 1895, at the age of 30, he conceived a plan to connect New York and Florida by rail. By 1900, the Seaboard Air Line Railway System was complete, and Williams was its president. Only three years later, the entrepreneur lost control of what he built in a bitter Wall Street battle with the financier Thomas Fortune Ryan.

The disappointed railroad builder kept up a running critique of the new Seaboard management. The interlopers spent too much, he charged. They borrowed too much, paid too high a rate of interest on the money they borrowed, paid too much in commissions and generally set about diverting the financial lifeblood of Williams's southern railroad to the coffers of Wall Street. And when, following the Panic of 1907, the Seaboard went bankrupt, Williams stood vindicated.

"In no spirit of boasting," the triumphant critic declared, "but as evidence for those who are interested in Seaboard securities that my opinion on the affairs of that system are well founded, I ask attention to the fact that my predictions on the course of the property and the results of its financial and operating management in recent years have been fulfilled exactly." [13]

While Williams was named a receiver of the bankrupt Seaboard, he was not among the capitalists who bought control of the rehabilitated railroad in 1912. "The Seaboard is distinctly a Southern property," the leader of the purchasing syndicate, S. Davies Warfield, of Baltimore, told the press, but Warfield's associates included such Wall Street titans as Frank Vanderlip of National City Bank, Albert H. Wiggin of Chase National Bank and Benjamin Strong of Bankers Trust.

As for Williams, cooling his heels in 1913 as president of the Bank of Richmond, he accepted an invitation to join the Wilson Treasury Department. In 1914, he was named comptroller over the opposition of the impressive number of enemies he had already accumulated.

In 1921, Comptroller Williams seemed not to notice the imminent turning of the political calendar. Certainly his examiners didn't. They had made a grand tour of City Bank branches in Europe, South America and Cuba. They had inspected the books at the bank's home office, at 55 Wall Street. Displeased, they summoned representatives of City's management to Washington to explain themselves and their methods, not least about Cuba.

By then the Cuban government had declared a debt moratorium. The American depression was deepening. City owed $144 million, or three times its required reserves, to the Federal Reserve Bank of New York. At 10 AM on Tuesday, February 22, Comptroller Williams, Deputy Comptroller Thomas P. Kane and three examiners, including Norris, set about interrogating three not very well informed representatives of the nation's largest depository institution.

There was no love lost between Williams and the bank whose affairs now engaged him. Upon taking office in 1913, the Wilsonians discovered that City had inserted a mole into the Department of the Treasury. A clerk on the City Bank payroll, Lotta M. Taylor, occupied a desk at the comptroller's office in the Treasury Building. From this strategic perch, she was able to copy confidential examiners' reports and forward them to City's Wall Street headquarters. The City front office was therefore as well informed on the state of the national banks as the comptroller was—and, apparently, as no other private institution was.

These highly irregular facts had come to light in the wake of a run on a Washington, D.C., bank, the United States Trust Company,* in November 1913. Williams, then assistant secretary of the Treasury, had mobilized $1 million of public funds to stop the panic. Strictly speaking, no trust company was subject to federal oversight, as none was federally chartered. But Williams judged that a failure would have rippled far and wide; with its five branches, $6.4 million of deposits and 50,000 depositors, the United States Trust was an integral part of the capital's banking scene. ("Financial conditions in this country at that time were nervous and more or less strained," as Williams subsequently explained, "and there was serious apprehension that such a disturbance as threatened in Washington might spread to other cities, with disastrous consequences.") So he sprinkled $1 million of federal deposits among the district's nationally chartered banks with instructions that the recipients redeposit the funds at the stricken trust company. The run stopped cold, and the affairs of the trust company were finally, and successfully, resolved.

For this aggressive stroke of public policy, Williams and the Wilson Treasury Department, including its secretary, William McAdoo, came under

---

*Not to be confused with today's U.S. Trust, a subsidiary of Bank of America.

attack by the *New York Tribune*, a Republican newspaper. When Williams became comptroller in 1914, he recounted the story of the run, of the *Tribune*'s attack and of City's penetration of a government office between the covers of the 1914 comptroller's annual report. "[U]nder previous administrations," Williams wrote, City Bank "had enjoyed special favors and privileges from the government, particularly in connection with the Treasury Department."[14] Pretty plainly, those privileges had expired. All this was preface to the 1921 interrogation.

Williams set the inquisitorial tone of the meeting.

"Mr. Brown," said the comptroller, directing his opening statement to the senior of the three City Bank officers, "we will take up the reports of the examination of European branches. Mr. Norris examined your branches at Antwerp, Brussels, Barcelona, Madrid and Genoa, Italy. The examiner advises that the supervision and management of the banks at the time of his examinations left much to be desired."[15]

That was among the least of the bank's transgressions. The comptroller and his staff had identified many dubious loans. Worryingly, Williams's men seemed to know more about the credits than the bankers did.

A loan to William B. Joyce,[16] long-serving president of the National Surety Company, in the sum of $600,000, was all too representative of the way City did business. The rate of interest to the borrower was 4.25 percent, well below the prevailing 6 percent rate. Besides, the comptroller observed, the maturity of the loan was unspecified, an unusual concession to the borrower. Could the bank not call the loan and reset the rate?

Yes, one of the defendants acknowledged, but City had chosen not to: "It is a matter of honor, that is all."

With his $600,000, Joyce had bought Liberty bonds, "and at that time we were loaning at the coupon rate," another one of the visitors from City said—that is, the bank was lending at the same rate of interest as the bonds paid.

"Encouraging people to buy Liberty bonds," Brown chimed in.

"Was he the only man you encouraged to buy Liberty bonds?" the comptroller asked.

"No; we encouraged thousands."

"I think it was very commendable to encourage customers to buy Liberty bonds," said the comptroller; " but I question the wisdom or the business acumen of making a loan for $600,000 forever."[17]

The examiners had discovered another loan struck at a below-market rate. George S. Mittendorf, of the American Debenture Company, had borrowed $29,500 at 5 percent. The comptroller wanted to know why he paid so little. "Mind you," Williams told the men from City, "I do not want to convey the impression that I am complaining of low rates. I should like to see very much lower rates than those that prevail, but I think that the rain should fall on the just and the unjust and that if you give a 4.5 percent rate to one customer, there are other customers who should be considered when 4.5 percent money is being loaned, and the same thing as to 5 percent money."

One of Brown's colleagues replied that these were exceptions and that the bank's interest rates were, as a rule, uniform.

The rate was not the only curious feature of the Mittendorf credit, the comptroller observed: "This 5 percent loan appears to have been carried on your books at that rate for 10 or 15 years, or, to be more exact, apparently since the year 1907. That is an old friend that you all ought to recognize easily, at least some of you. Do any of you remember him?"

None could recall.[18]

The comptroller next turned to a loan of $2,981,727 to M. Hartley Dodge, the very social and, by most accounts, very rich chairman of the Remington Arms Company. "It seems to have been carried for a long time," Williams observed. Was it a good loan?

"It is a good loan, but slow," one of the City Bank vice presidents answered.

"Could you collect it?" Williams asked.

"Yes, sir."

"Now?"

"Yes, sir."

"Don't you think it would be a good thing to collect it and pay back a little money to the Reserve Bank after having accommodated him for five years or thereabouts?"

"Well," the vice president replied, "we are collecting as fast as we can and paying our debts."

"I thought you said you could collect it now," Williams said.

"Yes, we could, but it would inflict a hardship, perhaps, like a great many others which we could collect."

To which Brown added, "We can collect a lot of loans by putting men out of business."[19]

Now the examiners turned to Cuba. One addressed the City Bank representatives: "Your managers taken as a whole throughout the Cuban branches are worse than incompetent; they are not proper men, most of them, to even make loans up to a limit of $2,000; they are not proper to analyze credits. Their credit information is in a great many instances incomplete and estimated. I found a number of your managers who, when they could not get proper financial statements from your clients, requested permission of the borrower to go to his office and go through his books and take a trial balance off, in order that he might get some idea of exact figures. You have so much money tied up in loans to cane planters who never render statements, who cannot show any liquid assets, who have borrowed largely from the banks, not only yours but other banks, and who have hypothecated their future crops up to the limit."

The visitors from City didn't have much to say when Norris condemned the lax security in the Cuban branches ($200,000 or $300,000 would be secreted in little safes that a competent burglar could crack in half an hour)[20] or the shabby appearance of City's "little hole in the wall" offices[21] or recurrent problems with collateral. In the city of Bayamo, the bank had extended a loan of $102,423 to a cattle dealer that was supposedly secured by 1,500 head of cattle. But the fact, said Norris, is that there were no cattle: The borrower had sold them before he gave the bank his lien, or—perhaps with the connivance of the loan registrar—he had sold them and kept the proceeds for himself. Anyway, there were no cattle.[22]

Norris said that he had talked to a Cuban banker who charged City Bank—and, as far as they went, the Royal Bank of Canada, too—with ruining his market. Local lenders knew who was who, Norris's informant said. They knew what the various plantations, or *colonas*, had on hand and what they were really likely to produce. Knowing these things, they were nowhere so free and easy with credit as the newcomers were. "That was the viewpoint of that Cuban banker," Norris diplomatically summed up, "and in going over your contracts, I was satisfied that in bidding for business you were possibly a bit liberal."[23]

Surveying the City of London a few years earlier, Hartley Withers had found not one thing to criticize: In monetary theory and banking practice alike, virtually nothing could be improved upon. Plainly, no such conclusion was possible concerning American banking in 1920.

To the City Bank representatives on the carpet, Comptroller Williams, too, leveled the charge of overly liberal lending. Against deposits of $500 million, they could show cash (including gold and silver coins, paper currency, clearing-house certificates based on gold and other lawful money and items in collection at the Federal Reserve) of only $9 million. Unpledged holdings of U.S. government bonds came to less than $150,000.

In self-defense, the City executives replied that the grand total of troubled loans in New York was only $40 million. "Would you regard $40 million as a large percentage of slow loans at this time," one of them asked the examiners, "in view of what we have been going through in the past year?"

Yes, he would, one of Williams's men replied, even if, as he believed, the grand total was in fact higher. But, yes, he allowed, the depression had had "a great deal to do" with the trouble. Besides, continued the reply from the examiners' side of the table, the National City Bank was no ordinary bank but America's largest. In keeping with its power and position, it surely had an obligation to keep itself more than minimally solvent.[24]

★ 7 ★

EGGING ON DEFLATION

Benjamin Strong, whose formal education stopped with high school, had little patience with scholarly speculation. But neither was the governor of the Federal Reserve Bank of New York inclined to remain silent when an academic bystander misconstrued his record or that of the Federal Reserve. Criticism that Professor E.L. Bogart had leveled against the Federal Reserve in a publication of the American Economic Association elicited from Strong early in 1919 a remarkably prescient 20-page letter to the monetary economist Edwin W. Kemmerer. After venting against Bogart, Strong presented his own analysis of current affairs.

"[O]ur strength is but slightly impaired and . . . our future tribulations arising therefrom will be, by comparison, moderate," Strong contended of the war-induced inflation. "I believe that the adoption of a somewhat changed policy by the Treasury and the Reserve System later on, and for which I am proposing to struggle, will insure during the next year or two a very considerable liquidation of our banking position, a discontinuance of government borrowings at a reasonably early date and a considerable decline in the price level."

The "somewhat changed" policy at which Strong hinted was no less than a plan to pull the rug out from under the American economy.

"I also believe, however," Strong went on,

> that this must be accompanied by some rather serious losses because our increased prices have occurred in a country enjoying exceptional prosperity in which merchants and manufacturers have unfortunately maintained too large stocks of goods as compared with their foreign competitors. I believe that this period will be accompanied by a considerable degree of unemployment, but not for very long, and that after a year or two of discomfort, embarrassment, some losses, some disorders caused by unemployment, we will emerge with an almost invincible banking position, with prices more nearly at competitive levels with other nations, and be able to exercise a wide and important influence in restoring the world to normal and livable conditions. One must have a theory of these things to work on, and at least the courage to practice and state it.[1]

Implicit in these words was a deep faith in the self-correcting nature of markets and in the strength and resilience of American finance. Nothing in the historical evidence suggests that Strong was a cruel man. He meant to inflict no pain on the unemployed. The depression he anticipated was a necessary evil. Wages, like prices, were distorted. They were too high and had to fall. They would fall to sustainable levels sooner or later. If the Federal Reserve could give them a push, so much the better for the timely return to sustainable prosperity.

In sensibility and training Strong and his contemporaries were bankers, not economists. Only one professional economist served on the Federal Reserve Board in the capacity of a governor, and he—Adolph C. Miller, for many years a finance professor at the University of California at Berkeley—was an economist of the practical sort. The governor—we would call him "chairman"—of the Federal Reserve Board, W.P.G. Harding, an alumnus of the University of Alabama, Class of 1880, was a commercial banker. John Skelton Williams, like Strong, had stopped short of college, studying business and finance on the job, not in the classroom.

At the age of 16, William Proctor Gould Harding was the youngest graduate in the 49-year history of the University of Alabama. After a three-year clerkship at the banking house of J.H. Fitts & Company, in Tuscaloosa, young Harding moved to Birmingham to become assistant cashier of the Berney National Bank.

In due course, the assistant cashier became cashier. Next, at rival First National Bank of Birmingham, he became vice president and finally president (in 2006, the First National Bank of Birmingham, rebranded as AmSouth, was absorbed by Regions Financial Corporation). Directorships came Harding's way, as did, in 1908, the presidency of the Alabama Bankers Association. A Democrat, Mason, Episcopalian and father of three, Harding was called to Washington in 1914 to become an original governor of Woodrow Wilson's new decentralized central bank. In 1916, he became the Federal Reserve Board's second governor—*the* governor.

In 2014, economists and bankers seemingly occupy different intellectual worlds. Bankers may speak in jargon, but it is a kind of English. Economists—monetary economists among the rest—communicate in jargon and in stanzas of higher mathematics. There was no such language barrier on Harding's Federal Reserve Board. Miller, the Berkeley economist; Williams, the autodidact; and Harding, the University of Alabama prodigy, did not always agree, but they seemed to understand one another's speech patterns.*

They shared a generally laissez-faire approach to economic and monetary policy. None expressed a doubt about a dollar defined as a weight of gold. None, with the exception of Williams, so much as intimated that the Federal Reserve had any business trying to override the structure of market-determined prices. Inflation had distorted those prices. Now deflation must set them right.

As Strong, the former president of Bankers Trust, had advocated lower prices, so did the former Flood Professor of Finance. "Where there has been inflation, there must follow deflation, as a necessary condition to the

---

*David F. Houston, Charles S. Hamlin, Edmund Platt and D.C. Wills filled out the 1920 Federal Reserve Board. Houston, an 1887 graduate of the University of South Carolina, earned a master's degree in political science from Harvard University. He served as Wilson's secretary of agriculture from 1913 to 1920 and as secretary of the Treasury until 1921. Hamlin, who graduated from Harvard in 1886, twice served as the assistant secretary of the Treasury, from 1893 to 1897 and from 1913 to 1914. Platt, another Harvard man, Class of 1888, was a newspaper editor and Republican congressman. Wills, a high-school graduate, worked his way up the ranks of Pittsburgh banking to become president of the Citizens' National Bank of Bellevue.

restoration of economic health," said Miller in an address to the American Academy of Political and Social Sciences on the topic of "After-War Readjustment" in 1919. Banks must reel in the inflationary increment of their wartime lending, he said. As for the rest of us, the economist added, more production or less consumption was the way forward. Work and save, he counseled.[2]

Those tough words aside, the Federal Reserve continued to suppress the interest rate at which it was prepared to lend and at which its member banks were all too happy to borrow. Between September 1918 and July 1921, the system's member institutions borrowed from the Federal Reserve more than 100 percent of the dollars they were required to hold in reserve. A year passed before W.P.G. Harding et al. made a decisive move to tighten policy. And when at last they did lower the boom, they took no half measures but raised the key interest rate by 1.25 percentage points, to 6 percent. It was one of the Federal Reserve's single most violent policy strokes from that day till this. Not entirely sure of themselves, the governors needed two votes to approve the 6 percent rate. Even then, the ballot was a close one, 4–3, the former fire-eating Miller voting with the majority but only after reversing his first vote.* The date was January 21, 1920.

The power of the monetary punch did not initially register on its intended recipients. Banks continued to lend, credit to expand and prices to rise. Short-term interest rates did push higher, as might have been expected or intended, and in so doing provoked the disapproving curiosity of the Senate. What was the cause of the "usurious" rates of interest lately quoted in the New York money market, the legislators demanded in March. Blame the impersonal forces of supply and demand, not us, the central bankers replied.[3]

But the central bankers were responsible for the condition of their own finances. By law, the Reserve banks were bound to hold reserves of gold and other eligible assets equal to a minimum of 40 percent of the Federal Reserve notes they issued. The trouble was that lending, borrowing and spending were racing ahead of the available collateral that anchored the dollar. In January

---

*"Miller has time and time again accused the Board of being dominated by the Treasury," recounted fellow Board member and diarist Charles Hamlin, in disgust of those proceedings, "and yet today he publicly announced that he changed his vote, against his convictions, because the Secretary of the Treasury and Governor Harding wanted the 6% rate. (He is a time server!!!)" The secretary of the Treasury was then an ex-officio member of the Federal Reserve Board. [Friedman and Schwartz, *Monetary History of the United States*, 230]

1920, the systemwide average reserve ratio stood at just 42.7 percent. Only by a dexterous juggling of collateral to deficient Reserve banks from better endowed Reserve banks did the system avoid the potentially panic-inducing embarrassment of announcing a temporary suspension of gold convertibility. The assistant secretary of the Treasury, Russell C. Leffingwell, warned the assembled officials at the January 21 Federal Reserve Board meeting that the country was perilously close to leaving the gold standard.[4]

In May 1920, Harding summoned representatives of each of the 12 Reserve banks to Washington for a conference on the worrying state of credit. Even so evidently punitive a rate of interest as 6 percent seemed unequal to the job of braking inflation. Actually, the inflationary bubble was already bursting—the Japanese silk market had crashed and Wanamaker's big department store had held its consciousness-raising clearance sale.[5] Unable to borrow from their frightened bankers, or even to arrange for an extension of loans previously extended, manufacturers were raising cash by dumping their war bonds.[6] The Fourth Liberty 4¼s of 1938 plunged to 82 cents on the dollar from 94 at the start of the year, to yield a tax-advantaged 5.82 percent. At the May lows, which would prove to be the bottom of the bear bond market, the solemn obligations of the U.S. Treasury promised a higher return than did the objectively less well-secured bonds of the better class of American railroad.[7]

Harding, watching the dwindling gold position of the Federal Reserve, could hardly assume that inflation had ended or that deflation had begun. So, addressing the emissaries from the regional Federal Reserve branches— each was a so-called Class C director, a commercial banker by trade—the governor opened the meeting with a recital of the grim facts. During the 19 months of the war, lending by the national banks advanced at an annual rate of 10.5 percent; in the 12 months to April 1, 1920, growth in lending was on the order of 25 percent.

"It is evident," Harding went on, "that the country cannot continue to advance prices and wages, to curtail production, to expand credits, and to attempt to enrich itself by nonproductive operations and transactions without fostering discontent and radicalism, and that such a course, if persisted in, will bring on a real crisis."

The job at hand was therefore a tricky one: "to bring about a normal and healthy liquidation without curtailing essential production and without shock to industry, and, as far as possible, without disturbance of legitimate commerce and business." That is, to brake without swerving and crashing.[8]

Nice work if one could get it—which, insisted Adolph Miller, one could not. "I have no hesitation in saying for myself that I do not feel at all optimistic about the outlook," the economist prophesied. "I do not for a moment expect that we are going to deflate in this country, and I think we are only deceiving ourselves if we talk about deflation."[9]

Williams, who, as comptroller of the currency, held an ex-officio position on the Board of Governors, now spoke. He favored low interest rates and was shortly to conceive an intense dislike for deflation. For the present, though, he sounded not much different than Miller or Harding.

"It seems to me," said Williams, "with the large wages that are being paid now in industrial establishments, that it offers a splendid opportunity for you to increase and build up the savings deposits in your banks. I was very much disgusted the other day to hear of my chauffeur buying about three silk shirts at ten dollars apiece."

How the audience received this indictment of high living by a man who had seated himself in a chauffeur-driven vehicle is unrecorded. Williams continued:

"I think that, when these individual cases of extravagance and luxury come to our attention, if we should call the attention of the spendthrifts to the importance of starting a savings account, it would be helpful." Not that America's difficulties were unique to America or that America could, solely by her own efforts, surmount them. Inflation was a worldwide bane. But if each individual bank would become a "missionary for thrift," a better steward of its own resources, how much better the situation would be.

Adolph Miller may have doubted that the United States could effect a real deflation. Williams had faith. "I think we should, and must, bring about a reasonable degree of deflation or contraction," he said.[10]

No more did Williams than most observers draw the properly downbeat inferences from the deflationary news in that spring of 1920. The year 1919 had delivered the lowest rate of business failure since the Civil War, he pointed out. As for his charges, America's nationally chartered banks, Williams emphatically asserted that "the record established for IMMUNITY

FROM FAILURE from January 1, 1918, to the close of the last fiscal year, October 31, 1919, is MANY times better than the best showing ever previously made." The Maine bankers had heard him make the same proud boast.[11]

The comptroller did not think to observe that artificially low interest rates flatter the financial strength of any borrower lucky enough to pay them. Bankruptcies were scarcer in early 1920 not because corporate managers were better; companies didn't fail as they once had done because easy credit allowed them to postpone the day of reckoning. The cheering business-mortality statistics to which Williams alluded would likely not have survived the new 6 percent interest-rate regime. It is a fact that they did not survive 7 percent, which rate the Federal Reserve Bank of New York first imposed on June 1, 1920. Other Reserve banks took New York's lead.

Williams had acceded to 6 percent. He warned against 7 percent. The bank examiners under his direction had, under his questioning, warned against it. With an exception for call-money loans in excess of $5,000, 6 percent was the maximum legal rate of interest in New York. Seven percent was abnormal. If adopted, Williams cautioned Harding, that aberrant rate of interest would punish the patriotic buyers of Liberty bonds. It would choke off credit to legitimate borrowers.[12]

Williams's criticism proved farsighted, though not immediately popular. Nor, to many, did it seem especially persuasive. Many market interest rates were already higher than 7 percent, the New York State usury ceiling notwithstanding. The Federal Reserve Board, stocked with, and advised by, some of the finest financial minds in America, had thrashed the matter out at its meeting on May 18. Besides, the consensus of expert opinion held, 7 percent would slam the door shut on the postwar inflationary bacchanalia.

"The people of the country have by no means realized as yet the necessity for economy, liquidation of loans and curtailment in the use of credits," A. Barton Hepburn, a former comptroller of the currency, told the *Wall Street Journal* on the occasion of the announcement of the 7 percent rate. "We will never be able to bring about the desired deflation until the general extravagance is curtailed." Extravagance, indeed: The average American was consuming 93 pounds of sugar a year, up from only 18 pounds in 1850. It was "only one instance of the heedless manner in which we are spending and consuming," Hepburn said.[13]

★ 8 ★

A DEBACLE "WITHOUT PARALLEL"

No stock-market crash announced bad times. The depression rather made its presence felt with the serial crashes of dozens of commodity markets. To the affected producers and consumers, the declines were immediate and newsworthy, but they failed to seize the national attention. Certainly, they made no deep impression at the Federal Reserve. "There are already indications that the transition period is nearing a halt and that an improvement of the general situation is in sight," the governors ventured at the end of August 1920.[1]

The slump began in staggered fashion; the effective starting point depended on one's place of residence and line of business. On average, wholesale prices peaked in March in Japan and the United Kingdom; in April in France and Italy; in May in the United States, Germany, India and Canada; in June in Sweden; in July in the Netherlands; and in August in Australia.[2]

For the American producer of pig iron, composite steel or beef, prices did not turn lower in May but kept rising until September. The producer of hemlock, Portland cement, bricks, bituminous coal or crude oil enjoyed rising prices until December. Newspaper publishers got no relief on contract newsprint until January 1921. Then, again, dealers in red cedar shingles and worsted yarn had an early reading on the change in the cyclical weather; prices of the things they bought and sold had topped out in February 1920.[3]

Cotton prices began their descent in April and May, in line with the average of American wholesale prices, but the violence and speed of the cotton-price collapse was something extraordinary. On April 16, the price of a pound of middling-grade cotton in New York fetched 43.25 cents. It tumbled to 30 cents in September, 20 cents in November and 12 cents in March 1921.[4] Textbooks teach that, other things being the same, low prices coax forth more demand than high prices do. But the vertical angle of descent of the cotton market seemed to paralyze would-be buyers. They could see for themselves that tomorrow's price would certainly be lower than today's, however ridiculously low today's might appear.[5]

In place of the 1919 buyers' panic—of cotton and most everything else— there began a 1920 sellers' panic. The authors of a congressional postmortem of the depression in agriculture studied records of price movements since 1800. They concluded that "the debacle of 1920–21 was without parallel."[6]

Personally, for W.P.G. Harding, the crisis of the cotton market was heartrending. As president of the First National Bank of Birmingham, he had ordered his credit department to take it easy on the cotton-growing borrowers in times of low prices or short crops. But, as the author of a national policy of deflation, he could hardly make a special exception to the general rule of stringency for the suffering cotton growers of his native state.[7]

On Wall Street, stock prices were tracing only a somewhat less precipitous decline than farm prices. The Dow Jones average of 20 industrial issues made its 1920 closing high on January 3, the second trading day of the year, at 109.88. It closed at 104.73 on April 16, the day cotton put in its high. By September 16—the day a bomb exploded outside the offices of J.P. Morgan & Co. on Wall Street—the average had dropped to 88.63. It made its closing low on December 21, at 66.75, representing a loss, from top to bottom in 1920, of 39 percent. Better, by far, to have invested in railroad equities, which marked time or traded slightly higher for most of the year, perhaps as an expression of relief at the close of the period of wartime government control of the nation's rail network.

• • •

Before a joint convention of the National Hardware Association and the American Hardware Manufacturers Association in Atlantic City, New Jersey, on October 20, 1920, a director of the Federal Reserve Bank of New York painted an upbeat picture of the deflationary future. As farmers and manufacturers had had the inflationary pins kicked out from under them, observed the speaker, Robert H. Treman, so would retailers and wage earners. Retail prices would be lower come next spring or summer, he said. Wages, too, must fall.

"So far as the moving of merchandise and liquidating of inventories is concerned, the deflation process has only really begun, and we must expect that it will be months and perhaps a few years before it is completed," Treman went on. "In this process we must expect some reduction in the wage scale. So large a part of the cost of articles may be traced to labor that there can be no real or permanent deflation completed until wage deflation takes place."

How the audience received this pitcher of ice water is unreported. When Major Frederick H. Payne, president of the Hardware Manufacturers Association, rose to speak, he lashed out not at the central bankers but at the "low ebb" of commercial morality, which found all too ready expression in the blight of cancelled orders. "An order should be as good as one's bond," said Payne. Money would be cheaper and easier to borrow in 1921, he predicted. Prices and wages would be "saner," as the *New York Times* paraphrased his remarks.[8]

Plunging prices were not John Skelton Williams's idea of sanity. The comptroller of the currency had changed his mind. He repudiated the Federal Reserve's move to a 7 percent discount rate on commercial paper, which had begun late in May 1920. No more did he support, as he had in the days leading up to that decision, a "reasonable degree of deflation or contraction" in monetary policy. Rather, he demanded lower interest rates.

The comptroller was no more inclined to keep his counsel in the matter of tight money than he had been on the subject of Thomas Fortune Ryan's railroad management. He blamed the decision to move to 7 percent for the plunge in stock prices and the shakeout in Liberty bond prices. Besides, he said, Wall Street banks earned unconscionable profits by lending overnight to brokers and securities dealers at interest rates well above the normal legal ceiling of 6 percent.[9]

Bankers, if they were listening to the talkative comptroller, just smiled. They knew that the kinds of outsize interest rates to which Williams referred—the anomalous 10 percent, 20 percent or even 50 percent—prevailed only in fleeting moments of stringency and accounted for a trifling share of the real business at the money post of the New York Stock Exchange.[10] If Congress wanted to improve the caliber of American finance, jointly urged the National Credit Men's Association and the Investment Bankers Association, let it pass a law to frustrate swindlers like the man named Ponzi, whose crimes, unmasked in August 1920, had threatened the stability of the Boston banking system.[11]

Other cities' banks were, if not teetering, then erecting defenses against the continuing drop in prices and business activity. This was just as it should be, contended George E. Roberts, vice president of National City Bank in New York. Some had mistakenly believed that the inflated, wartime level of prices and wages was permanent (perhaps City Bank's lending officers in Cuba were among that misguided contingent). He, for one, hoped that it wasn't.

"If the recent level of prices had been permanent," Roberts was quoted as saying in the *Wall Street Journal*,

> the value of all money and all obligations to pay fixed sums of money would be depreciated approximately one-half. It would mean that all the savings of the people which are in the form of savings bank deposits, promissory notes or life insurance are in large part, perhaps one-half, wiped out as with a sponge. It would mean that the retired farmer or business man who has converted his property into bonds or mortgages would find the interest as he received it, and the principal when it was paid back, approximately one-half of the purchasing power he bargained for and that he thought he possessed. The readjustment of salaries and wages has been only partially made. A great many salaried people and wage-earners are still losers by the change. The railroads and public utilities have been almost ruined by it. Nobody has gained anything by it except at the expense of some one else, and it has thrown the whole social and industrial organization into confusion.[12]

"Readjustment" was a very pretty word for "calamity," it must have seemed to Senator Robert L. Owen, Democrat of Oklahoma. As Carter Glass had shepherded the Federal Reserve Act through the House of Representatives, so Owen had guided it through the Senate. Owen and Glass were each born in Lynchburg, Virginia, in 1856 and 1858, respectively, but while Glass remained in place, Owen headed West to the Indian Territory. He taught school among the Cherokees, served as a federal Indian agent and, in 1890, organized the First National Bank of Muskogee. And when Oklahoma entered the union in 1907, Owen, a Democrat, became a U.S. senator.

In 1920, the senator's concern was not for the inflation-diminished saver but for the deflation-ravaged producer, and, like Williams, he took to writing letters of protest to the Federal Reserve Board. Inveighing against the "psychological effect of the policy of deflation," the senator deplored the contraction of credit. "The banks," Owen addressed Harding in October, "are exercising, naturally and properly, a discrimination against the speculator and the profiteer, but the man who produces and the man who distributes is entitled to credit against the value of the commodities which he handles."[13]

Glass, now himself a U.S. senator, saw things the Federal Reserve's way, not Owen's. And so did the *New York Times*, which, late in November, took notice of the dog that hadn't barked. As of yet, the paper observed, there had been no panic. The deflations or depressions of yesteryear, the *Times* pointed out, were invariably accompanied by a stampede for currency or credit. Solvent but illiquid banks and businesses were driven to bankruptcy in the trampling. Yes, "a baker's dozen of farmers' banks" had failed this time around, but these small neighborly institutions were not really banks in the Wall Street sense but investment institutions, or even "speculative pools"; they were managed to provide the farmer a year in which to market his crops. It was a well-intended and friendly doctrine, the *Times* conceded, but a dangerous one for banks whose depositors could reclaim their funds on demand. "What the farmers really need," said the editorial, turning the urban knife, "is more banking of the Wall Street sort."[14]

At the close of 1920, Daniel Guggenheim, a member of the fabulously successful mining family, made his contribution to the pro-deflation literature in an interview in the *Times*. His scouts had returned from a fact-finding expedition out west to report that the sons of the pioneers shared none of the easterners' gloom. "The farmer, rancher, miner and merchant have sustained severe losses," Guggenheim related. "They seem, however, to feel that this was inevitable after the boom times of war and that, prices now having reached a lower level and with reduced cost of supplies and labor, together with increased efficiency, they would be able to produce next year on a basis that would give them at least fair average profits."

Yes, many were unemployed, Guggenheim acknowledged, though, as the *Times* put it, they were "mainly among the itinerant, roving class." Guggenheim continued: "The good, steady married American is holding his job and has saved much during the period of high wages. He has raised his standards of living, ate better food, dressed better and his children had better educational opportunities. On the whole, the American worker is better off than I have ever known him to be. He realizes that his wages must be cut and is not blindly fighting reduction, so long as it does not go too far and is not out of proportion to the cost of living."

How many western wage earners saw things in just that enlightened way, Guggenheim did not venture to say. He did, however, take a stab at explaining the sources of the pessimism that was shrouding easterners. Taxation had "killed off enterprise," he said, while inflated wages had sapped the efficiency of labor. (Exulting in the fattest paydays they had ever known, employees had started giving themselves days off smack dab in the middle of the working week.) Deflation would cure some of these ills, the industrialist asserted. It would, "in a short time adjust the money market so that those who are in need of money can get it. This money will be largely invested in business enterprise, which will start the machinery into motion."[15]

When Comptroller Williams sat down to write an official letter, he stayed seated. And when he rose from his labors he had something to show for them. Ten or so single-spaced, typewritten pages, complete with statistical and documentary appendices, was a standard Williams production. It was one of these epistolary Big Berthas that the comptroller dispatched to Governor Harding on December 28, 1920.

Williams opened by recalling the warnings he had issued to Harding in October about the deepening slump in commodity prices. Two months later, the problem was only more acute and the need to relax the Federal's draconian policy only more urgent. Yes, Williams acknowledged, the Federal Reserve Board had been unanimous for tightening policy to stop the virulent 1919 inflation. And, yes, the subsequent depression was a worldwide slump (never before had the countries of the world been so intertwined, he paused to assert); it would be unreasonable to hope for an immediate recovery.

But though the Federal Reserve could work no miracles, it must not settle for doing nothing. "It is poor comfort," Williams wrote,

> to the man or woman with a family denied modest comforts or pinched for necessities each week to be told that all will be, or may be, well next year, or the year after. Privations and mortifications of poverty can not be soothed or cured by assurances of brighter and better days some time in the future. Our hope and purpose must be to forestall and prevent suffering and privation for the people of today, the children who are growing up and receiving now their first impressions of life and their country.

If it seemed as if he were advocating paternalism, Williams hastened to deny it.

> I am far from believing in a paternalistic government; but I also think there are emergencies when the power of government may very properly be used and ought to be used for the purpose of stabilizing business and averting financial panics when they threaten, and preventing commercial crisis.

The war had instituted a kind of paternalism, Williams continued. It had pushed the government into the position of directing and controlling the nation's commerce. That was the fact, like it or not.

> Sudden and violent abandonment of governmental direction, influence and assistance would be like seizing a vast and intricate and delicately adjusted machine, operating it at high pressure in new conditions and for new purposes and then dumping it, disorganized, disarranged and out of gear leaving its former managers to readjust it and run it as they can.[16]

It could not be said of a society that accepted Prohibition and, before that, Wilson's program of war socialism that it was unconditionally opposed to activist government. Nor was Williams so opposed. Why, he attested, recalling his own intervention in the 1913 run on the United States Trust Company, the Treasury had forestalled "many" a financial panic. And it was the Treasury that, in 1914, had organized a private lending pool to stabilize the sagging price of cotton (though a mere $28,000 had been drawn on a pledged sum of lendable funds of no less than $130 million).*

What, then, would Williams have Harding do? Cut interest rates, first and foremost: Lend against the collateral of Liberty bonds at a uniform rate of 4.5 percent, not 6 percent (the 7 percent rate applied to commercial paper); abolish the interest-rate surcharges on the member banks that, in the Federal Reserve's arbitrary judgment, loaned to excess. In one case with which Williams was familiar, a western bank had had to pay 19.5 percent to borrow from its local Federal Reserve bank in order, in turn, to lend to its suffering customers.

There was no reason for it, Williams continued. If, some months before, the Federal Reserve had tightened credit because it was running up against the limits of its own reserve position, that was no longer true, he reminded Harding. The Reserve banks, flush with gold and other eligible collateral, now could easily step up their lending to speed the nation's recovery. From the inflationary peak to the current deflationary depths, according to Williams's calculations, a grand total of between $12 billion and $18 billion had been erased from the value of America's mills, forests, farms, fields and factories. At the high estimate, it was very nearly as much as the amount of Liberty bonds outstanding.

"Pitiful tales come to me from National Bank Examiners in different parts of the country," Williams related.

---

*On the sensitive subject of cotton, Williams chose not to mention the failed price-support scheme that Nicholas Biddle, president of the Second Bank of the United States, a forerunner to the Federal Reserve, had orchestrated in the late 1830s. After some initial success, market forces prevailed, and the price of cotton once more sank, making Biddle and his bank the losers. The bank suspended payments in 1839 and closed for good in 1841. John A. Stevens, president of the Bank of Commerce, in New York, said good riddance. The close of Biddle's manipulations would "leave commercial affairs again to a regular and natural course," he judged. [Bray Hammond, *Banks and Politics in America from the Revolution to the Civil War* (Princeton, NJ: Princeton University Press, 1957), 522.]

The Chief Examiner from the Kansas City District told me recently that in parts of his territory the most heart-breaking tragedies were being enacted—farmers turned away from their farms, their cattle and implements sold and ruined families becoming wanderers on the face of the earth.

The same Examiner informed me of cases where farmers are being pitilessly sold out, and stated that in sections of the West the scarcity of money is such that their horses are being sold sometimes as low as $3 apiece, and purchased by impoverished neighbors who kill them and feed their flesh to their hogs and obtain some reimbursement by selling the hide of the horse.[17]

In the South, Williams pressed on (he was not quite halfway through), farm mules fetched 10 cents on the dollar at foreclosure sales. In Wyoming, there was a surplus of cattle feed but no cattle to which to feed it. In Oklahoma, cotton growers were leaving their fields unharvested because they couldn't afford to pay the hands. And in North Carolina, hopeless people were committing suicide, including "the President of a well-run and successful National Bank . . . apparently unable to stand the growing misery which he beheld around him."

In the circumstances, Williams was instructing his examiners to forbear. He told Harding he had given the banks he supervised "every proper means to prevent the selling out of honest debtors at sheriffs' sales and the ruin of their families, by extending their time and by giving them, wherever practicable, the opportunity to hold on to their farms and their farming implements, to the tools of their trade or to the equipment of their business, whatever it is; and that these debtors be given the chance to recoup, and to redeem their indebtedness and get again on their feet." In effect, the comptroller was promulgating his own personal credit policy with which to thwart the consequences of the Federal Reserve's high interest-rate policy.

Quoting from Alexander Pope's "Universal Prayer" ("That mercy I to others show, that mercy show to me"), Williams implored Harding to throw away the central banking rule book. "Such facts and conditions as have been brought so vividly before us can not be met with theories or removed by explanations and should not be dealt with by vague surmises and promises or unconsidered experiences," he wrote. *They demand definite and energetic action, even if precedent must be disregarded, accepted rules suspended or waived and new plans and methods devised.*"[18]

Usually, Williams wasted no opportunity to sing the praises of the banks he regulated and even of the ones he didn't. In May, to Senator Owen, he spoke of "the splendid condition and fine spirit" of America's banks, both state- and federally chartered, calling that circumstance "one of the most cheering and reassuring facts of the entire present situation." But he presented a very different appraisal to Harding on December 27. The big Wall Street banks were in a bad way, he now related. Some of the biggest presented risks not only to their depositors but also to the stability of the system.

Between May and December, business conditions and commodity prices had, of course, deteriorated. Banks that had seemed the picture of health in the spring of 1920 could very easily have tumbled to losses by Christmastime (any with exposure to sugar prices—National City Bank, for instance—were certainly feeling the cyclical chill). But Williams, in presenting his new and distinctly uncheering appraisal of the nation's banks, did not content himself with an update of his earlier reading of the situation. He rather let it seem as if Wall Street banks had always sailed too close to the wind, and now that a breeze had become a gale, some of them might founder. The people who ran them were none too savory, either, as far as that went.

The sheer scale of the lending and borrowing in lower Manhattan seemed to strike Williams as a moral problem as much as a financial one. Why, he informed Harding, some of these behemoths were borrowing $100 million from the Federal Reserve. That was "twice as much as the total loans some of the Reserve banks have been lending recently to *all* the member banks in their districts."[19]

Was it in any way relevant that a certain New York bank had borrowed more from the Federal Reserve—namely, $134 million—than the grand total of the advances that the Federal Reserve Bank of Kansas City had made its 1,091 member institutions (in a district encompassing the states of Kansas, Nebraska, Colorado, Wyoming and parts of Missouri, Oklahoma and New Mexico)? Yes, indeed, according to the comptroller. Such examples—he presented more than one—illustrated the malign power of the high interest rates in the New York money market. Usurious call-money rates redirected funds from the necessary business of agriculture to the gratuitous pastime of stock gambling.

"The inequalities and injustice in the distribution of these funds become apparent when we analyse the uses which big favored banks in the East sometimes make of the money they borrow from the Reserve System," Williams pushed on. The comptroller had a particular big favored eastern bank in mind. It was one that had made a specialty of self-dealing, and that had financed that questionable business with nine-figure advances from the Federal Reserve.

Though Williams discreetly withheld the name of this morally and financially dubious institution from the text of his letter, he did not scruple from appending an unredacted examiner's report. "Memorandum," the document was titled, "Regarding Indebtedness of Chairman Wiggin to the Chase National Bank and to the Chase Securities Corp."[20]

Albert H. Wiggin has come down through financial history as the hypocrite who quietly sold short the shares of his own bank during the 1929 Crash. But his reputation was unbesmirched in 1920 when the comptroller's office noticed a worrying pattern of insider dealing at Chase Bank (the second named unit of today's J.P. Morgan Chase). Wiggin was 52 years old. He had been chairman for three years. He was a director of dozens of corporations and—evidently—a very rich man. Certainly, he had a very large personal balance sheet, the liabilities of which his own bank was liberally funding.

Wiggin, his wife and their two grown daughters, along with their daughters' husbands, had borrowed $9.8 million from Chase, the examiner's memo reported. Another director, William B. Thompson, had borrowed $5.5 million. Between them, the examiner noted, Thompson and the Wiggins owed Chase more than Chase could show in capital—i.e., $15 million (surplus footed to another $15 million).

The companies on whose boards Wiggin sat were also, many of them, heavy borrowers, the memo pointed out. American Sugar Refining alone owed $8.1 million. And there were other loans to other officers and to other affiliated companies. The grand total of credits to officers, directors, and affiliated parties and companies came to just short of $40 million.

Nobody had to tell Wiggin that the bottom was falling out of American business. He could see it in the stock prices of the companies whose directors' meetings he attended. Shares of National Conduit & Cable Company fetched $24.75 in July 1919; on December 20, 1920, they were quoted at $2. Over the same span, shares of Inspiration Copper Company had plunged from $78.88 to $28. As recently as February 28, 1920, the stock of the Missouri Pacific Company had traded at $31.88; on December 21, it brought $11.50.

"It is unfortunate for the head officers of a National Bank to have his [sic] time and energies absorbed in the affairs of too many outside concerns," the examiner concluded his survey of Chase. "Furthermore, in disturbed times and falling market [sic], such connections become talked about, and are liable to react upon and offset unfavorably the credit of the bank."

9

THE COMPTROLLER
ON THE OFFENSIVE

Williams had written to Harding not in confidence but for the record. He had mailed copies of his letter to every other member of the Federal Reserve Board. Harding stiffly replied on behalf of himself and the rest of the board on January 13, 1921. "Dear Mr. Comptroller" was his subzero salutation.

Economists on both sides of the Atlantic were making the case for a new kind of monetary system. Under the prewar gold standard, exchange rates were fixed and inviolable. If something had to adjust, that something was business or employment or prices, not the gold value of money. Better by far in the postwar world, contended John Maynard Keynes and Irving Fisher, if prices remained stable while currency values were allowed to adjust. To achieve the great desideratum of "price stability," the theorists advocated a new style in central banking. It should now fall to the likes of W.P.G. Harding and Ben Strong to manage the currencies under their stewardship. The new mark of success in central banking was no longer a currency fully convertible into gold at a fixed and statutory rate. It was stable prices and lots of jobs.

Williams had seemed to hint about these new ideas with his demand for "definite and energetic action, even if precedent must be disregarded." But neither he on the offensive nor Harding on the defensive couched their arguments in economists' abstractions. They rather contended as practical men appealing to necessity and compassion (in Williams's case) and experience and common sense (in Harding's).

"I assume," Harding addressed his unfriendly colleague, "... that your object in addressing a written communication to the Board is to make a record of your views, for if it had been your purpose merely to have the Board consider the matter of changing discount rates, you could, in your capacity as a member of the Board, have had the subject put upon the docket at any time or you could have brought it up informally at any meeting of the Board."[1]

So if Williams chose to talk over the head of his addressee to unnamed others, so would Harding. There was the great preceding cause of the current troubles to be reckoned with, Harding noted. The inflation of 1919–20 required quashing, and the Federal Reserve, whose hands had been tied during the war, now took vigorous and appropriate action. As late as May 1920, the Senate had adopted a resolution directing the board "to advise the Senate what steps it purposes to take or to recommend to the member banks of the Federal Reserve System to meet the existing inflation of currency and credits and consequent high prices, and what further steps it purposes to take or recommend to mobilize credits in order to move the 1920 crops."*

But the crash had come, as it was bound to come. Like the wartime inflation, the commodity-price deflation was an event beyond the Federal Reserve's control. It was not an evil omen. "We hold," Harding averred, "that the shrinkage which has taken place is somewhat analogous to that which occurs when a balloon is punctured and the air escapes."

The "readjustment" was, of course, sharp and painful, but it was inevitable, and not even "the stimulus of inflation" could have delayed it for long. The Federal Reserve had, with the 7 percent interest rate that Williams opposed, forestalled a much worse problem. Indeed, Harding contended, "[W]e are of the opinion that the policies which were carried into effect by

---

* A notably poor piece of timing, as commodity prices were just beginning their record-shattering descent. The "existing" inflation of the currency was fast ending.

the Federal Reserve have prevented one of the greatest financial cataclysms of modern times."

And as for Williams's suggestion that the Federal Reserve replace the tried and true with the new and untested, why, Harding replied, he and the rest of the board would decline it, "especially if those new plans and methods are fundamentally unsound."

It only remained to answer Williams's provoking allegation that the Federal Reserve Bank of New York (and by implication, the Federal Reserve Board in Washington) had negligently allowed such extensive accommodation to so seemingly unworthy a supplicant as the Chase National Bank.

As a nationally chartered bank, Harding had the pleasure of pointing out to Williams, Chase fell under the comptroller's own regulatory purview. Admittedly, the Federal Reserve had the authority to examine any member bank it chose, but, reposing the confidence it had in Williams's examiners, the Reserve Board felt that any such duplication of effort would be unnecessary.

"We are surprised that such developments should have taken place in a National bank under your supervision," Harding wound up, "and wonder why it is that your examiners did not discover and report these conditions at an earlier date."[2]

Not many could outargue Williams, and fewer still could outtalk or outwrite him. The comptroller answered Harding's letter with four of his own. Each met the Williams standard in length, documentation (relevant or otherwise) and contentiousness, while the fourth rocket, dated February 28, hit a new mark in combustibility. In it, the comptroller proposed to show that the state-chartered Guaranty Trust Company of New York was on the rocks. He had so argued before, he reminded Harding, though mere repetition only slightly reduced the shock value of the allegations. So lofty was the reputation of the Guaranty Trust that Williams might as well have cast aspersions on the House of Morgan.

Because the Guaranty owed its legal existence to New York, it was the state's examiners who inspected its books. The Guaranty was functionally a bank; it took deposits, and it loaned and invested. Indeed, in deposits, it ranked second in New York only behind National City Bank, $481.9 million to $600 million. Among trust companies, only Bankers Trust, with deposits of $222.3 million, was close to the Guaranty.

As a trust company, the Guaranty was a kind of bank that could lawfully invest in real estate, a privilege (and a temptation) denied to Williams's charges. The Guaranty was advantaged, as well, in having to set aside fewer idle dollars—i.e., "reserves"—than its national cousins were required to maintain.[3] Before the advent of the Federal Reserve System, the New York trust companies had been more susceptible to runs than nationally chartered banks, a fact that had been amply demonstrated during the Panic of 1907. But now, a trust-company member of the Federal Reserve could borrow on the same terms as a federally chartered institution could. Certainly, the Guaranty Trust proved that to Williams's satisfaction.

A measure of the stature of the Guaranty was that its president, Charles H. Sabin, shared the rostrum with Governor Harding at an annual banquet of the New York State Bankers Association at the Waldorf Astoria on January 17, 1921. Expressing "conservative optimism, renewed courage and restored confidence," the Guaranty's head man reviewed the lessons that the banking industry had learned from 1920. At the top of his list was "the folly of extravagance in personal, business and governmental affairs." There were, of course, plenty of problems ahead, Sabin acknowledged—there always were after bouts of financial stringency. And there were plenty of crackpot ideas to deal with them, including punitive regulation and a tax on undivided profits. "Such perverted thinking and loose talking as have ruined Russia are now seeking to injure our private and public institutions," he said. "They are responsible for the false and absurd rumors circulated about solvent firms and sound financial institutions; they must be stamped out."[4]

On the star-studded board of the Guaranty sat, among others, Daniel Guggenheim of Guggenheim Brothers; A.C. Bedford, chairman of Standard Oil of New Jersey; Eugene G. Grace, president of Bethlehem Steel Corporation; Thomas W. Lamont, partner of J.P. Morgan; John S. Runnells, president of the Pullman Company; Harry Payne Whitney, heir, horseman and yachtsman; and Williams's old sparring partner, Thomas Fortune Ryan. A less likely collection of candidates for leading a bank into insolvency was hard to conceive of, though, as it surely must have occurred to Williams, Ryan had feet of clay.

Strictly speaking, the overseer of the nationally chartered banks had no official supervisory business with any trust company, especially—so it might have seemed—one so far above suspicion as the Guaranty Trust Company. But a governor of the Federal Reserve would have had every reason to interest himself in allegations of unsound practices at a member bank, especially one as large as the Guaranty Trust. While, in those days, no bank, officially, was "too big to fail," bankers and regulators alike were well aware of the risk that a shocking, conspicuous failure could pose to the banking system. The Guaranty's failure, if such a thing were imaginable (Sabin seems not to have considered it), would surely have rattled windows far from Wall Street. Late in 1919, the Federal Reserve Bank of New York was advancing that institution as much as $120 million, approximately twice as much as the sum of the Guaranty's capital and surplus and more than five times the average capital of the New York Reserve bank itself.[5]

That the Guaranty Trust was taking undue risk was one clear message of the examiner's reports from which Williams quoted. Just how serious was the trouble that the examiner identified, what that trouble signified for banks in general and what those difficulties might imply about the Federal Reserve's high interest rates, were questions without obvious answers.

When the New York examiners came calling on the Guaranty Trust late in May 1920, the depression was only beginning to leave its visible marks on American business. But there were signs of distress already in the Guaranty's books. Doubtful loans totaled $28 million. Under the heading of "Investment securities of doubtful value or not readily marketable," Williams quoted an examiner as saying, "Quite a large amount aggregating about seven millions. Not practicable to list here."[6] There were an additional $5 million of slow loans in the foreign department, and losses in market value of investment securities on the order of $2.9 million. Among such bruised and dented holdings were bonds of Seaboard Air Line, the railroad that Williams had lost to Thomas F. Ryan, for which the Guaranty had paid $1.3 million. They were quoted in the market at just $641,000, or 49 cents on the dollar. In about half of the $28 million in slow loans, President Sabin was said to have acted as guarantor or held some other personal interest in the transaction. Altogether, assets identified as slow, doubtful or impaired (including the mark-to-market losses just cited) made a grand total of at least $43.4 million, against which the Guaranty Trust showed capital and surplus of $66.3 million. "Quick," or highly liquid, assets amounted to just

$2.1 million, "or less than one-half of one percent of its deposits," as Williams emphatically noted.

"The rapid growth of this company has been such that it has often appeared to your Examiner that the management has not been able to keep pace with it, and things have not always appeared to be as well centralized or to run as smoothly as in some of our other institutions." So concluded the examiner in a report to the New York State superintendent of banks, dated July 7, 1920. Williams, having quoted this language to Harding, added his own astringent, upper-case summary:

THE REPORTS OF EXAMINATION WHICH WERE BEFORE THE FEDERAL RESERVE BOARD AND THE NEW YORK FEDERAL RESERVE BANK SHOW CONCLUSIVELY THAT THE GUARANTY TRUST COMPANY HAD BECOME AN ENORMOUS ENGINE OF SPECULATION; THAT IT WAS ENGAGED IN PROMOTING SPECULATIVE SCHEMES AND VENTURES NOT ONLY IN ALL PARTS OF THIS COUNTRY BUT IN FOREIGN COUNTRIES AS WELL.

First, they were investing their own funds in the stocks of highly speculative corporations, new and old;

Second, they were carrying syndicate [i.e., securities underwriting] participations on joint accounts in all kinds of speculative syndicates;

Third, they were furnishing money to borrowers who were engaged in promoting all sorts of speculative operations;

Fourth, these transactions were being largely financed on money borrowed from the Federal Reserve Bank of New York. The BORROWINGS at the time that I wrote my letter to you [i.e., one dated January 28, 1920] aggregated close to . . . . $131,000,000.[7]

And the Guaranty Trust had continued to avail itself of the openhanded accommodation of the Federal Reserve Bank of New York, Williams continued. Its monthly borrowings had ranged from $47 million (almost twice as much as the Guaranty's capital) to $129 million.

"I hardly think it necessary for me to discuss at this time the question as to whether the Board and the Reserve Bank of New York exercised reasonable and proper discretion in extending such credits," the comptroller added on page 10, though he appended five more single-spaced pages, quoting from his previous communication on the Guaranty, just in case Harding had forgotten them.

On its face, Williams's rendering of the findings of the New York State examiner was deeply troubling. If an institution as well reputed as the Guaranty was making such heavy weather of it—abusing the Federal Reserve's credit facilities all along the way—it was not unreasonable to suppose that other, less seaworthy banks and trust companies must be shipping water.

Yet what the comptroller asserted in one gesture, word or line of argument, he seemingly wiped away in another. He was collegial and not collegial. He was bearish and he was bullish. He damned the Federal Reserve and he praised it. He denounced deflation and he winked at it.

He had an office at the Federal Reserve Board, just as the other governors did.[8] If he had criticisms to make, Harding wondered, why didn't he just come out with it, man to man? Why didn't he air his demands for lower interest rates at regular meetings of the Federal Reserve Board, at which, as Harding did not neglect to record, his attendance was spotty? The comptroller did not do business in this courteous fashion but rather committed his often unsettling and sometimes bitter comments to paper and circulated copies of his letters outside the board, including to, among others, Senator Carter Glass.[9] Williams's correspondence radiated hostility toward the Federal Reserve, yet, early in 1921, he was pleased to invite the governors to spend the weekend at his country estate near Richmond (Harding, who accepted the invitation, along with two others, found Williams to be a most genial host).[10] And, even as he berated the management of the central bank in correspondence with Harding, Williams mystifyingly praised it in the pages of the newly published annual report of the comptroller of the currency for 1920, which he himself wrote.

It was Williams's final testament on the state of American banking before he resigned his office in March 1921. Reading it, one might have supposed that the comptroller supported the 7 percent discount rate policy, not opposed it. That America had avoided "the financial crises and complete disorganization which have made havoc elsewhere," according to Harding's bête noire, was "thanks largely to the splendid efficiency and stabilizing influence of the Federal reserve system."[11]

Neither, reading Williams, would one have supposed that the National

City Bank was drowning in sugar loans or that the Chase National Bank was riddled with self-dealing or that the Guaranty Trust Company of New York was an "engine of speculation." Banks had never been more profitable than they were in the 12 months through June 30, 1920, the comptroller attested. Moreover, since 1914—which happened to mark the start of his stewardship of the comptroller's office—the cumulative net earnings of the nationally chartered banks exceeded by $18 million the cumulative earnings of the nationally chartered banks during the 43 years from 1870 to 1913. As for failures, the comptroller pointed out, "The total capital of the five small national banks which failed during the year was $225,000, or seventeen one-thousandths of 1% of the total capital of all national banks," a showing "16 times better than the average of the entire period of 57 years, from the inauguration of the national banking system to the present."[12]

Nor, on the fraught topic of deflation, had the author of the comptroller's annual report evidently conferred with the man who badgered Harding. The singular, unprecedented and worldwide collapse in the prices of just about every commodity was, indeed, devastating, the comptroller's text allowed. But it was, after all, "inevitable," and, indeed, not altogether harmful, as "the country is now in many respects on a sounder basis, economically, than it has been for years."[13] Speed the day, Williams added, when "the private citizen is able to acquire, at the expenditure of $1 of his hard-earned money, something approximating the quantity and quality which that dollar commanded in prewar times."

So the personnel of the Federal Reserve Board were seemingly—astoundingly—in agreement. A continuing, drastic and perhaps violent rollback in prices, and therefore in wages, was the way forward.

10

A KIND WORD
FOR MISFORTUNE

American business, agriculture and labor were "readjusting." Prices and wages would fall, as they usually did following wars. Debtors would suffer, as would any holding overlarge stocks of crops or industrial commodities acquired at inflated prices. As there would—certainly—be no change in the gold value of a dollar, the burden of adjustment would have to fall on those who earned the dollars, owed them, loaned them or saved them. There was, however, one signal difference in this particular episode of postwar readjustment. No financial panic was in the cards: The Federal Reserve had seen to that.

Such was the narrative in the New York financial press in late 1920 and early 1921. The editors did not deny that deflation was underway. Nor did Governor Harding. All hands (i.e., those hands to whom the press accorded the privilege of a quotable voice) agreed that readjustment was necessary.*

---

*Among the dissenters was W. Jett Lauck, an economist who represented the railroad unions that were resisting deflationary wage reductions. In a 125,000-word brief he submitted to the Railway Labor Board in April 1921, Lauck contended that a "capital combine" of a dozen Wall Street financial institutions, under the baleful leadership of J.P. Morgan & Co., had "deliberately deflated the farmers and then

Harding gave speech after speech proclaiming that better times were at hand. This was not despite falling prices but because of them. He was on hand at Delmonico's in lower Manhattan on the evening of January 7, 1921, to honor the return to private business of the former secretary of the navy and unsuccessful Democratic vice presidential candidate, Franklin D. Roosevelt. Van Lear Black, publisher of the *Baltimore Sun* papers, saw to it that the honoree was rewarded with a private office and salary, even if the voters had denied him a public office. The Fidelity Trust and Deposit Company of Maryland, in which Black also had an interest, had just made the disappointed politician a vice president (the kind of vice president who could be spared from the bank to make a political speech).[1]

Addressing the diners through the postdessert cigar smoke, Harding reiterated his by-now-familiar optimism. There never had been much chance of a financial panic, he said, but now even that tiny risk was removed. He especially welcomed the recent acknowledgment by the Bank of North Dakota that it was futile to hold wheat off the market in hopes of realizing a price of $3 a bushel. Better, as the bank now advised its farmer clientele, to just sell their crops for whatever price the market would bear. As Harding spoke, a bushel of wheat commanded $1.49; at its lows in November 1921, it would fetch just $0.93.

"It is a source of gratification," opined the Federal Reserve Bank of Boston in a comment on the collapse in prices, "that as month follows month during this period, no general business disaster or widespread distress has yet occurred to shock the economic structure. On the contrary, we have been witnessing two important conditions precedent to the laying of enduring foundations for the future stability of business, namely, liquidation and deflation, which have been orderly, and an increasingly satisfactory banking situation with reserves augmented and loans decreasing."[2]

Assuredly, the wheat farmers of North Dakota, no more than the cotton growers of Alabama or the wool ranchers of Wyoming, were gratified by the course of liquidation and deflation. But one man's prices were another's

---

undertook by precipitating industrial stagnation to deflate labor." The railroads were pleading poverty, Lauck's brief contended, when in fact—even after the wartime interlude of government ownership and Interstate Commerce Commission–ordered rate suppression—they were rich. Capital was on strike against society, Lauck charged, and would remain on strike "until labor comes to its knees and consents to surrender its right to bargain collectively on a scale co-extensive with the organization of the employers." [*New York Times*, April 20, 1921]

costs. The railroads, heavy consumers of coal and steel, were naturally pleased by the declining cost of those critical inputs. Newspaper publishers similarly welcomed the opportunity to pay a nickel a pound for newsprint in March 1921, half the rate of the previous October, though not yet the good old pre-war price of two cents a pound.

Plunging prices were bane and blessing, all at once. They made American exports more competitive and American investments more alluring (certainly, more value laden). They made the governors of the Federal Reserve Board more amenable to considering a reduction in interest rates. They delivered relief to the inflation-weary shoppers, at least to those who still held jobs.

The gold-mining industry was a special beneficiary of cheapening commodity costs. Though the value of a dollar—i.e., the price of gold—was fixed by law, the cost of mining gold was variable. It had climbed during the war and for a year or more following the peace. Now it was plunging, and the miners' profit margins, in consequence, were rising. The higher the miners' margins, the greater their incentive to produce. And, of course, what they produced was money itself, the very article that, in a depression, everyone wanted more of.

Many were the uses of adversity, as a federally sponsored postmortem of the depression concluded. "Misfortune is not always to be appraised at face value," ventured the Columbia University sociologist Stuart A. Rice. "It drags down one person to ruin and despair. It serves another as a whetstone to point ambition and sharpen latent powers. . . . Unemployment, then, is sometimes good, generally bad and is frequently disastrous beyond repair for those concerned."

By averring that unemployment might be "good," even "sometimes good," Rice was not going off half cocked. He had a testimonial to that effect from S.R. Rectanus, director of employment at the American Rolling Mill, in Middletown, Ohio. Responding to a government questionnaire toward the end of the depression, Rectanus extolled the character-building dimensions of joblessness. "Within our experience," he related,

> there are no specific outstanding cases of disaster as the result of unemploy-
> ment nor can we say that this individual or that was particularly benefited,
> but our general impression gained through rather close observation is that

the moral fiber of our community was strengthened during the past fifteen months.[3]

Other respondents, hewing to the view that unemployment was "generally bad," or even worse than generally bad, noted that jobless people ate badly, dressed badly and lived without amenities. They sent their school-age children out to work, or away to live in foster homes. If they were able to keep their homes, they were often unable to heat them. "Unemployment is deadly in its effects," attested the personnel director of the Hammermill Paper Company, in Erie, Pennsylvania. "It breaks down morale, destroys courage, confidence and ambition, and finally produces poverty, than which there is no greater evil."[4]

David Mitchell, a western coal miner, lined up with the Hammermill man rather than with the one from the American Rolling Mill. Neither did he seem to share in Daniel Guggenheim's optimism about the business cycle. "A working man," Mitchell related,

> has sort of a treadmill existence. The treadmill sets on the edge of a cliff. You work for a while, pay your debts, unemployment comes, back you go into debt, each time a little farther. When work comes again it finds one a little weaker, and the battle against the mill is not as successful as before. Your creditors become alarmed; possibly a garnishment on your next earnings. The mill has got you over the cliff.[5]

America was engulfed in a "suicide wave," Dr. Harry M. Warren, president of the Save-a-Life League in New York City, reported in August 1921.[6] He said that 6,509 suicides were reported to the league in the first six months of 1921, up from 1,771 in the first half of 1920. "Month after month, the suicide rate is mounting over the corresponding figures for 1920," a mortality report by the Metropolitan Life Insurance Company corroborated. "It is an interesting problem to know whether the unemployment situation of the last year is, in fact, responsible for the observed conditions as to suicide."*[7]

---

*It was no easy question to answer. The war had ended three years earlier, and what we today know as post-traumatic stress disorder was a condition yet undiagnosed. Deaths from the 1918–19 pneumonia pandemic must surely have left many bereaved and despairing people in its wake. The national suicide

• • •

Tucked away in the John Skelton Williams archives is a newspaper cartoon that the comptroller did not draw but that he might have inspired. The scene is an operating room out of the blood-bucket era of orthopedic medicine. The patient, unanesthetized, is labeled "Business." The surgical subject is visibly sweating as he watches the doctor, named "Deflation," wielding an immense crosscut saw, start to amputate his right leg. It is more than concerning to Business that the doctor is oblivious to the ingrown toenail, designated "Speculation and High Prices," for which the patient had evidently sought treatment. "Gosh, Doc," implores Business, "couldn't you cut it off down a little nearer the toe?" The surgeon, too busy to listen, is ticketed "Federal Reserve Board." [8]

More than a few reputable economists agreed with the cartoonist. To Gustav Cassel, as well as to Fisher and Keynes, the Federal Reserve Board's deflation was a cruel and colossal blunder. If their language was less emotional than John Skelton Williams's, their conclusions were little different from the fiery Virginian's. Deflation was a bane and a curse, they judged.

Stability was the ideal, they urged, stability of prices most of all. The gold standard was yesterday's orthodoxy. A new century called for currencies, the gold value of which was not inflexible. Or, even if the world chose to return to fixed exchange rates, it should not fix them at prewar levels. To do so would institutionalize falling prices and unacceptably high unemployment.

There was something medieval about deflation to the sensibilities of the monetary reformers. In London, Barclays Bank wondered how it could possibly lead to anything except depression. Falling prices would deaden business activity and therefore reduce tax collections. It was a policy that,

---

rate, per 100,000 people, amounted to 12.4 in 1921. It had been higher in the panic year of 1907 (14.5) and would be higher still in the final full year of the Great Depression, 1932 (17.4). [*Historical Statistics of the United States*]

In fact, according to a consortium of major American life insurance companies, the overall death rate in 1921, 8.24 per thousand, made that year "the healthiest year on record." The flu had virtually disappeared, and deaths from pneumonia had fallen by 50 percent compared to 1920. The most menacing killer was a new, mechanized one, to which the actuaries referred as "bacillus automobilis." [*New York Times*, December 11, 1921]

"by retarding trade recovery and reducing the nation's productive capacity, will accentuate the very evils it is desired to cure," the bank concluded.[9]

Yes, Cassel acknowledged, the Federal Reserve sought a gradual deflation, but no such thing was possible. A central bank could set prices to falling, but it could control neither the rate of descent nor the depth to which the average price would finally tumble. Only consider the American experience. In October 1920, Harding et al. had drafted assurances that the "readjustment" in prices was nearing its end. At the time, the price level stood at 225 on the Bureau of Labor Statistics scale. By June 1921, the said index registered 148, a drop of 34 percent.[10]

· "By their energetic efforts at curtailing credits, and especially by their high discount rates," Cassel contended, "the Federal Reserve banks have brought about an extensive, and sometimes precipitate, realization [i.e., sale] of accumulated stocks [i.e., inventories], have severely cut down the demand for capital for all kinds of new construction and improvements, and have thus put a very effective check on enterprise."[11]

In conscience, the Federal Reserve could not have denied it. Indeed, Governor Harding, in commending the Bank of North Dakota in pushing for the immediate sale of wheat, had gone on the record for lower prices. Wielding words or interest rates, he was getting the deflation he wanted, if not more.

Like Cassel—and, certainly, unlike Harding—Keynes insisted that deflation was tantamount to depression. Modern business, "being largely carried on with borrowed money," would stop cold in the kind of environment the Federal Reserve was fostering. "It will be to the interest of everyone in business," he wrote,

> to go out of business for the time being; and of everyone who is contemplating expenditure to postpone his orders so long as he can. The wise man will be he who turns his assets into cash, withdraws from the risks and the exertions of activity, and awaits in country retirement the steady appreciation promised him in the value of his cash. A probable expectation of Deflation is bad enough; a certain expectation is disastrous. For the mechanism of the modern business world is even less adapted to fluctuations in the value of money upwards than it is to fluctuations downwards.[12]

Neither did the scholars cede the moral high ground to Harding et al., ground that the Federal Reserve Board had staked out on the eve of its deflation campaign in the autumn of 1919. "To accept the depreciation worked in the dollar by war conditions," the board had written, "and to standardize the dollar of the future on this basis, would be to ratify the inflation wrought by the War and the injustices it produced." [13]

Not at all, Fisher rebutted. By no means was the preponderance of debt outstanding in the early 1920s contracted in hard, 1913 dollars. Most of it was payable in inflated, wartime or postwar dollars. Contracts to pay money were forever being written, renewed, consummated. Some were very old, some very new, but most were (if prewar form still held) probably no more than one year old.

"When, therefore," wrote Keynes, seconding Fisher,

> the depreciation of the currency has lasted long enough for society to adjust itself to the new values, Deflation is even worse than Inflation. Both are "unjust" and disappoint reasonable expectation. But whereas Inflation, by easing the burden of national debt and stimulating enterprise, has a little something to throw on the other side of the balance, Deflation has none.*[14]

Williams had alienated the nation's bankers, particularly the city bankers, and he was *persona non grata* at the Federal Reserve Board. It could not have saddened Harding that he would leave office when President Wilson did. And because Williams was vacating the office of the comptroller, he was necessarily quitting the Federal Reserve Board. Each side, the board and Williams, was glad to see the other's back. On February 26, Williams wrote to condemn, among other things and people, Benjamin Strong for his "angry and mutinous language" while all but challenging the board to a duel by alluding to "unjust criticisms and observations unhappily close to limits beyond which I can permit no man to go." [15] The board, under Harding's

---

*There were respected academic economists on the other side of the argument. Thus, Professor E.W. Kemmerer of Princeton in June 1920, following the imposition of the 7 percent discount rate, in remarks to an audience of bankers: "We must have contraction; we must get it cautiously and carefully. We can't go ahead with our business and make much progress, however, until we get substantial contraction. If I were to summarize the rest of what I have to say in three words, I would say, 'work, save and pay up.'" [Chandler, *Benjamin Strong*, 182]

signature, fired back on March 2, charging that Williams had broken the law by failing to examine the national banks under his supervision at least twice every calendar year, as he was required to do (the comptroller had admitted as much in previous correspondence). "The Comptroller now claims that the Federal Reserve Bank of New York should itself have corrected these serious conditions," Harding et al. went on, "of which it had never been informed and of which it had never been put on notice. . . . Such a plea of confession and avoidance scarcely deserves being dignified with a reply." [16]

Detested though Williams might have been in the inner sanctum of American finance, he was reciprocally embraced by farmers and farm-state legislators. In an address to the Augusta (Georgia) Chamber of Commerce and the Georgia Press Association in July 1921, the excomptroller charged that the "losses and ruin which have attended the drastic shrinkage and deflation of values have been accentuated and made unnecessarily hard to bear by the stubbornly unwise and the unwise stubborn course of a majority of members of the Federal Reserve Board." He would resist these wrongs, Williams vowed, fighting "with all the fair means I can command, and with both fists, and to go on fighting." [17]

But it was W.P.G. Harding who threw the first punch, or tried to. Harding, Williams and Benjamin Strong had been summoned to testify before the Joint Agricultural Commission as to the causes of the deepening distress of the farmers. By then, the Federal Reserve Board and Williams had stopped talking to each other (though Williams had certainly not stopped talking *about* the Federal Reserve). It had fallen to Strong and Harding to answer the attacks of the monetary critics, Williams's most of all. During a preliminary exchange of unpleasantries, Harding lunged for Williams. The governor of the Federal Reserve Board failed to throttle his tormenter only on account of the timely intervention of his "struggling associates just in front of his adversary," as the *New York Times* reported on the encounter in a congressional hearing room on August 3, 1921.

The unpleasantries continued, though with no further recorded assaults. It came to light that Williams himself had supported the board's early deflationary policies. [18] Neither did the former comptroller score in his attack on the lending practices of the Chase National Bank (which discreetly went unnamed), nor in his contention that the board cruelly and ignorantly kept interest rates elevated even after prices had begun to cascade. Records showed that Williams had voted with the majority in imposing interest-rate surcharges, so-called progressive rates, on banks that borrowed over their limits; on those occasions, he had been ill informed, Williams lamely countered.[19]

The fact is that the Federal Reserve did set out on a program of deflation and that it did set constrictingly high interest rates. Not that Harding and Strong conceded much to their critics.

"There is a prevailing impression," Representative Ogden Mills, Republican of New York, addressed Harding when the governor took the witness chair, "that the break in general prices in 1920 was due to the restriction of credit, and that the Reserve board was responsible for the restriction."

"There is nothing in it," Harding replied. "Our efforts were devoted in 1920 to preventing a collapse of our banking system. It isn't our duty to enhance or reduce prices, but credit is based on prices, and in 1920 we had most significant signs a break was coming."

And if the Federal Reserve had not acted to tighten credit? asked a Republican senator from Wisconsin, Irvine Luther Lenroot.

"You can tell what happened in Cuba," Harding relied. "There would have come collapse, aggravated by banking insolvency."

"Suppose the board had restricted earlier," Lenroot said. "Would not the rise in prices have been lessened?"

Harding said it was likely. "I'll be frank with you. Had interest rates been put up earlier, the runaway movement in prices and speculation might have been checked. And it might have been better."

That much the Federal Reserve was willing to allow, but not much more. Strong made his rebuttal in three days of testimony that filled 367 transcript pages and was buttressed by 40 graphs and 47 statistical tables.[20] Yielding no ground to Williams, the governor of the Federal Reserve Bank of New York ventured a prediction: "For the benefit of those who are inclined to indulge in gloom, I want to say that we have entered the cycles of recovery."[21]

11

NOT THE
GOVERNMENT'S AFFAIR

The depression was something more than a rumor to the delegates to the Republican National Convention as they filed into the sweltering Chicago Coliseum on June 8, 1920. The Federal Reserve's index of industrial production had begun to weaken in March. Prices of sugar, cotton and wheat had peaked in May. Auto sales were softening. Common stocks were eight months into their bear market.[1]

The Republicans, presumptive beneficiaries of the economic difficulties of the Wilson administration, produced a platform in which business conditions were an afterthought. The only plank that seemed to animate the delegates was one that masterfully straddled the burning issue of the League of Nations.[2] As far as the political-economic mind of 1920 was concerned, there was no "U.S. economy." And as the economic totality was yet unimagined, so, too, was the government's role in directing, managing and stimulating it.

Looking backward, as committees are wont to do, the Republican platform drafting committee chose to condemn the inflation that was already ending. The 50-cent Democratic dollar was the prime cause of the high cost of living, the platform said; and the "gross expansion of our currency and credit" was the main cause of the halving of the dollar's purchasing power. There was no easy way out of the mess, and "much of the injury wrought is irreparable." The GOP, the party of "honest money and sound finance," pledged itself to "earnest and persistent attack on the high cost of living." It would achieve this goal by, among other things, "courageous and intelligent deflation of over-expanded credit and currency."*

Neither did the Democrats, convening in San Francisco on June 28, betray any inkling of what the economic future held. They, too, rounded on the high cost of living, which they blamed on Republican recalcitrance over the League of Nations and "conscienceless profiteering." Yet, despite Republican obstructionism, "the credit of the Government of the United States stands unimpaired, the Federal Reserve note is the unit of value throughout all the world; and the United States is the one great country in the world which maintains a free gold market." By reaffirming its commitment to the gold value of the prewar dollar, the Democratic Party, too, could be said to have chosen the deflation side of the monetary argument.

Ohio had produced six of the 10 presidents since 1869, and the odds were strong that it would deliver the 11th in 1920. Senator Warren G. Harding, the Republican nominee, was the former editor and publisher of the *Marion* (Ohio) *Star*. Ohio Governor James M. Cox, his Democratic opponent, had been the editor and publisher of the Dayton *Daily News*. No Buckeye was Eugene V. Debs, the Socialist candidate, though that was the least of Debs's political disadvantages. He was serving a 10-year prison sentence in Atlanta for obstructing the war effort.[3]

Debs's campaign was stationary of necessity. Harding initially clung to his front porch by choice while Cox barnstormed the country. Debs, naturally, spoke little for the record. Harding made soothing and conciliatory speeches in Marion, while Cox seemed to fly off the handle wherever he alighted from a moving conveyance. "Cox was arrested for speeding, was in a railway accident, was hustled, crowded, heckled and plagued by fatigue,

---

*William G. McAdoo, a Democratic presidential aspirant, in 1923 charged that this plank was the real cause of the deflationary collapse. People realized that the GOP would probably win. To prepare for Republican policies under an imminent Harding administration, they took anticipatory action. Bankers called loans and businessmen liquidated inventories. So contending, McAdoo scored more political points than financial or economic ones. The deflation was in progress well before the Republican platform writers sat down to work. [McAdoo to Glass, May 7, 1923]

hoarseness, and dyspepsia," wrote a historian of the campaign.[4] Few of the innumerable campaign words issuing from any political mouth concerned the fact that the bottom was falling out of business and agriculture.

Wilson had hoped that the campaign would be a "great and solemn referendum" on the League of Nations, which, minus the solemnity, it sometimes was. Cox, quick off the mark, led not with the League, but with the alleged corruption of the Harding finance committee. It was raising $8 million—no, Cox subsequently corrected himself, make that $30 million—to buy the White House. It was a "business plot" by conspirators seeking "the bayonet at the factory door, profiteering at the gates of the farm, the burden of government on shoulders other than their own and the Federal Reserve System an annex to big business."[*][5]

The contestants in the League fight resembled a circling pair of reluctant boxers. Candidate Harding, determined to prevent another schism like the one that, in 1912, had forced Republicans to choose between William Howard Taft and Theodore Roosevelt (the country wound up with Wilson instead), went out of his way to mollify pro-League Republicans. Cox extolled the League while also attempting to assuage the Democratic reservationists.

On August 10, Senator Boies Penrose, Republican of Pennsylvania, interrupted the foreign-policy debate to suggest that the voters probably cared less about the League of Nations than they did about the high cost of living.[6] Presently, the voters would be less concerned about inflated prices than a deflated labor market. As Penrose spoke, the prices of oats, sulfuric acid, structural steel beams, cattle, rye, shoe leather, flooring pine, common brick and newsprint had joined the lengthening list of free-falling commodity quotations.[7]

Neither Harding nor Cox seemed to notice. Certainly, neither presidential candidate—nor, for that matter, their running mates, Calvin Coolidge for the GOP and Franklin D. Roosevelt for the Democrats—rushed forward with a plan to stimulate consumption or investment or otherwise to anticipate modern macroeconomic management.

True to custom, both sides deplored waste and extravagance in the

---

*Republicans heavily outspent Democrats in 1920, perhaps by a margin of three to one, though the size of the respective dollar outlays is uncertain. According to Republican Senator William S. Kenyon of Iowa, the GOP spent $8.1 million, the Democrats $2.2 million, on all races, local, state and national. [Murray, *Harding Era*, 67]

federal finances. Each supported a more systematic management of government income and outgo. And each supported a balanced federal budget. Cox, a defender of Wilson's Progressivism and, as governor of Ohio, a leader in enacting a workmen's compensation law,[8] talked a more radical economic agenda than he seemed prepared to implement. Like Harding, Cox believed that business was better served with less government interference than with more.

In January 1919, a Kansas City newspaperman named E. Mont Reily composed a circular letter to "My Fellow Republicans" proposing Warren G. Harding as the party's standard-bearer in 1920. Consider Harding's assets, Reily mused: He was from that cradle of presidents, Ohio; he was a youthful 53; he had an oratorical gift surpassing even the great William McKinley's; he had remained regular and loyal to Taft in 1912; and he believed "in normal things, normal thinking and normal legislation." Anticipating success, Reily offered a campaign slogan: "Harding and Back to Normal."[*][†][9]

Reily had never met Harding, but he seemed to know him. "Normal," middle-of-the-road Republican things were what the candidate stood for. Good Republican that he was, Harding espoused a high protective tariff behind which American industry could produce good American jobs. He supported tighter restrictions on immigration, the elimination of the wartime excess-profits tax, the reduction of wartime surtaxes on upper incomes and more credit for the farmer. He endorsed collective bargaining and trade unionism, though not the unchecked power of organized labor.

Before his presidential career, Harding had been a regular on the Chautauqua lecture circuit. As early as 1904, for the consideration of 25 cents, one could hear him—he was then lieutenant governor of Ohio—hold forth at the Marion Armory on "Alexander Hamilton: Prophet of American Destiny." Harding seemed to imbibe the essence of the Hamiltonian doctrine, for he championed low taxes and minimum government economic intervention. "We need vastly more freedom than we do regulation," the presidential

---

*Albert D. Lasker, the advertising man who managed publicity for the GOP in 1920, popularized a shorter verison of the Reily inspiration: "Back to Normalcy." [Murray, *Harding Era*, 51]

†In recognition of his status as the "original Harding man," the president appointed Reily governor of Puerto Rico in 1921. Reily botched the job and resigned, much to Harding's relief, in 1923.

candidate declared in February 1920. "Less government in business and more business in government" was the ticket, he wrote in an essay that was published around Election Day. In it, Harding proposed the creation of a new federal agency to manage the government's finances.[10]

Harding's program, though, was chiefly himself. He was a candidate of disposition rather than ideas. Conciliatory, handsome, humble, tranquil, evidently ordinary—above all, "normal"—he was the antidote to the larger-than-life figures who had recently filled the White House to overflowing. If, to a caricaturist, Teddy Roosevelt was all brawn and Woodrow Wilson all brains, Harding was all smiles. Intellectuals sneered, none more so than the Wilsonians. "If we can beat anyone," Edward M. House confided to Brand Whitlock, "we should be able to beat Harding."[11] Cox, calling his Republican opponent a liar for something he had said about Wilson, added for good measure, "I suppose it is too much to ask that mediocrity pay to greatness the grateful tribute of truth."[12] "[A] third-rate political wheel-horse, with the face of a moving-picture actor, the intelligence of a respectable agricultural implement-dealer and the imagination of a lodge-joiner," sneered H.L. Mencken of the former Marion newspaperman.[13]

Harding readily conceded his intellectual limitations. He confessed that he couldn't understand the pros and cons of the tax question; the last person he listened to was the one he found the most persuasive.*[14] "Harding is nothing," said Wilson of his soon-to-be successor.[15] "[O]ne of the most intellectual figures of a century and a half," said Harding of Wilson.[16]

Harding was the binder up of wounds, the mediator of old quarrels and the salver of damaged egos. Progressive Republicans had wanted nothing to do with him, but now, in droves, they signed up to campaign for him.[17] They were disarmed by the man who wouldn't speak ill of them—would not, in fact, speak ill of anyone, including the reviled Democratic incumbent. In response to an early suggestion that the Republican campaign zero in on the sick and pathetic figure of Woodrow Wilson, Harding demurred. "I guess you have nominated the wrong candidate, if this is the plan, for I will never go to the White House over the broken body of Woodrow Wilson," he told his handlers.[18]

---

*I can't make a damn thing out of this tax problem," Harding once confided to an aide. "I listen to one side and they seem right, and then—God!—I talk to the other side and they seem just as right."

Harding intuited how tired was the country of Progressive experimentation and great crusades. "America's present need," he declared in May 1920, the month before he was nominated, "is not heroics but healing; not nostrums but normalcy; not revolution but restoration . . . not surgery but serenity."[19]

Like Mencken, McAdoo gagged at the Harding style—"an army of pompous phrases moving over the landscape in search of an idea," he called it.[20] But Americans warmed to the calm man with "no beads on his forehead, no dust on his shoes, no red in his eye," as a less partisan observer perceived the candidate.[21] "It got no rise out of Harding when Cox called him a standpatter," the journalist and historian Mark Sullivan reported. "Harding was a standpatter, a genuine one, his temperament made him one."[22]

"This subject of the League of Nations, frankly, has possessed my very soul," said Cox in the heat of the campaign.[23] It was not something that Harding would have said.

Reliably Republican Maine, which voted early, had been tipped to go for Harding with 20,000 votes to spare but instead delivered a margin of 66,000 votes.[24] Cox concluded his Marathon of vote chasing at Chicago and Akron on the eve of the national election. There he reiterated the Wilsonian theme that the campaign was really a moral referendum, a test as to "whether the civilization of the world shall tie itself together into a concerted purpose to prevent the tragedies of war." After which he said, "Every traitor in America will vote tomorrow for Warren G. Harding."[25]

The scale of the Republican victory was astounding. Harding won 16.2 million popular votes to Cox's 9.1 million (and to Debs's 942,000); he won 404 electoral votes to Cox's 127. To complement this presidential triumph, the voters handed the GOP 303 House seats to the Democrats' 131 and fattened the Republicans' majority in the Senate to 22 seats, a gain of 10. "It was a landslide, it was an earthquake," allowed Wilson's aide Joe Tumulty.[26]

It happened that Election Day, November 2, was also Harding's birthday, and the imminent president-elect topped off dinner with a big slice of celebratory cake. Just then, as Boyden Sparkes of the *New York Tribune*, reported, "A small group of people straggled up the front walk and into the porch. One of the women in the party stepped over to the bell, hesitated a moment and then rang it."

Harding rose to meet them, "his table napkin still in his hand."

One of the group stumbled through a carefully prepared presentation speech and then—it was old Luther Miller, a long-bearded printer, oldest employee of the *Marion Star*—fairly poked a gift into the editor's hand. It was a printer's rule, made of gold. Then the old printer delivered the last line of his speech. He said that everybody on *The Star* knew that the country was going to have a good President.

It was the editor of the *Star* who tried to speak then. His face twitched. The lines behind his nose and mouth deepened and then tears streamed from his eyes. He tried again to make some kind of reply and then he just began to shake hands with all of them.[27]

★ **12** ★

CUT FROM
CLEVELAND'S CLOTH

By the time President Harding got around to mentioning economics in his inaugural address of March 4, 1921, he had already ruminated on America's Founders, the Great War, the League of Nations, American sovereignty, war profits, "the aspirations of humankind" and the commanding necessity of the United States to resume its "onward, normal way." He did not say the words "depression" or "recession," although the slump was already 15 months old. Neither did he propose a government plan to stop it. Rather, he seemed to trust in the curative powers of supply and demand.

"The economic mechanism is intricate and its parts interdependent, and has suffered the shocks and jars incident to abnormal demands, credit inflations and price upheavals," Harding shrewdly observed. War, and the inflation induced by war finance, had upset that mechanism, and it fell to the people to fix it. "Prices must reflect the receding fever of war activities," he said, with a seeming tip of the hat to the Federal Reserve–sponsored deflation. "Perhaps we shall never know the old level of wages again, because war invariably readjusts compensations. . . . All the penalties will not be light, nor evenly distributed. There is no way of making them so. There is no instant step from disorder to order. We must face a condition of grim reality, charge off our losses and start afresh. It is the oldest lesson of civilization."

Government would do its part, the president continued, though he could not seem to specify how. What it should not, and would not, do was tinker with the market system. To be sure, Harding acknowledged, there were alternative approaches, but none was better: "Our best assurance lies in efficient administration of our proven system," the president said.

Mencken flayed the Harding speech as "rumble and bumble," "flap and doodle" and "balder and dash." This was a rhetorical judgment. On the economic substance, the president was unassailable. It was through the price mechanism that millions of Americans would retune the misaligned economic machinery. Dealers and manufacturers who withheld their inventory in hopes of realizing higher prices at some future date were not merely deluding themselves but also delaying recovery, contended *Nation's Business*, the United States Chamber of Commerce's house organ, in January: "The sooner, within a reasonable time, both of them take their medicine, the sooner we will return to normal times."[1]

President Harding might have failed to appreciate the depth and persistence of the depression. Not so Harding's nominee for secretary of the Treasury, the banker and industrialist Andrew Mellon, one of the wealthiest men in America and, from his vantage point as a director of no fewer than 60 companies, one of the commercially best informed. He subsequently described the crisis of 1921 as "one of the most severe this country has ever experienced."[2]

To Harding and Mellon, it was the very gravity of the situation that demanded reduced federal spending as well as lower tax rates—and, in Mellon's personal view, lower interest rates, too. In none of the 12 years up until 1912 had the federal government spent as much as $700 million, which outlays it financed by consumption taxes derived from the tariff. In 1917, the first year of America's participation in the war, spending leapt to almost $2 billion; by 1919, it topped $18 billion. To Harding, these sums were as disturbing as they were vast. His first fiscal priority was to restore something like prewar order and balance in the nation's finances.

There was, in fact, no way back to the Eden of nine-figure federal budgets. Before the war, the public debt had barely topped $1 billion.[3] Now the annual interest cost on debt on the order of $23 billion came in at around

$1 billion.[4] The means were at hand to reduce the levels of government intake and outgo, the new administration decided. Happily did Harding sign the Budget and Accounting Act on June 20, 1921, legislation to create a Bureau of the Budget to put the government on a businesslike basis. On June 29, with the new budget director, Charles Dawes, at his side, the president looked out at a hastily summoned meeting of the government's top managers, about 1,200 anxious faces.[5] Said Harding:

> The present administration . . . is committed to a period of economy in government. This statement is made not with any thought of criticizing what has gone before. It is made in a new realization of the necessity of driving out the loose, unscientific expenditures of government. There is not a menace in the world today like that of growing public indebtedness and mounting public expenditures. There has seemingly grown up an impression that the public treasuries are inexhaustible things, and with it a conviction that no efficiency and no economy are ever to be thought of in public expense. We want to reverse things.[6]

Dawes was as good as the president's word. In the fiscal year ended June 30, 1922, the can-do budget director presided over a reduction in federal outlays to $3.3 billion, from $5.1 billion the year before. The budget had shown a $291 million surplus in fiscal 1920, Wilson's last year at the helm. The surplus fattened to $509 million in the depression year of 1921 and $736 million in the recovery year of 1922.

Though Harding wanted no part of revolutionary economic systems, he was keen to sabotage the world's established naval and diplomatic order. The means to this attempted subversion—and to an even trimmer federal budget—was the Washington Naval Conference of November 1921, an event convened to head off a race for naval supremacy in the Pacific. Secretary of State Charles Evans Hughes amazed the assembled delegates with a call for the scuttling of 66 capital ships, 30 by the United States Navy, as well as a 10-year cessation of naval construction. The conference produced seven treaties, even if it did not usher in the universal peace to which Harding aspired.[7]

• • •

If, inconceivably, Harding and Mellon and Dawes had sought to encourage business activity by spending the taxpayers' money rather than by saving it, four million voices, at least, might have cheered them on. Those voices belonged to the veterans who, according to the American Legion and its friends in Congress, had never received their just desserts for serving their country. Talk of a soldiers' bonus—or, a more palatable term to the veterans, "adjusted compensation"—began to crop up in Congress before the 1920 elections. It was as quickly batted down by Russell C. Leffingwell, the former Wilson administration official. Harrumphed Leffingwell: "Instead of telling the young men who were drafted to fight the war, and who came back better and stronger and more fit to fight their own battles than they ever were before, to go to work and save their money and look out for themselves as any self-respecting man should, we listen complacently to their organized demands for a bonus."[8]

Leffingwell was, of course, a Democrat, while Representative Joseph W. Fordney of Michigan, who introduced the first bonus bill in 1920, was a Republican.[9] Senator James Alexander Reed, a Missouri Democrat, supported the bonus scheme, while Senator John Sharp Williams of Mississippi, another Democrat, denounced it. Advocates and detractors spoke in language heated to a temperature appropriate to the dollars at stake; estimates of the cost of cash payments to each and every former member of the wartime military and naval forces of the United States ran into the billions of dollars.

Late in the 1880s, the ruling federal fiscal problem was the surplus: Tax receipts annually piled up in the Treasury. Eager to ameliorate that difficulty was James "Corporal" Tanner, President Benjamin Harrison's commissioner of pensions. Tanner, who had suffered the amputation of both legs below the knee at the Second Battle of Bull Run, had more sympathy for the veterans than he had for the Treasury's creditors. "God help the surplus," he cried.[10]

The Harding administration had cause to worry about the resurgence of the Tanner spirit. A tailor-made vote getter, the bonus idea was especially popular in the Senate. Enactment of such legislation would scuttle any hope for the restoration of fiscal order, Mellon's and Harding's first priority.

Candidate Harding had opposed the concept of a bonus well before President Harding did. In September 1920, a reporter from the army newspaper *Stars and Stripes* had visited Marion to solicit the view of the Republican nominee on the bonus question. Harding was forthright. While he was all for helping the wounded and disabled, he could not support plans for any general disbursement. Among the considerations, he cited the sagging market in U.S. Treasury securities. It was overburdened enough as it was, he said.[11]

In early July 1921, the administration decided to take its case against the bonus bill directly to Capitol Hill. Mellon wrote to Republican Senator John S. Frelinghuysen of New Jersey to plead the case for restraint. Enactment of such legislation would saddle the taxpayers with "a stupendous indeterminate liability" and "virtually defeat the Administration's program of economy and retrenchment," he said.[12] While there was no telling exactly how much a bonus would cost (that would depend on which options veterans selected from a proposed menu of federal assistance), the tab would likely be in the neighborhood of $3 billion and could range above $5 billion. Bear in mind, the secretary pointed out, that this prospective drain would coincide with the maturity of $5 billion of short-dated Treasury notes.*

On July 13, Harding took the calculated risk of presenting his case in person to his former colleagues in the Senate chamber. Senators, the gallery jam-packed with visitors and the odd assortment of representatives, rose to applaud the president as he strode in at 2 PM.

Of course, Harding began, the bonus bill was the Senate's business, but the executive branch of government owed the legislative branch an unvarnished accounting of the nation's finances. And what the administration had come to understand during its four months in office was that conditions would "stagger all of us were it not for our abiding faith in America."

Three things should be done immediately, Harding went on: Reduce taxes, refinance the war debt and straighten out the debts that America's wartime allies owed to the Treasury. The bonus bill, whatever its merits— and Harding proceeded to deprecate them—had no claim to first place in the legislative queue.

"It is unthinkable," Harding continued, "to expect a business revival and

---

* America's national output in 1921, measured in nominal dollars (i.e., without adjustment for purchasing power), totaled $69.6 billion.

the resumption of the normal ways of peace while maintaining the excessive taxes of war. It is quite as unthinkable to reduce our tax burdens while committing our Treasury to an additional obligation which ranges from three to five billions of dollars."

The expedient of just printing up dollar bills then being unavailable, Harding reminded the senators of the constraints inherent in the gold standard. "Our Government," he said, "must undertake no obligation which it does not intend to meet. No Government fiat will pay our bills. The exchanges of the world testify today to that erroneous theory. We may rely on the sacrifices of patriotism in war, but today we face markets, and the effects of supply and demand, and the inexorable laws of credits in time of peace."

What the uncounted millions of unemployed people needed was prosperity. Tax cuts and spending reductions would hasten prosperity. The bonus bill would set it back on its heels. "Stabilized finance and well established confidence are both essential to restored industry and commerce," Harding continued.

> The slump which is now upon us is an inevitable part of war's aftermath. It has followed in the wake of war since the world began. There was the unavoidable readjustment, the inevitable charge-off, the unfailing attendance of losses in the wake of high prices, the inexorable deflation which inflation had preceded.
>
> It has been wholly proper to seek to apply Government relief to minimize the hardships, and the Government has aided wherever possible, and it is aiding now, but all of the special acts ever dreamed of, all the particular favors ever conceived, will not avoid all the distresses nor ward off all the losses. The proper mental state of our people will commit us resolutely and confidently to our tasks, and definite assurances as to taxation and expenditure will contribute to that helpful mental order. The only sure way to normalcy is over the paths nature has marked through all human experience.[13]

Harding, then at the peak of his popularity—he had just announced his plan for the naval disarmament conference—got his way, and the Senate shelved the bonus bill. In the House, the great Democratic orator Bourke

Cockran smoldered at the president's trampling of the "sacred rights" of Congress.[14] For facing down his former friends and colleagues in the Senate, the editors of the *New York Times* paid Harding the very handsome compliment of comparing his moral courage with that of a Democratic predecessor, the indomitable Grover Cleveland.*[15]

---

*The bonus bill was reintroduced in the summer of 1922. It passed both the House, 333 to 70, and the Senate, 47 to 22. Harding vetoed the measure, not long before the off-year congressional elections. The House voted to override Harding's veto, while the Senate upheld it. [Sullivan, *Our Times*, 211]

★ 13 ★

A KIND OF
RECOVERY PROGRAM

Andrew W. Mellon looked nothing at all like the business giant he was. To one newspaperman he rather resembled "a tired double-entry bookkeeper who was afraid of losing his job." His hooded, unlit eyes gave fair warning of his unhearty handshake: Only the fingertips were proffered. Mellon's hair was white, and so was the mustache that fringed his unsmiling mouth. When his little cigar went out, he relit the stub. His dark suits hung loosely on his thin frame.

Like Harding, with whom he seemed to share not one personality trait, Mellon was a Hamiltonian. In his 1924 book, titled *Taxation: The People's Business*, he espoused, on the authority of the first secretary of the Treasury, a balanced budget and the repayment of the public debt: "Both are in line with the fundamental policy of the Government since its beginning," he wrote.[1]

In the croesus who didn't look the part, the administration had a one-man force for economic recovery. Mellon's strategy was one of growth through reduction. Shrink tax rates, interest rates and public spending, he urged.

Market interest rates had in fact been falling since the bond market put in its lows in price (which is to say, its highs in yield) in May 1920. Mellon sought a corresponding reduction in the Federal Reserve's administered interest rates. An ex-officio member of the Federal Reserve Board, he weighed in for lower interest rates at his first opportunity, at the meeting of April 4, during which he urged all Reserve banks with 7 percent discount rates to reduce them to 6 percent.*[2] When Harding objected that such a policy might revive bullish speculation in the stock market, Mellon replied that a little speculation might not be a bad thing. Better to wait, Benjamin Strong urged, until wages and prices settled at more acceptable, lower levels.[3]

Boston lowered its rate to 6 percent from 7 percent on April 15.[4] New York trimmed to 6.5 percent from 7 percent on May 4 and Atlanta followed, with a reduction to 6 percent from 7 percent, on May 5. "The changes in discount rates do not indicate any change in policy," W.P.G. Harding hastened to say, "but merely the recognition of the fact that the emergency which justified a 7 percent rate has passed."[5]

Mellon exactly wanted a "change in policy." And when, on June 4, the *New York Times* ran a gossipy bulletin from Washington speculating that a further reduction in rates was on tap for the summer, it did not seem unreasonable that the secretary himself was among the "Treasury officials" who had whispered in the paper's ear.

Strong reluctantly fell in with the easing program. On the one hand, a central bank ought not to lead the market but to follow it, he believed (that was classical doctrine), and the market had not yet spoken, in his opinion. "On the other hand," Strong wrote to his friend Montagu Norman, governor of the Bank of England, on May 5, "a bullheaded resistance in this situation is always liable to invite political retaliation, and I finally concluded that the wisest course was to meet, at least in part, the demand for lower rates."[6] Norman had lowered his own discount rate, to 6.5 percent from 7 percent, on April 28.

Mellon, in his capacity as financier of one of the world's foremost

---

*In official meetings, unless the topic touched on his expertness, Mellon was one to keep his counsel. "What has the Sphinx here got to say on the subject?" Harding jocularly demanded of his Treasury secretary at one cabinet meeting following a wide-ranging discussion of a matter on which Mellon felt he had nothing to contribute. "Well, Mr. President," replied the perplexed financier, "I think there is a good deal to be said on both sides." [Murray, *Harding Era*, 181]

borrowers, might have cheered the news of the falling cost of borrowing, if he were the cheering kind. Some $7.5 billion in short-term Treasury obligations would soon have to be repaid or refinanced. Immediate repayment was, of course, out of the question; the government didn't have the money. The debt would have to be refinanced—that is, repackaged in securities in staggered maturities at what the secretary hoped would be lower interest rates. The Mellon refinancing got underway on June 7, 1921, with the sale of $500 million of three-year notes yielding 5.75 percent and of one-year certificates yielding 5.5 percent. No immediate savings in interest cost was realized, but investors clamored for the new paper.

Along with that gratifying news, Mellon could announce that the Treasury would likely be able to report a $500 million surplus in the fiscal year ending June 30, 1921. He added that the gross debt of the government had been shrunk by $350 million, to about $24 billion, in the previous 11 months. As for the prospective surplus, it would not be spent but "applied for the most part to the retirement of the short-dated debt, chiefly through the operation of the cumulative sinking fund, the current redemptions of war-savings securities and the miscellaneous retirements of the public debt to be made by law." This Hamiltonian update met with the hearty editorial endorsement of the *New York Times*. The editors were especially admiring of the Treasury's reduction in the outstanding volume of short-dated obligations; it called it one of the leading achievements in postwar finance. "There are blemishes on our practice," the paper conceded, "and there are those looking backward who think we ought to have done better. But we have done wonderfully well. Our conditions are the world's best and growing better, even if the Treasury is too much in the money market."[7]

Without uttering the then-unspoken phrase "gross national product," the Harding administration was pushing its plan to restore prosperity. By the summer of 1921, it had tackled the federal budget, announced its plan for a world disarmament conference and enacted an emergency tariff to protect the farmers from imported produce (which was not, in fact, the farmers' problem; the legislation helped them not in the least). Still to be achieved was the apple of Mellon's eye, a comprehensive revamping of the wartime federal tax code. It proved a much more difficult trick.

Leaders of each party were in broad agreement on what had to be done. Mellon's immediate predecessors at the Treasury, David Houston and Carter Glass, had been no less committed in 1919 and 1920 to abolishing the excess-profits tax and the surcharges on the incomes of relatively well-to-do taxpayers than Mellon was in 1921. Leaderless, the Wilson administration could not convert those hopes into action.

Neither did Harding take prompt and decisive action. Let the House take up the emergency tariff fig leaf, he decided, while the Senate began work on tax reduction. But the Senate could seemingly agree to nothing except the soldiers' bonus bill, a fiscal abomination, in the administration's eyes. So, in August, the House began the hard and contentious work of rewriting the tax code.

In 1921, the income tax was not even 10 years old—it shared a 1913 birth year with the Federal Reserve. Those who taxed and those who paid were still testing each other's strength and cunning. Most Americans paid nothing; fewer than 18 percent of the nation's wage earners were required to file a return for 1920. The code in place laid a 4 percent tax on the first $4,000 of income and an 8 percent tax above it. Surtax rates ranged from 1 percent on incomes greater than $5,000 to 65 percent on incomes above $1 million. Corporations paid a 10 percent rate, as well as a tax on profits deemed "excess." Mellon, in testimony before the House Ways and Means Committee on August 4, urged repeal of the excess-profits tax and a halving in the top surcharge rate on personal incomes to 32 percent. Combined with the basic 8 percent tax rate on incomes over $4,000, the maximum federal tax rate would therefore fall to 40 percent from 73 percent.

Joe Fordney, chairman of the Ways and Means Committee, a self-made Saginaw lumber man, was himself a Hamiltonian. It made eminent sense to him, as it did to Mellon, that lower marginal rates would yield not less revenue but more. Lower rates would stimulate enterprise and risk taking while discouraging passive investments in tax-free state and municipal securities, in which many of America's wealthy savers found refuge.

The rich proved vexingly hard to soak. In 1916, before the imposition of high wartime surcharges, 1,296 tax filers had admitted to incomes of more than $300,000. In 1919, only 679 did; as the number of overall tax filers soared by 12 times, the number of filers in the over-$300,000 bracket tumbled by half. The Senate Finance Committee, when it finally turned its attention to the tax question, concluded that a 32 percent top surcharge rate would yield more than the 65 percent rate. Sky-high marginal rates, the committee said, were driving capital into municipal bonds and "encouraging taxpayers to avoid the tax through the device of gifts, division of their income, refraining from profitable sales and placing their money in investments which promise well for the future, but yield no immediate return."[8]

Then, too, the American taxpayer did not file his or her declaration of income with a hand on the Bible. "To many the taxes seemed—as indeed taxes are—a seizure of the individual's property by force majeure exercised by the government," in the words of the journalist and historian Mark Sullivan.

> The ethics that would be recognized and lived up to in private transactions between man and man, voluntary on both sides, did not seem compelling in transactions in which the government demanded arbitrarily, and the citizen paid involuntarily. Men were willing to evade, in situations in which the risk attending evasion—while serious, being fine or imprisonment—nevertheless did not include any wound to the evader's conscience. The amounts involved were large.[9]

The tax bill that emerged from Fordney's committee was approximately the one that Mellon wanted. Its pleasing features included a new, reduced surtax rate (a maximum of 32 percent) and the elimination of the excess-profits tax, each as of January 1, 1921.

Reception of the measure in the full House was wary. Some doubted the wisdom of cutting taxes when enormous bills were still falling due for the Great War. Others objected to the rich paying less under any pretext. "Less than 5,000 persons, most of them war profiteers, pay the higher surtaxes on incomes of more than $100,000 annually," protested Oscar E. Keller, a Minnesota Republican (or, rather, as clear enough from his politics, "Independent" Republican), "yet Secretary Mellon wants to cut in half the $500 million which they contributed to the upkeep of the Government, and throw the additional burden upon small manufacturers, jobbers, merchants and workers and farmers."[10] Another Republican, Alfred Michaelson of Chicago, announced that he would vote for the bill only if his two proposed amendments were adopted: No. 1, the exemption from tax of all incomes under $5,000; No. 2, a 100 percent surtax on all incomes above $1 million.

The cartoonist Ding Darling weighs in on the monetary question, September 1920.
Courtesy of the Jay N. "Ding" Darling Wildlife Society

John Skelton Williams,
comptroller of the currency.
*John Skelton Williams papers, Albert
and Shirley Small Special Collections
Library, University of Virginia*

Comptroller Williams picks a fight with
the banking industry, 1914. *John Skelton
Williams papers, Albert and Shirley Small Special
Collections Library, University of Virginia*

CAN HE MAKE IT? ASK THE TRIBUNE.

Elihu Root of New York, arch opponent of the Federal Reserve Act. *Bettman/Corbis*

Personnel of the original Federal Reserve Board sit for a portrait, August 1914. Seated from left to right: Charles S. Hamlin, W. G. McAdoo, F. A. Delano. Standing: Paul M. Warburg, John Skelton Williams, W.P.G. Harding, Adolf C. Miller.
Bettman/Corbis/AP Images

Benjamin Strong, first chief of the Federal Reserve Bank of New York, in 1917. *Bettman/Corbis*

Wartime price controls produce a New York coal queue, 1918. *Bettman/Corbis*

President Woodrow Wilson, fresh from the Versailles Peace Conference, makes landfall in New York aboard the SS *George Washington*, July 1919. *Bettman/Corbis/AP Images*

President Wilson on his special train in Saint Paul, Minnesota, September 9, 1919, two weeks before the stroke that incapacitated him and his presidency. *Bettman/Corbis*

A. Mitchell Palmer, President Wilson's energetic attorney general. *Bettman/Corbis*

Striking steelworkers make their case to a photographer, September 1919. *Bettman/Corbis/AP Images*

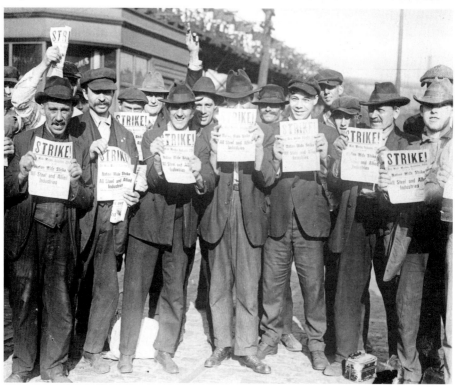

Passage of the Quota Act of 1921 bars would-be immigrants from disembarking from SS *Aquitania* in New York Harbor. *Bettman/Corbis/AP Images*

Striking mill workers take to the streets of Pawtucket, Rhode Island, February 1922. *Bettman/Corbis/AP Images*

Samuel Gompers, president of the American Federation of Labor. *Bettman/Corbis/AP Images*

Socialist Eugene V. Debs, the 1920 election's least conventional presidential candidate, poses in prison garb while clutching a botanical prop. *Bettman/Corbis/AP Images*

Harry S. Truman, foreground, at the Truman & Jacobson haberdashery in Kansas City, January 1921. *Bettman/Corbis/AP Images*

Horse-drawn machinery cuts a swath through a Cuban sugarcane field, January 1920. *Bettman/Corbis/AP Images*

Jobless women throng New York's Free Employment Agency in lower Manhattan, August 1920. *Bettman/Corbis*

Aftermath of the Wall Street bombing of September 16, 1920. *Bettman/Corbis/ AP Images*

President Harding's new secretary of commerce, Herbert Hoover, arrives at the White House for his first cabinet meeting, March 1921. *Bettman/Corbis/AP Images*

Urbain Ledoux, "Mr. Zero," crusader for the unemployed.
Bettman/Corbis/AP Images

Hungry men file through a breadline at the Labor Temple in Cincinnati, February 1921. *Bettman/Corbis*

British unemployed march on Downing Street, October 1920. *Bettman/Corbis*

Labor leader Samuel Gompers, left, and steel magnate Charles M. Schwab uncharacteristically stand together at Hoover's 1921 Unemployment Conference. *Bettman/Corbis*

Judge E. H. Gary, head of U.S. Steel, takes the witness stand, June 1922. *Bettman/Corbis*

Acclaimed a genius: the Yale economist Irving Fisher. *Bettman/Corbis*

President Harding throws out the first pitch on opening day in Washington, D.C., April 13, 1921. *Bettman/Corbis/AP Images*

William "Billy" Durant begins his post–General Motors career with a foot on the running board of the new Durant Star, June 1922. *Bettman/Corbis/AP Images*

Chimneys smoke again at the River Rouge Ford factory, Dearborn, Michigan, December 1922. *Bettman/Corbis/AP Images*

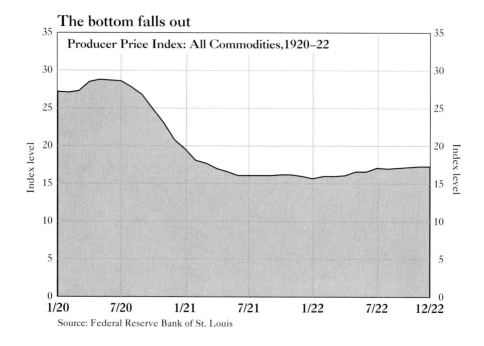

The bottom falls out

Producer Price Index: All Commodities, 1920–22

Source: Federal Reserve Bank of St. Louis

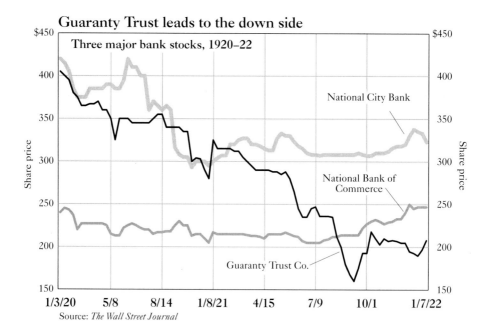

Guaranty Trust leads to the down side

Three major bank stocks, 1920–22

National City Bank

National Bank of Commerce

Guaranty Trust Co.

Source: *The Wall Street Journal*

Michaelson did not, finally, get his way, but neither did Mellon. The Revenue Act of 1921 that President Harding signed just before Thanksgiving held disappointments for all. The excess-profits tax was repealed, but the corporate income-tax rate was raised to 12.5 percent from 10 percent. Surcharges on high earners were capped, though at a rate of 50 percent, not Mellon's preferred 32 percent. A special rate on capital gains was instituted; for many investors, it would be 12.5 percent, with no specified holding period.[11]

For an administration that controlled every branch of government, the new tax law fell far short of a political victory. But it did reveal the Hamiltonian lineaments of that administration, if any still doubted them. Less government in business and more business in government was, indeed, the Harding plan.

WAGES CHASE PRICES

The Dow Jones Industrial Average put in its closing high at 119.62 on November 3, 1919. It was a notable and ominous fact that the Dow Jones Railroad Average failed to confirm the industrials' record with a closing high of its own. It was all very well if a certain stock was on the boil, as the American Bank Note Company was (it could hardly keep up with the public's demand for new share certificates) and as the high-flying Coca-Cola Company also was (an early beneficiary of Prohibition, Coke was preparing to list on the New York Stock Exchange). But these glad tidings concerned companies, not nations. They said nothing about the American economic future.

"As a standing rule," pronounced William Peter Hamilton, astute editor of the *Wall Street Journal,* "it may be taken that the stock market is always many months ahead of business conditions and is moved by the sum of everybody's real knowledge."*[1] There was nothing illegal about insider trading in

---

*John Moody, founder of the eponymous credit-rating service, denied it. "Close study reveals the fact that the stock market is a creature of trade, and a trailer after it, and not a leader or a maker of trade

those days, and corporate disclosure was sparse. In those circumstances—and in the absence of today's superabundance of economic data on production, employment, prices, consumer and business sentiment, et cetera—real knowledge was embedded in stock prices. Especially significant, according to the theory of stock-price movement developed by Charles Dow, a founder of the *Wall Street Journal*, were coordinated movements in the industrials and rails. When a new high, or a new low, in one index was validated by a corresponding move in the other, American enterprise in the aggregate was likely trending in the direction so indicated, either up or down. In the case of the November 3, 1919, nonconfirmation, the direction was down.

One did not have to understand Dow's theory to intuit that the postwar boom was ending. Anyone could see that money was getting tighter. Margined speculators were paying up to 20 percent to "play with stocks," as the *Journal* put it, and they paid it gladly. The market was going up, was it not? That much was evident to the miscellaneous company of lay investors who were knocking down Wall Street's doors. Hotel chefs, undertakers, union officials and leisured ladies were among the latecomers to the frolic.

Was the stock market too high, or, at least, was it overly speculative? Benjamin Strong's branch of the Federal Reserve did not scruple to say so. "On the whole," declared the Federal Reserve Bank of New York on November 1,

> the market seems to have moved according to the rules of speculation rather than of investment. Purchasers appear to have been guided by matters of expectation rather than by performances in the way of earnings and dividends. The steel strike was rather the reverse of a depressing influence, because current market opinion exaggerated the appearances of victory won by the steel companies at the outset. Moreover, high rates for call money, precipitated to a considerable degree by the activity of the market, did not act as a deterrent to the traders, but were regarded merely as an incidental and minor offset to expected profits. Throughout most of the period, urgent liquidation has been notable for its absence.[2]

---

conditions," he contended. A century or so later, it seems that Hamilton was right, and Moody was wrong. [Friedman, *Fortune Tellers*, 89]

Up went the discount rates of the New York Federal Reserve Bank on November 3, by one-quarter of one percent to three-quarters of one percent, depending on the nature of the collateral behind the advance; in the case of 15-day loans against commercial bills, the rate jumped to 4.75 percent from 4 percent. The reason, Strong explained, was the misdirection of "some part of the great volume of credit" into "speculative" channels.[3] A fair reading of Strong's message was that the monetary authorities were not at all afraid of a deflationary liquidation. On the contrary, they meant to sponsor it.

This ambition they presently realized, at least as it pertained to stock prices. From November 3 to the third week in May, the industrials fell by 27 percent, to 88. The rails, which had put in their cyclical high in May 1919, at 91.13, lost 23 percent, to 70. Perhaps, as William Peter Hamilton had posited, the stock market had anticipated the bad medicine of rising bond yields and falling commodity prices.

The Federal Reserve's final turning of the discount-rate screw in the 1920–21 era—the rise on June 1, 1920, to 7 percent from 6 percent—had no direct immediate impact on prices. People had seemed to expect it, and high-level financiers gave the new 7 percent rate their public blessing. Then, too, the commercial pulse of a vibrant nation still seemed to be beating. Examples abounded. Thus, between January 1, 1919, and May 15, 1920, the New York Telephone Company had hired enough operators to expand its staff to 14,000 from 8,600; these fast talkers were answering calls in half the time it had taken them even at the start of 1920. New York Telephone's capital spending in New York City alone in 1920 would top $32 million.

The industrial average was still in the high 80s on September 16, 1920, the day of the Wall Street bombing. The editorial page of the *Wall Street Journal* breathed defiance. "Columns will be written about the incident," the newspaper said. "They will be largely wasted. It has been crudely said that you can't kill an idea. You can kill a bad idea, like slavery or the closed shop. But you cannot dynamite the Constitution of the United States."*[4]

---

*The Governing Committee of the New York Stock Exchange met at 3.30 PM on September 16 to decide how to respond to what the minutes of the meeting referred to as the "trying" events of the day. When one of the governors moved that the exchange should open for business the next morning, the president, William H. Remnick, responded that no such resolution was necessary. As a matter of course on any given business day, the exchange would be open. The next day—carnage, shock and blasted windows notwithstanding—would be no different. [New York Stock Exchange Governing Committee minutes]

• • •

Election Day, November 3, 1920, happened to fall on the first anniversary of the 1919 high of the Dow Jones industrials; in the succeeding 12 months, the industrials had shed 29 percent. The market had long since sniffed out a Harding victory, if not the immensity of the GOP landslide, and the averages had had an upbeat October. Was the bear market therefore ending? To many, it seemed so. After all, 139 big industrial companies had not paid out all of their inflationary windfall; over the previous six years, they had, in fact, added $3 billion to their working capital. Besides, Harding was from Ohio, one of the great steel-producing states. Surely, he and the Republican Congress would protect the home industry from its enemies, domestic and foreign.[5]

Among the usual garland of optimistic pronouncements to mark the New Year's season appeared a table of share prices comparing 1920 year-end quotations with the highs and lows of the preceding 12 months. In dozens of cases, the compilers were able to demonstrate that blue-chip equities had recovered from their worst levels of the year. Thus, International Paper, which had traded as high as 91¾ and as low as 38½, had bounced back to 46⅜. The once-beloved Cuba Cane Sugar, which had plunged to 16½ from 59⅜, had come all the way back to 23⅜. Sears Roebuck, which had made a high of 243 and a low of 85¼, was back at the threshold of 100. General Motors, which had been as high as 42 and as low as 12¾, had recovered to 14½.

"There is no need for pessimism," advised former comptroller A. Barton Hepburn, one of the grand old men of Wall Street. "The money market is easing; credit is being strengthened under the general administration and inspiration of the Federal Reserve Board. What we need is confidence, economy, patience and persistent industry."[6]

Besides, America was a paradise compared to the former European belligerents. More than a half-million French houses were wrecked in the war. Germany was to have financed the reconstruction of those dwelling places, but the Germans too often remitted their reparation payments in kind, rather than in cash—when they remitted at all. French contractors went unpaid and French families, especially in the northern, battle-trampled department of Aisne, went unhoused.

Wall Street could count its lucky stars that American stock prices were falling in terms of the honest gold dollar, rather than skyrocketing against the inflation-ravaged German Mark. There was cold comfort in the 100 percent gain recorded by German share prices in 1920, when the reciprocal of that advance was the depreciation in the German exchange rate. And if American capitalists feared a socialist fifth column in the United States, German capitalists didn't have to imagine it: A collectivist revolution in Germany was actually underway. Neither had the German Republic found her Andrew W. Mellon: Between the Armistice and October 31, 1920, Germany's floating public debt had more than tripled.[7]

Things were not measurably cheerier in Britain. "Seldom," the *Economist* magazine appraised the situation at year-end 1920,

> have the outstanding features of our economic position been more unfavorable at this season of goodwill and festivity than they are this year. With unemployment rife, short time general, demoralized stock markets, stocks of goods that are difficult to sell—or even unsaleable—when offered below cost of production, and a consequently uncomfortable feeling on the part of all who own them or have lent money against them, we have a most depressing setting.[8]

In the United States, the forces of economic and financial gravity that had pulled down the prices of commodities, consumer merchandise and common stocks seemed to have no effect on the price of labor. Wages had fallen in previous depressions. There seemed no *a priori* reason why they shouldn't fall in 1921—except, that is, for the expressed determination by the leaders of the heavily unionized American work force that wages would fall over their dead bodies. "We will tolerate no reduction of wages," Samuel Gompers, president of the American Federation of Labor, served notice in July 1920. "Even yet, we have ground to cover before we restore to all the purchasing power of 1913."[9]

Falling prices cut the ground out from that uncompromising position. Business couldn't operate for long in the red. To return to profitability, or to a satisfactory level of profitability, corporate management had to find ways to reduce costs, of which wages were among the biggest. According to a survey conducted by the *New York Herald* in 1921, 85 cents out of every dollar of cost in both the steel-making and construction trades was earmarked for labor.[10] "All costs, including wages, will have to be reduced," a steel manufacturer in Youngstown, Ohio, was quoted as saying a week before Christmas. "The money now being lost on steel production at reduced prices makes continuance of present costs impossible."[11]

The wage knives were already out in the Massachusetts textile towns. Operatives in the mills at Lowell, Lawrence and New Bedford faced reductions in pay on the order of 20 percent. In Lowell, that meant a rollback in pay to the level at which the mills had earlier granted raises to compensate for the postwar spike in inflation.[12] Fall River, Massachusetts, home of 111 mills, had ordinarily set the pace for wage trends in the coarse-goods segment of the cotton trade, but the city's employers were hanging back in 1920, happy to let others set the new deflationary tone. With the Fall River mills running at 25 percent to 40 percent of capacity, with the products of those mills fetching less in the market than they cost to produce and with 10,000 of the city's 35,000 mill employees already out of work, wages were plainly on the chopping block.[13] In the cases of many western copper miners and midwest steel producers, compensation had already been chopped.

"The wave of wage reductions is disagreeably familiar," the editors of the *New York Times* commented.

> It recurs as often as there is business reaction, and that is as often as there are "booms," say every ten years, but sometimes at intervals of twenty years. Those who think that such alternations are an indictment of our institutions and signify that capitalism should be abolished would be listened to with more attention if they should first solve some simpler problem. If they tried to make a clock run without the swinging of the pendulum in opposite directions, they would learn that the excess in either direction is a necessity of the case, unless what is desired is rest at the dead center. In economics, the dead center is abhorrent to labor and capital alike.[14]

The *Times* did not choose to distinguish between "wages"—the sum total of American employee compensation—and the rate at which businesses paid those wages. By adjusting downward the hourly rate of pay to bring costs into alignment with prices, a loss-making business had a chance, at least, to return to profitability. And by returning to profitability, it would have a reason to invest and hire and thereby to grow. Wage rates frozen at inflationary levels would find favor among the dwindling remnant of fully employed workers. But society's overall income would be lower at that uneconomic level of compensation than it would have been if wage rates had been properly realigned with prices.

Whether or not Samuel Gompers would have found persuasive the critical distinction between "wages" and "wage rates," he fired back at his critics. "I have lived to see many industrial depressions and panics, so-called," the labor leader said in a talk before Harvard students on March 11, 1921, a few weeks after the publication of the *Times* editorial. "I have seen the pendulum swing both ways, through depressions and revivals as well. I want to say in all earnestness that it will not do, it bodes no good, for the enemies of bona fide national labor unionism in America to drive the bargain too hard. . . . [W]hat with the cutting of wages and profiteering still going on, the pirates of finance and of business have much to answer for."[15]

The guilty parties in Gompers's eyes included the American Woolen Company, the Colorado Fuel and Iron Company, the Steelton division of Bethlehem Steel, the United States Steel Corporation and the meatpacking industry in toto. All had imposed—or, in the case of the packers, were in the process of trying to impose—wage reductions of between 10 percent and 20 percent.

In anticipatory fashion, Gompers might have called out, too, the Wisconsin Steel Works of the International Harvester Company. On top of a 20 percent wage cut in May 1921, management imposed additional reductions of between 27 percent and 32 percent in August, for a grand total of about 44 percent. Without these concessions, the plant would probably have to close, said the front office. "[B]etter starve without working than to starve and work, too," some of the employees retorted. Management got its way.[16]

The Hardings had barely moved into the White House when the butchers and meatcutters' union requested the president's good offices to mediate its struggle with the meatpackers. Because the war was technically still on (there was yet no peace treaty), the union men demanded that wartime wage

and hour agreements between them and the big meat concerns—Swift &
Company, Armour & Company, and Wilson & Company—remain in effect. This meant no wage reductions and no extension of the 40-hour work
week, both of which the packers were trying to implement. If the employers
refused to abide by the law, the government should seize the packing companies and "publicly brand the present owners and managers of the industry
as menaces to the government and society in general." So the Amalgamated
Meat Cutters and Butcher Workmen of North America urged the president. For their part, replied the packers, plucking a rhetorical string of the
Republican presidential campaign, their object was "a definite part of the
whole nation's campaign to get back to normal."[17]

The Harding administration, though pledged to keep the government
out of business, readily offered the services of three of its new cabinet officers in arbitration: the secretaries of labor, agriculture and commerce. The
last-named, Herbert Hoover, won over the union men with his quick and
sympathetic understanding: "I want to say that in the past I have never
considered Herbert Hoover friendly toward labor," attested the labor lawyer Redmond S. Brennan, " but I was gratified at the way he grasped the
justice of our claims." Still, along with the other two Harding arbitrators,
Harding urged the union side to accept that lower wages were inevitable.
Reluctantly, the butchers and meatcutters agreed to a reduction that, for
piece work, amounted to 12.5 percent, while the employers agreed to abide
by the 40-hour week; the wartime labor contract would remain in force
until September 21, 1921. There was no love lost between the sides—"What
we have really done is to sign a truce to prepare for war," said Brennan in
parting—but the fact was that wages, too, had entered the gravitational field
of the depression.

★ 15 ★

SHREWD JUDGE GARY

The United States Steel Corporation was the largest industrial enterprise in the world. It was America's first billion-dollar company and the undisputed leader of the iron and steel business. The company employed more than a quarter million people, to whom it paid, in 1920, a total of $581,556,925, or an average of $7 a day. In that year, U.S. Steel generated sales of $1,755,447,025 and net income of $109,694,227. On December 31, 1920, its impregnable balance sheet footed to $2,430,546,963.[1]

The company was a union of 11 operating businesses joined together in 1901 by the capitalist visionaries J.P. Morgan, Elbert H. Gary, Charles M. Schwab and Andrew Carnegie. Like some immense, modern industrial subsistence farm, the Steel Corporation was seemingly self-sufficient. It consumed its own coal, iron ore, coke, natural gas, crude oil, gasoline, water, dolomite, limestone and manganese. It fed these raw materials into its own blast furnaces, Bessemer converters, open-hearth and electric furnaces, slabbing mills, sheet-bar mills, rail mills, universal-plate mills, sheared-plate mills, wire-rod mills, beehive ovens, skelp mills, merchant mills, nail mills, barbed and woven-wire fence departments, spring works, rope and electrical works, welding-pipe furnaces, seamless-tube mills, bridge and structural plants, nut and bolt factories, brass foundries and cement plants. And from this immense and farflung capital stock, the company manufactured its own steel rails, rail joints, structural shapes, bars for reinforced concrete, merchant bars, bolt and nut rods, wire rods, plates, sheets, black plates, skelp, hoops and bands, axles, nail and tack plate, angles, spikes and spelter.

If the Steel Corporation fit the legal definition of "monopoly," as the Federal Trade Commission had alleged and the company denied, the reason was unrivaled efficiency. The company's own rail network operated 1,063 miles of main line and total trackage of 3,780 miles, over which 1,501 steam locomotives pulled company freight cars numbering 62,221. A water-borne corporation fleet comprised 35 ocean-going steamers, 78 Great Lakes steamers, 13 river-going steamers and 818 steel barges.

As for the people of U.S. Steel, some worked seven-day weeks and 12-hour days, and—once every two weeks—a 24-hour day. Would the company not fall in with other enlightened employers and consent to a six-day week and an eight-hour day? The company would not. Nor would it discuss the matter. Especially would it not discuss the matter with representatives of the trade unions.

At the head of this mighty enterprise sat Gary—or, as he was addressed, "Judge" Gary, an honorific he had earned for eight years' service on the DuPage County (Illinois) bench in the 1880s. The judge had conceived an interest in the steel business while listening to testimony in commercial cases in his own courtroom. In 1898, he left the law—he had practiced before and after his time on the bench—to become president of the Federal Steel Corporation, which the new steel combine absorbed in 1901.

At 74 years of age, Gary had lived through the Chicago fire, the boom of the 1880s and the depression of the 1890s. He had helped to instigate the great wave of corporate consolidation at the turn of the 20th century and had built, in 1906, the model Indiana steelworker town that took his name. In the business downturn of 1914, he had chaired a New York City municipal committee to study the unemployment problem. In 1916, he was riding another boom—by June 1917, the price of steel had almost tripled from its depressed 1914 level.[2] In 1919, he had faced down the Steel Workers Organizing Committee and come out on the winning side of a three-month strike. Mrs. E.H. Gary, invited to become an honorary member of the

Women's Steel Striker's Auxiliary of Gary in November 1919, telegraphed her regrets. To reporters she explained, "I am entirely in sympathy with the stand Judge Gary has taken against the steel strikers, not because he is my husband, but because it is the only right stand to take if we do not want to get in the grasp of the Bolsheviki and have labor override the country with unreasonable demands."[3]

In October 1920, the judge allowed that some prices and some wages would have to fall.[4] By December, many independent producers—i.e., the ones not affiliated with U.S. Steel—had shut down. The independents still in operation were cutting their prices below the leader's. Some were cutting wages, too, the eastern plate mills by as much as 25 percent. Gary's behemoth was operating at full tilt, but the business on which it was feasting was its own backlog.

Would the Steel Corporation fire back with price and wage reductions of its own? As late as the first week of February 1921, Gary denied it. This remark of Gary's—he had stated it publicly—enflamed none other than the lame-duck comptroller of the currency. Steel prices must fall, John Skelton Williams admonished Gary in one of the comptroller's trademark open letters, dated February 15. In a time of general suffering, all should contribute his or her mite of discomfort. For U.S. Steel, that meant lower selling prices and smaller profits. No Bolshevik propagandist could do the American system more harm than corporate profiteers like Gary already were, Williams charged.[5]

Gary did not immediately favor Williams with a reply, though other steelmen expressed surprise: Was Williams not comptroller of the *currency*? Then, too, they observed, if the mighty Steel Corporation cut its prices as much as Williams demanded—namely, by $25 a ton (on a base of $63.49 a ton)[6]—even the more efficient independent producers would be driven to the wall.[7] Gary's reply, published on March 3, marshaled figures that exploded the comptroller's "profiteering" allegation. In the same communique, the judge asserted that the most important problem facing America and the world was not deflation but the high cost of living, which, he declared, "should and must be promptly and radically further reduced."[8]

Gary needn't have worried about high prices. On March 30, 1921, the average price of eight principal iron and steel products was quoted at 27.4 percent below the level of the year before. And, while in 1920 the

independent producers had charged prices pitched 27 percent above the
Steel Corporation's, in 1921 the independents were charging prices some
8 percent less than the ones Gary's company quoted.[9]

Copper prices, too, were in a tailspin. At 11 or 12 cents a pound at the
end of March 1921, they had fallen by 37 percent from their 1920 peak. Anaconda, the world's top copper producer, said it was suspending production
indefinitely. It seemed to make no difference that the price of the red metal
was below the cost of producing it; surplus stocks piled up anyway. Demand
was dying the world over, said the president of Anaconda, John D. Ryan,
"on account of the general cessation of business activity in this country, the
industrial collapse in the Orient and the general unsatisfactory business and
political situation in Europe."[10]

Though Gary—as the industry's leading statesman and head of its
low-cost producer—had a vested interest in stability, the deepening slump
pointed to a business situation that was deeply unstable. Perhaps the judge's
eye was drawn to a suggestive item in the March 30 edition of the *Wall
Street Journal*:

LIVING LOWER IN STEEL DISTRICT

Youngstown—For the benefit of its 12,500 employees Youngstown Sheet and Tube Co. has prepared
a compilation, showing that living costs have been
reduced by 37.8% in the Mahoning Valley [home to
dozens of mills, including Youngstown's] within the
past 12 months.

Even if Gary had failed to pick up on the broad hint from Youngstown,
he would probably have been reading the news about the spread of wage
reductions in the packing industry and the railroads. And even if he never
opened a newspaper, he would certainly have heard the bearish news from
his own subsidiaries. When the depression struck and new orders dried up,
the Steel Corporation had the luxury of 10.4 million tons of unfilled orders
to work through; between April 1920 and March 1921, that backlog had
dwindled to 5.8 million tons.[11]

The nation's steel consumers had not put much store in the judge's
denials about price reductions, and on April 12, the doubters were proved

correct. Gary announced cuts sufficient to bring the Steel Corporation's prices back into line with the independents'. Now eight principal iron and steel products fetched an average of $58.54 a ton. On the one hand, this was 31 percent below the 1920 high of $85.03 and 51 percent below the all-time record of $119.69, set in July 1917. On the other, it was more than 60 percent above the typical $35 a ton average price prevailing before the war.

Lacking the scale and financial strength of U.S. Steel, the independents suffered deep losses. From the November 3, 1919, market peak to the immediate aftermath of the Gary price announcement, on April 13, 1921, Bethlehem Steel's share price was cut in half; Crucible Steel's was down by 66.3 percent and Republic Iron and Steel Company's was lower by 56.2 percent. In comparison, the Steel Corporation's share price suffered a mere flesh wound: down by 27.4 percent. Over the same span, the Dow Jones Industrial average gave up 37.3 percent.

But Gary's relative success was still a far cry from prosperity. In the first three months of 1921, the corporation earned $32.3 million, down from $42.1 million in the same period in 1920. In the second quarter, ended June 30, it earned $21.9 million, compared with $43.2 million in the like span of 1920. The second quarter's profit was the smallest for any quarter since the first three months in 1915.

The judge saw better times ahead. "Just at present," he addressed the stockholders, "there are many reasons for believing our conditions are improving, even though we may not as yet have experienced, to a large degree, the good results. Readjustments were necessary and they have been and are progressing with beneficial effect." The war was all about waste, starting with government waste, Gary went on. But

> [n]ow we are witnessing a contrary disposition, also from the Government down, although not every man, woman and child is yet included in the effort to reduce, to economize and to save.

The financial situation, too, declared the judge, looked bright. Echoing the public pronouncements of former Comptroller Williams, he appraised America's banks as sound. "We need not shout in triumph," the judge concluded, but we are not compelled to feel despondent. The world has been very sick. Therefore full recovery is longer delayed. The further we proceed in the direction we are now going the faster will be the pace. With the continuous maintenance of law and order, securing individual freedom of action in legitimate effort, the economic position of this country will be invincible.[12]

A little less than invincible was the immediate economic position of the Steel Corporation's employees. The judge, hewing to the anti-union line that his wife had seconded, elicited a blast from Matthew Woll, vice president of the American Federation of Labor: "He will give the last stockholder's nickel to preserve the right of the steelworker to work 12 hours a day."[13]

Effective May 16, 1921, the Steel Corporation—to the unions, Steel "Trust" was its name—slashed wages and salaries by 20 percent. The rollback was the company's first since 1904; raises had rather been the rule. Since 1915, compensation had been bumped up on nine separate occasions, in amounts ranging from 9 percent to 15 percent, which had cumulatively lifted the average wage for a day laborer on a 10-hour shift to $5.06, from $2. It was a gain twice as great as the increase in the Consumer Price Index.[*] If there was any consolation to be found in the deflationary news, it was that there were many fewer Steel Corporation employees to be disappointed by it. In January, the company had employed 263,208; in July the headcount stood at only 157,083.

Before the coming of federal and state unemployment insurance benefits many years later, the jobless had to fend for themselves. Judge Gary, though he wished his employees well, put the financial position of his company before the family finances of his workers. That the Steel Corporation was a pillar of financial strength[†] was a fact visible enough on its balance sheet. One could infer a degree of financial strength, as well, from the caliber of its shareholders. Gary himself, in conjunction with the secretary and treasurer of the corporation, Richard Trimble, held 321,408 common shares, or

---

[*] The average Steel Corporation employee's real compensation looked more or less favorable depending on the starting and ending dates of the computation. The company itself calculated that, between October 1913 and December 1921, the average daily wage had increased to $4.60 from $2.93, or a rise of 57 percent. Over the same 10 years, the CPI had jumped by 75 percent. [1922 Annual Report cited in the *Wall Street Journal*, March 21, 1923]

[†] Even in 1921, earnings before interest and taxes covered interest charges by more than 4:1.

6.3 percent of the 5.1 million shares outstanding. George F. Baker, head of the First National Bank of New York and one of his era's most successful investors, owned 57,300 shares. Harvard College and Pierre S. du Pont, recently retired president of E.I. du Pont de Nemours and Company, were major owners, as were William H. Crocker, the San Francisco banker; Cleveland H. Dodge, the copper entrepreneur; A.A. Housman & Company, which counted among its customers the investor Bernard M. Baruch; and the former president of the United States—with 45 shares of Steel preferred—Woodrow Wilson.

Cheap stocks in bear markets always go begging, a *Wall Street Journal* editorialist in March 1921 observed. Investors don't want them and never have. If it were otherwise, "there would be an active market today, with an interested and even excited public."

The public was obviously unexcited. In the first three months of the year, New York Stock Exchange trading volume had barely reached 44 million shares, down by 38 percent from the same interval in 1920. Did it matter that shares in the Steel Corporation were quoted at one third of book value and at four times trailing net earnings, or that they were priced to deliver a dividend yield of more than 6 percent?

It did, at least, for the patient, long-term investor, that rare bird of plumage. As recently as year-end 1916, some 41 percent of Steel common "floated" in the custody of brokerage houses; as of March 31, 1921, only 24.3 percent was so earmarked. The reciprocal—75.7 percent—was registered in the presumably stronger and steadier hands of dividend-seeking, value-minded investors. It was the highest such percentage on record.[14]

Judge Gary's inspirational message in his second-quarter report to shareholders did not exactly mark the bottom of the cycle, though it came close. In July 1921, as steel prices continued to fall, the industry briefly operated at less than 15 percent of capacity. Looking back unfondly at the full 12 months, John A. Topping, president of Republic Iron and Steel, one of the larger independents, pronounced 1921 the worst year in his company's 22-year history. Republic had operated at an average of just 25 percent of capacity, had laid off more than half of the 13,230 workers whom it had employed in 1920 and could point to not much good news except some relative strength in the demand for sheet—a sign of the recovering automobile market.[15]

At low ebb in the stock market in the third week of August 1921, Wall Street paused to marvel over the resilience of the Steel Corporation's share price.* At 72¾, it had fallen by 34.3 percent from the November 3, 1919, market top, compared to a 46.6 percent loss in the Dow and declines of 57.5 percent and 68 percent in the shares of Bethlehem Steel and Republic; Crucible was down by 79.6 percent. Judge Gary had earned his success. In the boom, the Steel Corporation had had the foresight to lay in a $95 million inventory reserve; it was clear to the front office that the ruling inflated values would sooner or later come back down to earth. A second source of strength in the company's share price was the dedication of the workforce, shrunken though it was. In that depression year, 81,722 employees had subscribed to purchase 255,326 shares. The cost of a single, $80 share to a steelworker earning $5 a day was 16 days' labor. A third source of resilience was the public's confidence in Gary. The number of holders of record of Steel common stock stood at 105,310 in the second quarter of 1921, up from 73,456 in the third quarter of 1919.

"The fact is," the *Wall Street Journal* noted, "that notwithstanding what the speculator may think about Steel common, the investor regards the corporation as the country's strongest industrial concern and feels little doubt about the safety of its dividend." That confidence proved well placed.[16]

---

*"Every other trader in the Street seems to be short of Steel common," the *Wall Street Journal* reported. "They have watched other stocks go down, but Steel refuses to follow. The strength of the stock is uncanny."

★ 16 ★

"A HIGHER SENSE
OF SERVICE"

Fatalism was the bipartisan mainstream attitude toward the depression. Democrats and Republicans agreed that the slump was inevitable, unstoppable and even salutary. But whatever its conceivable merits (for instance, in rebalancing wages and prices and in correcting the errors that investors and entrepreneurs had committed under the influence of federally suppressed interest rates and false, inflated prices), many Americans were suffering. How would the government respond?

Here, too, there was a degree of political comity. The government ought not to make things worse by costly or ill-conceived intervention, it was widely accepted. "We have demobilized many groups," David F. Houston, Woodrow Wilson's secretary of the Treasury, had dryly remarked in the election season of 1920, "but we have not demobilized those whose gaze is concentrated on the Treasury."[1] A few months later, from the libertarian left, the *Freeman*, a weekly journal published in New York, scorned "the growing tendency to hold Governments accountable for all modes and degrees of prosperity and adversity. . . . This is an acute absurdity."[2]

President Harding, too, espoused laissez-faire. But above all things—and above any ideology—he was for kindness. As he held out the hand of friendship in private life, so he did in the Senate and at the White House. And if the extension of that hand seemed to violate the boundaries between the public and private sectors, he seemed untroubled by the fact, even unaware of it. The president was one of the rare people, eulogized a political critic of Harding's after the president's death in 1923, who "sweeten life. Come to analyze them and it is discovered that they give out love. . . . That is what Harding seemed to do; he gave out love."[3]

One of the top items on Harding's legislative agenda was the creation of a new, cabinet-level department of public welfare. After all, the president said, the government's obligation to "develop the highest and most efficient type of citizenship" is "modernly" accepted. Perhaps so, his critics replied, but the government was under a prior obligation to live within its means.* The Harding proposal went nowhere.

The administration was more successful in its push to reactivate the War Finance Corporation. A creature of the national emergency, the WFC was capitalized in 1918 with $500 million of public funds. It spent $1 billion to support the prices of Liberty bonds. After the Armistice, it found a temporary new mission in export finance. With Treasury Secretary Houston, ex-officio chairman of the WFC, leading a drive to kill it, the agency was demobilized in 1920.

The collapse in farm prices brought demands to remobilize it, this time with an emphasis on agricultural credit. A resolution by the Senate Agriculture Committee to that effect, dated December 6, 1920, cited "unprecedented and unparalleled distress" on the farm.[4] Wilson sent it back unsigned: "I am of the opinion that now, more than two years after the Armistice, the Nation should resume its usual business methods," said the veto message, which Houston drafted.

Harding saw no reason why the government should not do something for the suffering farmers. The WFC deserved a new life, he urged Congress in July 1921; there was, after all, another "nation-wide emergency." From

---

*"To a multitude of Americans the thought of a lady in the Cabinet, specially charged with the duty of making us all healthy and good, will no doubt be alluring," the *New York Times* editorially commented. "But Congress also has a duty in relation to the public welfare, and it is to make the Administration as efficient and economical as possible." The American Federation of Labor, under Samuel Gompers, was no happier with the idea. Gompers rather preferred that any available federal resources be directed to the Department of Labor. [*New York Times*, April 14, 1921, May 13, 1921]

this political acorn presently sprang the Agricultural Credits Act of 1923, which created a dozen farm intermediate credit banks (which exist to this day as the Federal Farm Credit Banks). Eugene Meyer, the Wilsonian who had headed the WFC, worked with the Harding administration to enact the legislation.[5]

No one could doubt Herbert Hoover's generosity of spirit, even if the secretary of commerce had none of Harding's personal warmth. A geologist trained in the first class at Stanford University, the Class of 1895, Hoover went to Australia, developed gold mines, married his childhood sweetheart, Lou Henry, and, with her, moved to China to pursue a career as a mining consultant. Together, they escaped the clutches of the rebelling Boxers in 1900. By 1908, Hoover was an independent consultant with investments on every continent and offices in San Francisco, New York and London, a Russian base in St. Petersburg and a Burmese one in Mandalay. In 1912, Lou and he presented the fruits of their joint intellectual avocation, an English translation of the 16th century mining classic *De re metallica*. She had worked out the Latin, he the metallurgy. In August 1914, his reputation was the purely private one of a successful corporate restructuring consultant, a "doctor of sick mines." Living in London, they were rich—he was worth $4 million—and content.

The war plunged them into public service. An estimated 120,000 Americans had been stranded in Europe by the outbreak of fighting. The Hoovers devoted themselves to the costly and complex logistical task of getting the travelers home. When it came to light that millions were hungry in German-occupied Belgium, Hoover became a *pro bono* battler against starvation. Later, after America joined the war, he headed the U.S. Food Administration. With the peace, he led the American Relief Administration. Millions owed their health, if not their lives, to the man who now served as Harding's secretary of commerce.

In the years before the invention of countercyclical macroeconomic policy, what should a secretary of commerce of the United States do about a deflationary depression? No one was less temperamentally suited than Hoover to do nothing. He abhorred suffering. He hated it as a man, as a member of the Religious Society of Friends and as an engineer. That a country as rich as the United States could just stand by in the face of the pain and waste and mass unemployment was, in his word, "inconceivable."[6]

Hoover laid out the Harding economic program in an address to the National Association of Real Estate Boards in Chicago on July 15, 1921. The administration was committed to tax reform, government-spending reduction and tariff revision, the secretary of commerce announced. It was seeking reductions in armaments, enhancements to the American merchant marine and assistance to exporters and farmers. It intended, as well, to discharge the government's wartime debts to the seminationalized railroads and to streamline the federal bureaucracy.

The current depression was the 14th since the Civil War, Hoover observed. As the country had survived the other 13, so would it surmount this one, especially with the Federal Reserve on the job. Something else was new and improved in America, Hoover went on. This was "a higher sense of service, a wider-spread willingness to give aid to the injured in business. Thousands of firms whose cases seemed hopeless are on the road to safety." (Bankers, too, had remarked on something of the kind: Benjamin Anderson, economist at the Chase National Bank, judged that lenders were more inclined to work with a troubled borrower—not to force that debtor into bankruptcy—than they had been in times past.)

Hoover would go only so far in advocating for government action. Deflation was a tribulation, but a necessary and constructive one, the speaker told the real estate men. Booms did more than precede busts; to a degree, they caused them. It was during the champagne-and-confetti phase of the business cycle "that we speculate, over-extend our liabilities, slacken down in effort, lower our efficiency, waste our surplus in riotous living instead of creation of new capital, drive our prices to vicious levels, lose our moral and business balance." The comeuppance phase of the cycle was therefore unavoidable. Though some would resist it, said Hoover, everyone would "have to come into the cold water in the end."

Of course, Hoover went on, many in Washington *would* resist. The capital was chockablock full of crackpot ideas:

The purpose and place of the Government in expediting economic recovery is raised in Washington every hour of the day. We are flooded by economic patent medicines that would evade the stern laws of economic hygiene. The question of what the Government can do becomes in part a question of our whole attitude toward social and economic questions. Unless we would destroy individual initiative and drive ourselves straight into nationalization or paternalism, the Government can not undertake to reduce or raise wages, to deal in commodities or fix prices, no matter how it is camouflaged.[7]

On Boston Common on September 8, 1921, lunchtime passersby stopped to stare at a re-creation of an antebellum slave auction. A certain "Mr. Zero" prodded and harangued the spectators to bid for an unemployed man. Each of the volunteer chattels was able-bodied—they had stripped to the waist—and some had served in the war.

Mr. Zero, otherwise known as Urbain Ledoux, styled himself a philanthropist for the unemployed.[*] He had staged this political theater to awaken Boston's conscience to the plight of the jobless, he said. He succeeded, at least, in awakening the curiosity of the press. A week after the Boston Common event, the New York City Police Department announced it would refuse to issue a permit for a replay of the Boston spectacle in Bryant Park.

In Britain and Wales, the jobless had rioted and marched.[8] In Montreal, they had pushed their way into restaurants to demand food. In Chicago, they were poised to rally in support of a demand, put forward by the Amalgamated Sheet Metal Workers of America, that the government pay unemployment compensation equal to 75 percent of prevailing wages. To finance these prospective jobless benefits, the union demanded that taxes be laid on unearned incomes of more than $5,000.[9] "What could be more reasonable than that the idle should support the idle in idleness," the editors of the *New York Times* sarcastically replied. "Why should anybody be denied anything which tax money can supply?"[10]

Serious unemployment, there obviously was. But in the absence of reliable figures, no one knew how much. The 1920 census counted 106 million Americans, of whom 41.6 million were classified as working "in gainful occupations." Manufacturing, with 12.8 million, or 30.8 percent of the workforce, was the most prolific employer, followed by agriculture, forestry and

---

[*]The philanthropist admitted he had abandoned his wife and two children. "I've got a bigger family than that one," Ledoux told reporters in reference to his adopted family of the jobless. [*New York Times*, September 10, 1921]

animal husbandry, with 11 million (26.3 percent); retail and wholesale trade, with 4.2 million (10.2 percent); domestic and personal service, with 3.4 million (8.2 percent); and transportation, with 3.1 million (7.4 percent). But not all of these working Americans were immediately susceptible to layoff or firing. The census takers counted 6 million farmers, 1.5 million merchants or shopkeepers, 275,000 manufacturers and "officials," and 2.5 million professionals. This cohort of more or less self- or steadily employed persons topped 10 million, which left 31 million or so Americans under the general heading of "employee."

The 21st century financial world huddles around computer monitors on the first Friday of the month to hear the U.S. Department of Labor announce a temporarily definitive (though oft-revised) estimate of the number of nonfarm payroll jobs added or subtracted in the prior month. There was no such guiding light in 1921. The U.S. Employment Service, the Federal Reserve Board, the Commerce Department, various state employment offices, chambers of commerce and the Metropolitan Life Insurance Company all weighed in with their own incomplete reckonings of employment. As there was no one standard set of survey criteria, results of these canvasses widely differed. Thus, the Commonwealth of Massachusetts, a longtime and well-regarded reporter on the statewide labor market, reported that, in the first quarter of 1921, joblessness had reached 30 percent, vastly in excess of the previous top reading of 18.3 percent, which had been set at year-end 1914.[11] Nonsense, the Massachusetts State Chamber of Commerce shot back a few months later. On the authority of 21 local chambers of commerce, joblessness was not much worse than usual and, in any case, was "correcting itself through natural channels of increasing activity and brisk business."[12]

Matters were hardly clarified when, on August 18, the U.S. Secretary of labor, J.J. Davis, announced that 5,735,000 Americans were out of work, up from a reading of 3,473,446 in January.[13] At least, Davis added, the situation was not so dire as in 1914, when seven million were jobless. (Exactly where the secretary got that figure he didn't say; no such official tally was conducted at the time.) "Now while we have our unemployed," he added, "let us not forget the . . . people who are still at work." Then, too, the secretary noted, the government's own statisticians had detected evidence of an economic turnaround. Not all of the message encoded in those data might be self-evidently encouraging. "But," Davis affirmed, "one must have his head very much in the air these days not to notice the growing prevalence of silk hosiery and the use of silks in general."[14]

Some contended that what was out of kilter was not the number of the currently unemployed but, rather, the number of the previously employed. "Every man, woman and child who could possibly be influenced by the highest wage ever offered and by the patriotic slogan 'We must produce, produce, produce to save Europe!' were dragged into the factories," one such skeptic argued. "As soon as the slump came the women and children went back into the homes they never would have left except under these extraordinary circumstances, and the men went back to the jobs that they had previously held."[15]

The Harding administration was not so sure. It was worried by the sheer number of America's jobless—there *seemed* to be a lot of them—and by their evident suffering. The White House was spooked by the Boston "auctions," by the "rumblings of discontent among the unemployed abroad"[16] and by the onset of winter at home. What to do? Not nothing, Hoover was quite certain. Private property was inviolate; so, too, was the enterprise system of economic organization, as Hoover understood that system. But these strictures did not preclude innovative action. Needed was a national conference on unemployment, Hoover decided (a "war on unemployment," he presently styled it).[17] A panel of economic experts would determine the number of unemployed. Facts in hand, the economists would propose solutions to the problem. Representatives of labor and capital would weigh their conclusions. Invitations to prospective participants went out in August 1921.

Deferentially, Hoover styled his summit the "President's Conference on Unemployment," though no one could doubt who had dreamed up the idea and furnished the motive power to bring it to fruition. The secretary of commerce gaveled down the opening session on September 26.

To a citizen who had asked him in 1908 what an unemployed man should do, the as-yet-unannounced presidential candidate William Howard Taft replied, "God only knows." Harding, along with Hoover, did not say that the government knew what such a jobless man should do, only that the government should find a way to lend him a hand. It should make its contribution by the force of ideas and leadership, not through spending. Unemployment or not, debt reduction remained at the top of the administration's fiscal agenda.

The depression was a "war inheritance" and a worldwide scourge, said the president in opening remarks to delegates seated in the auditorium of the Department of the Interior. Then, too, "There is always unemployment. Under most fortunate conditions, I am told, there are a million and a half in the United States who are not at work."

"Frictional unemployment," economists have learned to call this residual of joblessness. What Harding said was this: "The figures are astounding, only because we are a hundred millions, and this parasite percentage will always be with us."

Depressions followed inflation "just as surely as the tides ebb and flow," the president went on, "but we can mitigate, we can shorten duration," though not by spending the taxpayers' money. "The excess of stimulation from that source is to be reckoned a cause of trouble rather than a source of cure," he said. [18]

The delegates, summoned by telegram, included Charles Schwab, the Bethlehem Steel chief; Ida Tarbell, the famed investigative journalist; William C. Procter, cofounder of Procter & Gamble; Samuel Gompers, among other labor leaders; also mayors, trade association men, mining executives, railroad executives, a lumber man, a shoe manufacturer and miscellaneous public servants. There was a black man, George E. Haynes, Ph.D., a member of the Commission on Race Relations of the Federal Council of Churches of Christ. "Mr. Zero," who was not summoned, dropped by the White House to talk to the president. "Most kind and courteous," the beaming agitator praised his host as he emerged from the interview to speak with reporters; Harding had given him 25 minutes.

For Hoover, the conference was to be no mere temporary gathering of experts, but a long-range project to attack unemployment by ironing out the business cycle. As best as Hoover's panel of experts could determine, there were 3.5 million unemployed (nothing close to the 5.5 million that some had claimed). To help these unfortunates get through the winter, a targeted plan of public works spending was in order. Cities and states would bear its financial burden. The federal government would neither command nor spend but rather cajole and coordinate. For the long run, there was a crying need for better economic statistics; this the Department of Commerce could and would supply.

Was that all there would be? Why, yes, some believed—and more than enough. Markets should be left to their own devices, classical economic doctrine had it. As prices had fallen, so must wages fall. In the language of the day, labor must be "liquidated."

To "liquidate" means to throw on the market—to sell. To liquidate labor means to rid oneself of a portion of the overpaid help. Bankrupt businesses paid poorly and hired not at all. By realigning inflated wages with deflated commodity prices, businesses could reduce costs, restore profit margins and resume hiring. Less than a week before the delegates to the conference took their seats, the front page of the *Wall Street Journal* approvingly reported on the steel makers' progress in this regard. "Liquidation of Steel Industry May Be Ended," the headline said. "In Addition to Disposing Of Materials, Drastic Cuts Have Been Made in Labor Costs." In some districts, according to the dispatch, 25 cents an hour was the new going rate, down from 50 cents or 60 cents an hour during the war.[19]

This was not Hoover's preferred approach. Critically, he opposed wage reductions. "[H]e still looked upon individual creativity as the mainspring of progress and still called for 'healthy competition' within a cooperative framework," as a student of his economic thought has written, "but in its main outlines, the type of system he envisioned was closer to the NRA program of the early New Deal or to corporate liberalism in general than it was to the competitive model of classical economics."[20]

The modern businessman, equipped with timely statistics, would make better decisions, Hoover believed. Better decisions would render depressions less frequent and less severe. To provide this critical information, Hoover's Commerce Department created the *Survey of Current Business*, a monthly compendium of economic data; the first issue appeared in July 1921.*

John L. Lewis, president of the United Mine Workers of America, was

---

*There was nothing very new in the credo that rational people could manage economic fluctuations more sensibly than the seemingly uncoordinated forces of the marketplace. "It is now administratively possible . . . ," the Majority Report of the British Royal Commission on the Poor Laws and Relief of Distress concluded in 1909, "to remedy most of the evils of unemployment to the same extent, at least, as we have in the past century diminished the death rate from fever and lessened the industrial slavery of young children." [Mallery, "Long-Range Planning of Public Works," 260–261] Peeking ahead a couple of years,

quite sure that Washington, D.C., could do more than it was accustomed to doing. The unemployed should get government credits, he demanded; corporations should be compelled to build up a reserve labor fund equal to one half of their annual payroll; the mines should belong to the people, or, at least, be heavily regulated by the government. Mayor William "Big Bill" Thompson of Chicago would have certainly agreed with Lewis had he been present. He was not present. "This is a capitalistic move with the following objects," Thompson had written Hoover in protest after the conference disbanded: "A blacklist, a refusal of charity to American union laboring men, a drive against union labor, a conspiracy to lower wages."

There was, in fact, nothing like a conspiracy. The Chicago Association of Commerce made no bones about it in its correspondence with Hoover. The members wanted to liquidate labor.[21] Fiscal conservatism was another nonsecret priority of the business interests. "We do not think our fellow citizens sufficiently appreciate the value of the insistence of the president and secretary of commerce that neither government relief nor public doles shall be considered as a means of meeting unemployment," said Ernest T. Trigg, president of the National Federation of Construction Industries, speaking for the employers.[22]

Before adjourning on October 13, the delegates directed a standing committee of 14 to oversee the work of emergency relief that was underway in cities and states nationwide. Hoover and his minions assembled a network of mayors' coordinating committees, private charities and state and county officials. It was this volunteer force that would see to implementing the conference's action agenda, Hoover expected. Capital spending programs would be accelerated. Road building would be pushed ahead to the winter months from the customary springtime start date. Businesses would "give a job for a Christmas gift."[23]

In November, at the conferees' urging, Congress enacted, and Harding signed, a $76.4 million highway bill; 150,000 jobs would be directly created. State and local governments, prodded by Hoover, borrowed record sums of money in the tax-exempt bond market in the nine months following the conference.[24] In February 1922, Senator William S. Kenyon, Republican of

---

John Maynard Keynes would contend that, owing to sharp advances in "economic science," a central bank might assure that average prices would be forever stable. [Skidelsky, *John Maynard Keynes*, 152]

Iowa, introduced a bill to empower the president to start and stop federal spending (on worthwhile projects only, it was stipulated) as a counterweight to the ups and downs of the business cycle.

The delegates could not have known that, even as they took their seats, the economic recovery was entering its second month—the National Bureau of Economic Research, organized in 1920, would so declare well after the fact. Perhaps the upturn in business activity helps to explain the conference's lack of tangible achievement. City and state public works spending did, indeed, increase in 1921, but likely not by enough to make a measurable difference. Kenyon's bill died in the Senate. Some opponents charged that the White House, by declaring the time had come to fend off an anticipated depression, might inadvertently start a panic. Another critic, Senator Harry New, Republican of Indiana, demanded what business the federal government had in trying to override the biblical injunction that seven lean years would follow seven fat ones. Though Hoover succeeded in expanding the statistics-gathering role of the Commerce Department, he failed at procuring the money with which to enlarge the work of the Bureau of Labor Statistics; that would have to wait until his own presidency during the Great Depression.

The unemployment conference left an intellectual mark, if not a legislative one. *Recent Economic Changes,* the encyclopedic study of the growth and evolution of America's economy, which appeared in 1929, was among its publishing achievements. The secretary of commerce and his cadre of experts established to their satisfaction that the public sector could play its part in shearing the sharp edges off the American business cycle, even if that shearing entailed a critical loss in the downward flexibility of wage rates. To Hoover, the conference was a "milestone in the progress of social thought." [25]

As testament either to Hoover's stage management or to the mellowing of the relations between capital and labor, the delegates declared themselves satisfied with the overall results and delighted with the facilitating work of the chairman. On the fraught question of wage reductions, trade unionists and businessmen agreed to disagree. "Conference Ends Without Clash," was, for the *New York Times,* the essential news at the conclusion of the summit. [26]

As the delegates went their separate ways, the British unemployed were marching. Twenty thousand demonstrated in London on October 13, demanding either jobs or the dole (or, rather, an enhanced dole, as Britain shared none of America's scruples against mobilizing the exchequer to address the problems of the labor market). They carried banners saying "Bread or Revolution" and "Work or Maintenance." In Manchester, it was reported that "several thousands" converged on town hall, where they sang "The Red Flag."[27]

"In England," the editors of the *New York Times* pointed out, "there is a mixture of politics and economics not to be observed here. The unemployed are leaning on the State there because they have been encouraged and even taught to do so, both by the authorities and by the labor leaders. Our unions have a small minority which mix social reform with labor questions, but the large number are not revolutionists and keep their politics and economics apart."[28]

Britain's government, like America's, was running a budget surplus. Britain's monetary policy, like America's, had been suffocatingly tight. Britain's wages, like America's, had fallen during the 1920–21 slump. "Yet," related Keynes's biographer, Robert Skidelsky, "they had not fallen far enough to restore equilibrium, and for the rest of the 1920s remained rigid, despite further deflationary pressure."[29]

The "liquidation of labor" turned out to be a paradoxical secret of American success. Wages rates had fallen—evidently, far enough to make industry profitable again. Optimists resumed hiring first. Realists followed—simply to compete, they had to pay market wages, or higher than market wages, to attract the better cut of employee. By and by, the 1920s roared.

GOLD POURS INTO AMERICA

J ohn Skelton Williams was out of the government—succeeding him as comptroller in March 1921 was Warren G. Harding's old boyhood pal, Daniel R. Crissinger, with whom the president had stolen watermelons— but that didn't mean that the Federal Reserve's most argumentative critic had lost his voice. Early in July Williams repeated to the secretary of the Treasury, Andrew Mellon, the warnings he had earlier delivered to W.P.G. Harding about the alarming deterioration in the position of Guaranty Trust Company of New York.

By this time, shares of the Guaranty Trust were quoted in the vicinity of $240 apiece. They had topped $400 in the first week of 1920 and $300 as recently as March 1921. Stock prices were broadly falling, bank stock prices among them, but Guaranty Trust's shares were falling faster and farther than those of its big-city peers.*

---

*From top to bottom, 1920–21, shares of the Guaranty Trust Company declined by 60.5 percent, those of Chase National Bank by 47.4 percent and of National City Bank by 30.2 percent. Shares of the National Bank of Commerce, on whose board Mellon had sat before he joined the Harding administration, were down by just 16.3 percent. "A clean, well-managed bank," a federal examiner had appraised the

A notorious promoter "of all sorts of schemes and enterprises" and an outsize borrower from the Federal Reserve, the Guaranty was an accident waiting to happen, Williams alleged. Nor would one likely have to wait long for the ugly denouement. Compounding the Guaranty's home-grown difficulties was the overextended position of the Mercantile Bank of the Americas, of which the Guaranty Trust was a principal shareholder. Williams was writing to warn Mellon of the risk that the Mercantile Bank might bring down the Guaranty, and that the failure of the Guaranty might precipitate a general panic.

The Mercantile Bank of the Americas was organized in 1915 to conduct a trading and banking business in South America. The 1920 collapse in commodity prices had caught a subsidiary of the Mercantile with large stores of suddenly unsaleable inventory. Williams knew the story firsthand, he advised Mellon; his examiners had gone to South America to get the facts. And now, as the excomptroller observed, the Mercantile's shareholders were very publicly raising a $20 million rescue fund.[1]

Williams seemed unable to collect an audience for his concerns about the Guaranty Trust. Governor Harding of the Federal Reserve Board had waved him off. *Barron's*, the new Dow Jones financial weekly, denounced the critics as rumor mongers.[2] Surely, Williams pressed Mellon, the time had come to prepare for the worst. By the letter of the Federal Reserve Act, a bank in need of a loan to forestall a depositors' run was required to post collateral—eligible collateral only, consisting of Treasury securities or a specific kind of commercial bill. State and municipal bonds, senior railroad obligations and even high-grade corporate debt were ineligible.

So Williams, repeating a proposal that he had floated in his final annual report from the comptroller's office, asked Mellon to support a rule to liberalize the collateral requirements to prevent the failure of "important" banks, the kind that might induce systemwide disturbances. Some of these institutions had eligible collateral only to the extent of a quarter of their assets.

National Bank of Commerce in June 1920, when the sum total of its slow and doubtful loans came to $527,000 against overall loans and discounts of $313.8 million; estimated losses were zero. But the depression told even on that estimable institution. In March 1921, the examiner tallied $20.6 million in slow and doubtful loans and $900,000 of estimated losses. "This condition is a result of the general business situation," said the examiner's note to Washington. "The management closely checks credits before taking them and constantly reviews existing credits, both with considerable ability and efficiency."

Was it not the better part of wisdom to permit them, in an emergency, to stump up alternative assets?

The excomptroller was suggesting that some banks were too big or important to fail. He had so classified the United States Trust Company of Washington, D.C., in 1913, as we have seen. The too-big-to-fail idea would have its time, but that time was not 1921. Williams was right about the Guaranty Trust: Something clearly was wrong. What he underestimated was the determination of private initiative to set things right.

Rushing to the aid of the Mercantile Bank—and thus of the Guaranty Trust—in August 1921 was not the government but the House of Morgan. Beyond the $20 million it had helped to raise in June, J.P. Morgan & Co. organized a bankers' syndicate in August to furnish another $35 million. Altogether, the *Wall Street Journal* speculated, as much as $80 million in new investment might have found its way into the Mercantile.

And how discreetly and efficiently it was done, the *Journal* marveled: "With the exhibition of as little linen as possible, a distressing bank situation has been—in the case of the Mercantile Bank of the Americas, Inc.—washed out, dried, and is now in the process of ironing."*[3]

So would the federal finances be overhauled, if the Harding administration got its way. Mellon, in his first week in office, had enunciated the new fiscal program: "The people generally must become more interested in saving the Government's money than in spending it." To which he added the admonition, "The nation can not continue to spend at this shocking rate."[4] Such thoughts were balm to the fretful capitalist. Soothing, too, was the administration's friendlier posture toward business, its announced intention to reduce taxes and its expressed ambition to bring about worldwide disarmament.

---

*The rehabilitation of the Guaranty Trust involved the shrinkage of its lending, the reduction of its borrowing from the Federal Reserve Bank of New York, the charge-off of its losses, the reduction of its dividend and the evident kicking upstairs of its president, Charles H. Sabin, to the office of chairman. Sabin had been recruited into banking on account of his prowess in baseball—he was signed as a clerk in 1887 to an Albany bank that needed a pitcher for the company team as much as it did a bookkeeper. So it was, on October 5, 1921, that the departing president of the Guaranty Trust Company made his valedictory comments to the financial press as he was leaving the bank for the Polo Grounds to attend Game 1 of the 1921 World Series between the Yankees and the Giants. [*New York Times*, October 6, 1921]

In 1929, Sabin was again in the news, this time for arranging a merger of the Guaranty Trust with the National Bank of Commerce; the merged entity, which retained the name Guaranty Trust, formed a $2 billion institution, the largest in the country. Thirty years later, there was another mighty union, and Guaranty Trust became the Morgan Guaranty Trust Company.

None of these aspirations was actually realized when, on June 20, 1921, the Dow Jones Railroad Average put in its low for the cycle. There was nothing in the day's price action to suggest that the rails were about to begin a strong bull market. On the contrary, the closing level of the index, 65.52, was the lowest since 1898. Nor was it obvious that the railroads, still staggering from the aftereffects of government management during the war, would win the rate relief they sought from the Interstate Commerce Commission or the wage relief they sought from their employees. If there was one glimmer of sunshine, it was the cash position of the New York, New Haven and Hartford Railroad. In 1920, the bleeding New Haven had shown a deficit of $4.6 million on record-high revenue of $123.5 million. Now it looked as if the carrier would, after all, be able to meet its July 1 interest payments.

Public policy made one signal contribution, at least, to the improvement in American finances. This was in the all-important matter of interest rates. It was welcome news when the Federal Reserve Bank of Boston cut its main discount rate to 6 percent from 7 percent, effective April 15.[5] It was the first easing move by any Federal Reserve bank since the previous spring. The Federal Reserve Bank of New York followed on May 4 with a reduction to 6.5 percent from 7 percent. This move the market correctly interpreted as the beginning of the end of the era of ultrahigh interest rates (high enough in nominal terms, extra lofty when adjusted for the declines in prices and wages).*[6] Bond yields, which had been gently falling since May 1920, now began to nosedive.[7]

A more important source of relief for the formerly straitened American money market was the persistent flow of gold into the United States. It came by steamer, mostly from Europe, and especially from Britain and France—for instance, the unannounced arrival on May 9 of $12 million of bullion on the Cunard liner *Mauretania* consigned, in part, to J.P. Morgan from the Bank of England.[8] Not just any seaworthy craft was up to the job of hauling a multimillion-dollar gold shipment. Twelve million dollars of

---

*In the light of falling prices, even a 6.5 percent rate was asphyxiating. Using estimates of the rate of change in prices cited by Allan H. Meltzer, one finds that real money-market interest rates near the bottom of the 1920–21 depression ranged between 13 percent and 26 percent. This is the 21st century view of the situation. To judge by the contemporary financial press, the practitioners of 1921 did not yet think in terms of real rates, only of nominal ones. [Meltzer, *History of the Federal Reserve*, 117–18]

gold, at the prevailing value of $20.67 to the ounce, weighed 36,284 pounds, or more than 18 tons.*[9]

The United States was by now a great creditor. It exported more than it imported, and it loaned more than it borrowed. Foreigners could satisfy their debts to Americans in gold, securities or merchandise. Sending merchandise had appeal, but Britain or France or Germany would have had to send the goods that Americans wanted at the prices Americans wanted to pay. Not every war-weary European country was competitive in this regard, even with their cheapened postwar currencies. In 1920, Americans imported $6.7 billion worth of merchandise but exported $10.3 billion worth; in 1921, they imported $3.4 billion worth but exported $5.5 billion worth. So the foreigners had to send something else besides goods and/or services. Many sent stocks and bonds—and gold. Some of the *Mauretania*'s treasure was destined for the Treasury in payment of a $150 million war loan that Britain had floated in the United States in 1916; the debt would come due on November 1, 1921.[10]

Under prewar monetary arrangements, gold was relatively evenly apportioned among gold-standard nations. It did not roll, like so many marbles on a tilted surface, into one set of national hands. Too much of it would lead to inflation—which, in turn, would tend to drive money away. Too little of it would lead to deflation—which, in its turn, would tend to draw money in. Gold, being footloose and opportunistic, went where it found high real returns.

There were few such synchronous tendencies in the postwar world. Central banks tended to manage the currencies they oversaw. No longer was gold a free agent in search of a good home and a competitive rate of return. So more and more gold came to America to stay. The United States, alone among the major nations, adhered to the basic prewar monetary conventions, to wit: Gold could freely enter and leave the country, and anyone could exchange dollar bills for gold, and vice versa, at the longstanding statutory rate of $20.67 to the ounce. Then, too, the United States was productive, stable and enterprising. Its politics were conservative and its prices were cheap and getting cheaper. The war had left it relatively unscathed. So the

---

*At $1,400 an ounce, the value at this writing, $5 million of gold weighs only 223 pounds.

gold flowed west across the Atlantic in volumes that left journalists reaching for synonyms for "immense."

Lugged out of cargo holds and on to the New York City docks, the coins and bars made intermediate stops at various Wall Street banks. Their final destination was usually the Federal Reserve Bank of New York. Gold was money—that hadn't changed—but it no longer circulated as it used to.*

One of the important changes in monetary organization since 1914 was the centralization of the nation's gold in the vaults of the Federal Reserve system. It was change for the good, the Federal Reserve Bank of New York patiently tried to explain in a July 1921 bulletin.[11] Stacked in the vaults of a commercial bank, a gold ingot was idle, the exposition said. On deposit at the Federal Reserve, it was procreative; it became "reserves." A big-city bank was required to hold back a dime out of every dollar in deposits. Those fallow 10 cents were the reserve. Once the minimum was satisfied, the bank could lend a multiple of its reserve balances—in the case of a big-city bank, up to nine times the amount of the money it had on deposit in its reserve account at the Federal Reserve. It didn't have to lend to that degree—prudence, not arithmetic, was the ultimate consideration—but it conceivably could.[12]

On deposit at the central bank, moreover, the gold contributed its mite to America's financial strength. This was because of the law that required the nation's principal paper currency, the Federal Reserve note, to be supported by a certain volume of the metal into which the note was convertible. At the low point, in the summer of 1920, just 40 percent of the face amount of the Federal Reserve notes in circulation was supported by gold, the bare legal minimum. How to protect the supply of currency against a shortfall in gold coverage? One could shrink the supply of Federal Reserve notes or increase the supply of gold. Painfully high real interest rates achieved both objectives. They set in train a contraction of bank lending and, thus, of the

---

*In January 1914, when the Federal Reserve existed in the statute books but not yet as an institution, the money supply totaled $3.215 billion, of which gold coins made up $329 million, or 10.2 percent. By July 1921, the stock of gold coins had dwindled to $157 million, representing 3.5 percent of the $4.510 billion money supply. [Board of Governors of the Federal Reserve System, Banking and Monetary Statistics: 1914–1941 (Washington, D.C., Federal Reserve, 1943), 409 and ff.]

stock of money.* And they helped to entice an inbound movement of gold. By May 1921, 80 percent of the volume of Federal Reserve notes was supported by gold. At the Federal Reserve Bank of New York, 100 percent were so collateralized.

Gold was making a beeline for America. Between the start of the depression, in January 1920, and the trough, in July 1921, foreign bullion augmented the American gold stock by some $400 million, to $3 billion.[13] The vast importation put a spring in Wall Street's step. It was, the speculative community correctly reasoned, the augury of lower interest rates and easier money. "One banker expressed the opinion that as much as $500 million more gold might reach here before the movement reaches the crest," the *Wall Street Journal* reported in May 1921. "Should this possibility actually eventuate, it would result in approximately half of the world's gold stock being accumulated in this country and would lay the foundation for a business expansion that would even eclipse the record performance that amazed the world during the Great War."[14]

The unnamed banker underestimated America's monetary drawing power. Five hundred million dollars' worth of additional gold arrived by February 1922. Another $500 million's worth was landed before the close of 1923.

The perpendicular plunge in commodity prices was something new in post-Napoleonic history. Never before had they fallen so far and so fast. So the recovery, when it came, was a tonic for any who had suffered in the liquidation. Silk prices, which had led to the down side, were the first to revive, starting as early as July 1920. By March 1921, lead, pig iron, red cedar shingles and calfskin hides had scraped bottom and started back up. Cottonseed oil, hides, red brick, cattle, sheep, cotton sheetings, burley tobacco, and crude oil followed suit by midsummer.

In the halcyon days of the lingering postwar inflation, cotton had fetched more than 40 cents a pound in New York. By June 1921, it was quoted at

---

*Between March 1920 and January 1922, the sum of currency and bank deposits—the basic money supply, or M1—dropped to $20.45 billion from $23.91 billion, a decline of 14.4 percent. Between October 1920 and January 1922, the sum of currency and bank reserves—the "monetary base"—dropped to $6.08 billion from $7.33 billion, a decline of 17 percent. [Meltzer, *History of the Federal Reserve*, 121]

less than 11 cents a pound. Planters, bankers, merchants and fertilizer manufacturers, among other numerous dependents on that staple southern crop, wondered if they would live to see 20 cents a pound again. They did, within 90 days. Still, the economic damage to the South was done.

Senator Thomas E. Watson, Democrat from Georgia, could not undo it, but he could call to account the men who caused it. Who might the guilty parties be? Watson blamed the governors of the Federal Reserve Board (for other problems at other times, he blamed Catholics, blacks and Jews).

The senator had entered politics as a Democrat in the 1880s. Switching to the Populist Party, he was William Jennings Bryan's vice presidential running mate in 1896. He was the Populist candidate for president in 1904, after which he returned to the Democrats. At length, he switched to the Theodore Roosevelt wing of the Republican Party, then back to the Democrats. An archopponent of Woodrow Wilson and the League of Nations, he was elected to the U.S. Senate in 1920.

Watson had a monetary agenda, too. Any and all government obligations issued during and after the war should be transformed into currency at par value, or 100 cents on the dollar (as opposed to the then-prevailing discount from par at which government bonds were quoted). The Federal Reserve should lend directly to farmers on approved collateral at the concessionary interest rate of 5 percent. Watson promised that his reforms would light up the country "like an electric current." [15]

On July 19, the senator introduced a resolution to replace the Board of Governors with "competent and honest" men who are neither bankers nor the "servitors of the Morgan interests, the Standard Oil Corporation, the packers, the Steel Trust or any other legalized marauders upon the common people of the Republic." Watson charged that, in the previous year, the "secret, unlawful and ruinous" policies of the Federal Reserve had saddled "the helpless American people by the sudden and colossal contraction of the money in circulation" with losses of no less than $21 billion. [16] He charged the governors with helping themselves to $18 million of the Federal Reserve's funds.

Senator J. Thomas Heflin, Democrat from Alabama, embellished that fabrication on August 15. "I am not advised as to whether or not any of the friends of the Federal Reserve Board were speculating in cotton at that time"—i.e., when the cotton price caved in, said Heflin. "The senator from Georgia [Mr. Watson] reminded us the other day that they loaned to themselves in the System the sum of $18 million. I want to say just here, Mr. President, that if they invested any of that $18 million in speculating on the bear side of the cotton market in the month of August last year, they made a lot of money." Neither Watson nor Heflin had a shred of evidence to substantiate those fanciful claims, and the Senate declined to call the slanderers to account for them, as an aggrieved W.P.G. Harding had demanded.[17]

Lost in the senatorial windstorm was news of a broad-based rise in commodity prices, the first since early 1920. Indices produced by Dun and by Bradstreet (the two were as yet unmerged) and by the U.S. Labor Department all pointed in the same novel direction: up. The tide was turning, even if nobody then living could be positively sure of that fact. Deflation was on the way out.

★ 18 ★

"BACK TO BARBARISM?"

In the unhappy 12 months of 1921, E.I. du Pont de Nemours and Company, maker of explosives, dyestuffs, paint and cellulose products, earned $5.7 million, or $2.35 per common share, down from $14.6 million, or $16.96 per common share, in 1920. Net sales dropped to $55.3 million, from $93.9 million in 1920 (and from $329.1 million in 1918, the year before the Armistice knocked the demand for explosives for a loop). In that depression year, DuPont eliminated its bank debt and sacked more than half of its employees. It wrote down the value of its inventories to $24.9 million, from $52.1 million.

"The stockholders of this company are anxious to know whether this represents a new era of reduced business or whether the depression will quickly pass," Irénée du Pont, president, wrote to his investors.

No attempt can be made to answer this question, which does not start with an endeavor to determine the reasons leading up to the low volume of business. The writer believes immediate cause of the low volume of business was the endeavor, in latter part of 1920 and during 1921, on the part of those engaged in industry and commerce to liquidate inventories. Your company is probably a fair example of average conditions. Of raw materials used in products sold during the first eight months of 1921, approximately one-half came out of the storehouses and one-half was purchased. This means that those who sold to the du Pont Co. suffered a reduction of 50% in volume of materials needed by this company for its already reduced operations. This condition must cease when inventories are exhausted.

It seems reasonable to suppose that marked reduction in buying has resulted in intense competition to sell and that this has been a large factor in the reduction of prices.[1]

The breakneck rate of decline, especially of prices, was one defining characteristic of the 1920–21 depression. The relatively strong showing of the American banking system—which John Skelton Williams, in his official utterances if not his private ones, had often noted—was another. What distinguished the subsequent recovery was likewise its uptempo pace. From 1921 to 1922, industrial production jumped by 25.9 percent and residential construction by 57.9 percent. Manufacturing employment increased to 9.0 million from 8.2 million, a gain of 9.5 percent (though, as had been amply demonstrated, employment was a somewhat fuzzy datum).[2] Real income per capita rose to $553 from $522, a gain of 5.9 percent.[3]

In 1921, 356,000 American corporations showed a cumulative net profit of $458 million, which was down from $5.9 billion in 1920. In 1922, such profits rebounded to $4.8 billion.*[4] In 1921, Detroit produced 1.453 million cars and trucks. In 1922, it turned out 2.372 million, a leap of 63 percent.[5] "In 1921," to quote the Hoover-commissioned volume *Recent Economic Changes*, "more than 300 articles appeared telling of methods used in cutting wages and speculating as to how far they would fall. By 1922, articles of this sort had disappeared and those about wage increases had taken their place."[6]

Irénée du Pont had hit the nail on the head. At the crest of the inflation of 1919–20, businesses had laid in all the inventory they could prudently (and sometimes imprudently) afford. As prices rose, so did the value of the

---

*Another line of sight on profits: The number of corporations reporting net income in excess of $100,000 was as follows: 1918, 9,634; 1920, 9,737; 1921, 5,330; 1922, 8,864; 1923, 10,206. [*Recent Economic Changes*, 180]

items stacked in warehouses. These valuation gains the companies duly recorded on their financial statements.

In the ensuing deflation, businesses unburdened themselves of those stocks at a loss, which valuation losses they recorded in turn. On the way up, inventory accumulation had contributed to the panicky sense that the world was running out of everything. On the way down, inventory destocking helped to enflame the fear that the world was oversupplied with everything.

"Inventory accounts mirror the savage cut to even below pre-war values for many commodities," the *Wall Street Journal* related in a survey of 1921 corporate financial results. "What appeared to be huge profits built up during war prosperity have in many cases turned out to be but inflated inventory values and these have been punctured by the fall in prices of both raw and finished products during 1921. To absorb these losses with sales running far below normal has been the problem."[7]

White Motor Company, a leading truck manufacturer, had had a typically tumultuous experience in the 1920–21 inventory cycle. The company closed its books on 1920 with $23 million of goods on hand. It was an extraordinary bulge in the inventory account (up from $15.7 million in 1919 and from $10.2 million in 1918), but the inflation- and war-induced boom had taught management never to be caught short. In 1921, the bottom fell out—or, rather, two bottoms fell out, as sales and prices alike collapsed.

In 1920, White had generated gross revenue of $52 million; in 1921, it did but $30.3 million. In 1920, the company had produced an operating profit of $2.3 million, in 1921 an operating loss of $4.4 million, almost half of which was owing to a writedown of inventory values. At least, management could console itself, White had not fully shared in the miserable results of the average truck maker. National truck sales in 1921 had fallen by 68 percent, White's by a mere 43 percent.

Then, too, Walter C. White, president, advised the stockholders, there was something to be said for the occasional spell of downtime. "After years of constant effort to increase our output to a maximum, we, in order to reduce the stock on hand, reduced our factory production to a minimum."

This afforded an opportunity to put into effect many of the economies of manufacture and selling, the importance of which had long been appreciated, but the adoption of which had been precluded by the necessities of peak production.... With our inventories largely reduced, and priced at present values, with our selling expenses as nearly commensurate as possible with the volume of sales reasonably to be expected, with our plant and man-ufacturing organization in the best condition they have ever been, we, today, are in a better competitive position than ever before.... We feel justified in hoping that a profit will be shown at the end of the year.[8]

Management did not hope in vain: The year 1922 delivered a net profit of $3.8 million, against a 1921 deficit of $4.8 million.[9]

Constructive shrinkage were the business watchwords of 1921. Inventories had to go, even with the attendant losses. So, too, would have to go the bank debt that financed the redundant and overvalued stocks. They were opposite sides of the same cyclical coin.*

Not every company could emulate the shining example of White Mo-tors. Sears, Roebuck & Company, the even-then venerable mail-order house, could not. Its sales were weak, its inventory position was outsize and the loans that financed that slow-selling merchandise were likewise excessive. Like the other great Chicago mail-order house, Montgomery Ward & Company, Sears sold to rural America, which remained economi-cally moribund. And, like Montgomery Ward, Sears struggled against such fast-rising chain stores as F.W. Woolworth, S.S. Kresge, Piggly Wiggly and J.C. Penney.[10]

Sears was in the corporate minority. In 1921, American business in toto reduced its overpriced inventories by $627 million, to $1.8 billion from $2.5 billion, a decline of more than 25 percent. A sample of 23 big industrial companies examined by the *Wall Street Journal* revealed an overall purge of $485 million, to $715 million from $1.2 billion, a drop of 40 percent. In the way of all mass financial movements, this one would carry at least a little too far. Come the return of prosperity, penny-pinching managements would

---

*In the 18 months leading up to July 1, 1921, 3,676 companies, each with a capital of more than $250,000, sold promissory notes in the open market. And of this cohort of borrowers, according to the National Credit Office, only 89 failed to meet in a full and timely fashion their obligations to their credi-tors. Of $4 billion borrowed, only $104 million wound up in default. In a time of deflation and inventory liquidation, it was a superb record. [*Wall Street Journal,* July 23, 1921]

discover the need to restock depleted shelves. They would discover, too, that they were shorthanded. And so the deflationary process described by Irénée du Pont would swing into reverse. It was bound to happen—it always had happened—though no one could be certain when it would start.

One commodity of which there was evidently too little in the United States, even in 1921, was the standard, detached single-family home. In 1910, 110 American families had occupied every 100 houses. In 1920, 117 families had had to squeeze themselves into every 100 houses. As Secretary of Commerce Hoover did the arithmetic, the country was short 1.5 million houses, even by the 1910 standard. Perhaps 60 percent of the population rented their dwelling places, he estimated, an elevated level by world standards. A rate of home ownership on the order of 40 percent he called shockingly and unacceptably low (the census would put the figure closer to 45 percent; today it is just shy of 65 percent). "Nothing is worse than increased tenantry and landlordism in this country," Hoover declared.*[11]

What Hoover implied, although he did not say, was that the deficit in American residential real estate was an opportunity waiting to happen. By the close of 1921—he spoke in July—the outlook for construction had brightened. By the close of 1922, statisticians could gasp at the accomplished fact of the biggest building boom in American history.

Interest rates had fallen, and so, too, had the cost of building materials (erected structural steel in early 1922 was being sold at prices below the prewar average level). Labor was plentiful. Superimposed on these bullish facts was a large, unmet demand. If nothing is inevitable, the eruption in building was at least unsurprising.

In 1922, $3.5 billion of residential construction was put in place, up from $2.2 billion in 1921, a jump of 59 percent. Total construction in 1922 amounted to $7.6 billion, up from $6 billion in 1921, a gain of 26.7 percent. In 1922, 160,000 buildings of every description were constructed, up from 110,000 in 1921 and 80,000 in 1920. By the middle of 1923, the *New York*

---

*To advance the cause of home ownership, the secretary of commerce urged a relaxation of the regulations that prohibited nationally chartered banks from making mortgage loans. "I wish to say," said Hoover, in response to proposals that Washington lend a hand, "that the federal government has no notion whatever of getting into the housing business, either directly or indirectly."

Times could pose the question; How long can this rate of building construction progress be maintained (for 1923, too, was shaping up as a year to remember)? W.J. Moore, president of the American Bond and Mortgage Company, had an answer. He replied that the upswing was constrained chiefly by the shortage of skilled labor. In the depths of the depression, who could have imagined it?[12]

There was no scarcity on the farm. In American agriculture in the early 1920s, surplus was rather the rule. Crops were too big, debts too heavy and prices too low. Export markets were clogged and domestic demand was weak. "Back to Barbarism?" queried *Wallaces Farmer* in its edition of September 1921, to which the editors replied, "It really is unthinkable that the present situation can continue for more than a few months longer, but if it should continue for as long as two years, the farmers would be forced into the situation which they occupied in the '70s, and if it should continue for as long as five years, the United States would find herself in much the same plight as Russia is at present."[13]

"The situation" in fact persisted for many years, though with consequences less dire for the country than for the undercapitalized and over-encumbered marginal farmer. American agriculture had produced and improved itself into a crisis. It planted not much less in 1921 than it had in 1920, but the land under the plow represented 20 million more acres than the average of 1910 to 1914. As for the economic return to that colossal effort, the U.S. Department of Agriculture had kept records going back to 1866 for the average value of crops per acre. And never before had that value plunged more steeply than it did from 1919 to 1921, from $35.74 per acre to $14.52 per acre, a decline of 59 percent. By January 1922, the purchasing power of the farmer's dollar was "probably at the lowest point ever known," according to Henry Wallace, now Harding's secretary of agriculture.[14]

What the farmer needed was what the world was not then offering: stable currencies, fixed exchange rates, strong foreign demand and rising per capita consumption of wheat, cotton, veal, beef, potatoes and the like.[15] What was on offer was rather monetary disequilibrium, stunted European demand and a flattening trend in American food consumption. On average, the 1921 harvest yielded a return somewhat lower than the cost of producing it.[16] The huge disparity between what farmers earned and what they paid sent researchers to the history books. In terms of what it availed the grower, reported the 1921 *Agriculture Department Yearbook*, the price of wheat on December 1, 1921—94 cents a bushel—was actually lower than the price of wheat on December 1, 1894—49 cents a bushel.[17]

Nationally chartered banks acquitted themselves just as Williams had publicly promised they would. In the 12 months prior to June 1921, only 28 failed, and not one with capital more than $100,000. The full brunt of the agricultural depression rather fell on small state-chartered banks; 330 suspended over the same 12 months, the most since the panic year of 1893.[18]

Angry farmers could have blamed progress. It was perhaps no coincidence that 1919, the peak year of the farmer's postwar earning power, coincided with the highest number of horses and mules in agricultural service in America, 26.4 million. Tractors were just coming into their own; trade groups counted none in 1917, 80,100 in 1918 and (here was a census tabulation) 246,139 in 1920. By 1925, there were half a million tractors and 22.3 million horses and mules. The cost of growing food and fiber was inexorably falling.[19]

Land values, too, were on the skids. Between 1914 and 1920, the cost of an acre of farmland in South Carolina and Iowa had doubled. By 1922, those peak prices were lower by 45.2 percent and 23.9 percent, respectively. Much of this property was mortgaged, and much of that fell into foreclosure (though typically not before some deadline stretching by sympathetic creditors). Forced sales eventually followed. "The significant thing in all this, however," wrote the agricultural economist Edwin G. Nourse, looking back from the late 1920s, "is that prices have shown but little tendency to recover, and meanwhile a very large number of involuntary owners are still holding on to this property. . . . There is probably not a single large insurance company, if it loaned on real estate in the Middle West, which does not have substantial holdings of farmland in some of these states, and the total runs to many millions." At the Metropolitan Life Insurance Company, the stewards of foreclosed farmland formed a unit that came to be known as the "Department of Agriculture."[20]

★ 19 ★

AMERICA ON THE BARGAIN COUNTER

By the *Wall Street Journal*'s telling, it was no coincidence that so many business and financial leaders took to making public professions of op-timism starting in the middle of September 1921. "It is known," the paper reported on September 19, less than a month after the Dow Jones industri-als had put in their low, "that this change in attitude followed conferences between prominent bankers and men of high standing in finance." And what had these great men decided? "It was agreed that bottoms for good securities, prices for commodities and business had about been reached, and that the situation warranted the spreading of optimistic propaganda."*

The unsigned *Journal* dispatch imputed mighty powers to the unnamed financiers. It was they who were behind the recent strength in stock and bond prices, the story said. Nor had they invested to scalp a few quick

---

*A week later, in political counterpoint, the People's Reconstruction League summoned an all-day con-ference to promote the cause of "economic justice." Planks of the league's program, according to the *New York Times*, included "Prompt restoration of the railroads to unified Government operation; legislation to control the meat-packing industry; taxation of privilege instead of poverty; making banking and credit system serve the people; control of natural resources, and the defeat of the universal compulsory military training project." [*New York Times*, September 26, 1921]

dollars of profit, as the professional traders on the floor of the New York Stock Exchange were wont to do. They rather bought for the long term because securities were cheap and because the country was on the upswing. Thus, "the stock market passed the control of professionals to what Wall Street terms 'big constructive interests.'"

The public-spirited big men wanted no new boom, the story hastened to add: "What they are working for is a gradual, safe recovery, that will put back to work the several million men out of employment. In this they have the cooperation of Washington, and constructive railroad and tax legislation is looked for before the end of the year."

At this point in the article, the reporter yielded the floor to an anonymous prominent banker. In direct quotation, the moneybags vouchsafed anyone with the price of the *Journal*—seven cents—the information required to get rich. The banker first went over some old ground by explaining how the country got into the mess it was in. Then he came to describe the necessary, if painful, phase of readjustment, which was still underway. "[F]ew people can fully realize what has been accomplished in this direction over the last year in correcting an economic situation which in its seriousness was without a parallel. In this direction we have made great strides of a constructive character," the informant said. "We are on the verge of a period of prosperity that will be backed by rigid economy. There will be no wild inflation. The day of the silk shirt millionaire has passed into history."

By this time, an attentive *Journal* reader might have wondered if the unidentified mogul was actually the *Journal*'s own editor, William Peter Hamilton. On page one of the same September 19th edition of the newspaper, the editorial voice of the *Journal* reproved the National City Bank and a competing paper, the *New York Herald*, for warning against "false booms." It was gratuitous advice, Hamilton (at least, it certainly sounded like Hamilton) countered. The critics ought to stop lecturing the stock market and start listening to it instead:

There is a bull market impending in stocks. The stock market is doing what it always does, if people could ever understand. The volume of trading is controlled by no manipulation. Business is discounted as far ahead as the total knowledge of the country's financial center can see. Practically all news is discounted when it is published. The stock market today is discounting a return to normalcy which will not be apparent to any worker, or to many employers, for months to come. The National City Bank, which did not foresee the decline in business when the stock market had foreseen it, at the end of 1919, will realize a return to firm ground somewhere about next May and congratulate itself that it warned us against "false booms."

This is the thankless business of the stock market, and it is attending to its business while the conductors of the country's business are taking time off for talk.

The *Journal*'s interviewee, in any case, could not have agreed more with the *Journal*'s editor. All conditions were ripe for revival, the big man went on: The vast accession of gold had restored American banking and credit, industrial inventories were negligible and production was depressed (the steel industry was on a "starvation basis"). The railroads were in crying need of new equipment: "Although the country is today on a 40 percent productive basis, more than 80 percent of our freight cars are in use."*

Stocks were commandingly cheap, the *Journal*'s capitalist source concluded. "Scores" of companies were valued in the market at less than their working capital—as if the business itself, apart from the net cash, was worthless. The shares of "large numbers" of industrial companies were selling at "one-third of their respective intrinsic values."

It was just as he said—America was on the bargain counter. The lyricist of the 1921 hit "Ain't We Got Fun?" had famously written that "the rich get richer." A more accurate, if less sing-able, formulation would have been "the liquid and financially flexible rich get richer." The depression had driven the overencumbered rich, like Billy Durant, founder and president of General Motors, into the swelling ranks of the formerly rich. But for any with cash to invest, the opportunities in 1921 were boundless.

Deflation took its toll on real estate as well as on stocks and bonds, to judge by a perusal of the *New York Times* classified advertising pages. Thus, in the edition of June 26, 1921: "BARGAIN; $1,500 cash investment will

---

*As prophesied: In 1922, American railroads addressed the equipment shortage by ordering the most freight cars since 1912 and the most locomotives since 1918. In 1921, the carriers placed orders for 239 locomotives; in 1922, they bought 2,456. [*Wall Street Journal*, June 1, 1923]

return over $5,000 per year net. I will sell my five-story modern walk-up apartment house near Washington Heights for less than five times the rent."

Or, on November 9, 1921: "Corner Business Building, vicinity 34th Street-8th Av., recently rebuilt; all leased; present income over 25 per cent. on investment: excellent proposition for a conservative investor: principals only."

Or, more plaintively, on December 6, 1921: "New Jersey—For Sale or To Let, I will lose my home and every dollar put into it by foreclosure in few days because I can't pay balance due on mortgage; to save something from the wreck, sacrifice for $6,500 cash purchase to assume mortgage of $17,000; house is worth twice this amount; I'm willing to take big loss, rather than all I have put into it." This was a 12-room house with three-car garage, set by a lake.

Possibly, the sellers of these properties were exaggerating. If, however, the auditors and managements of America's leading industrial companies were telling the plain truth, the stock market was as cheap as any illiquid Manhattan corner office building.

Thus, at the August 24 low in the Dow, General Motors changed hands at 9½. The company was on its way to showing a 1921 loss of $38.7 million—compared to a 1920 profit of $37.9 million—and to selling just 215,000 cars, trucks and tractors, down from 387,000 in 1920. Management was in the process of writing down $55.9 million of inventory (from a 1920 starting point of $164.7 million) and of eliminating $33.1 million of short-term indebtedness.[1] The dividend, too, was on its way out. Liquidation had been the order of the day in 1921, the chairman and president, Pierre S. du Pont, reminded the stockholders early in 1922. But that chapter in the company's history was closed: "The year 1922 opens with inventory accounts reduced to current basis and old commitments provided for or adjusted. The opening months of the year show substantial increase in demand and sales, not only with respect to corresponding months of 1921, when business was nearly at a standstill, but also as to several divisions even in comparison with the record year 1920."[2]

In the depths of the slump, some had speculated that the automobile market was "saturated," that the Ford Motor Company itself was broke and that the best days of the evidently now mature industry were behind it. Roaring sales in 1922 hushed that discouraging talk. By late March, Ford was finding work enough to keep its employees busy for five days a week instead of the depression-shortened three.[3] By late in April, there were reports of a developing labor shortage in Detroit. At least one automobile supplier, Michigan Copper & Brass Company, was recalling its salesmen from the road; the company had more business than it could handle.[4]

November 16 brought news that GM would resume paying a dividend, though the directors had not forgotten the company's near-death experience over the preceding year. They would authorize a payout of 50 cents a share just this once and defer a decision on a permanent rate of distribution. In 1920, the company had produced an average of 31,867 cars a month, with an investment in inventory equal to about $5,548 per car; in 1922, monthly production averaged 45,000 cars on an investment in inventory of only $2,530 per car. "In other respects," the communique concluded, "the corporation has materially fortified its position and the outlook for the year 1923 is considered entirely satisfactory."[5]

More than "entirely satisfactory," in fact, the results proved to be. At a price of 9½, at the depression lows of 1921, GM shares were valued at just 4.3 times 1922 earnings and 3.6 times 1923 earnings—that is, at what those earnings would prove to be (only a clairvoyant, and an optimistic clairvoyant at that, could have predicted it in August 1921). At 14⅞, the closing price on the day of the dividend announcement, the stock was valued at 6.8 times 1922 earnings and 5.6 times earnings for 1923.

As General Motors prospered, so did the fortunes of GM's largest shareholder, E. I. du Pont de Nemours and Company. In cars and trucks, the one-time leading outfitter of the ordnance departments of the Allied armies had found a business steadier and faster growing even than human conflict. Of the 20 million GM shares outstanding in 1922, DuPont owned 7.4 million. In that year, a gifted young investor took the trouble to compare the value of this single DuPont holding with the overall quoted value of DuPont company shares. The arithmetic revealed an anomaly. Just about all of the quoted DuPont value was attributable to the value of the GM stock, and none to DuPont's own nonautomotive earnings and assets. So the investor—he was Benjamin Graham, widely regarded today as the father of modern American security analysis—bought DuPont while simultaneously selling GM. In Wall Street parlance, Graham performed a relatively riskless arbitrage operation, correctly reasoning that DuPont would sooner or later appreciate relative to GM.*

Then, again, like so many other stocks at the bottom of the market, DuPont was cheap on its face, without reference to recondite techniques of valuation. Closely held, the shares rarely traded in 1921; at the 1922 low price of 105, they were valued at 6.3 times 1922 earnings and 4.0 times 1923 earnings (as those earnings were subsequently recorded).

On August 24, 1921, the low point of the Dow, many stock prices translated into multiples on 1923 earnings of less than five times. That held true of the steel companies but also of the kind of consumer-products companies that had enjoyed a relatively prosperous depression. Thus, Coca-Cola, at $19 a share—500,000 shares were outstanding, providing a stock-market capitalization of all of $9.5 million—was valued at what would prove 1.7 times 1922 earnings and 2.5 times 1923 earnings; the shares provided a dividend yield of 5.26 percent. Gillette Safety Razor Company, which was selling as many razors and blades in 1921 as it had in 1920, was quoted at a little more than five times forward earnings and yielded 9.23 percent. Radio Corporation of America, not yet revealed as one of the great growth stocks of the 1920s, could be purchased in the market for about as much as the company earned in 1923: $1.50 a share.

As a matter of course on Wall Street, bargains hold no appeal at the bottom of the market. In August 1921, stock prices had been sliding for almost two years. At such junctures, the memory of losing money is usually more vivid than the imagined prospect of making it.

It didn't take much imagination to recognize the value of F.W. Woolworth Company, the five-and-dime chain merchandiser that was finishing its tenth year as a fused corporate unit. Frank W. Woolworth himself, founder and builder of the gothic corporate headquarters tower at

---

*The first thing he did upon founding Graham Corporation in the early 1920s, Benjamin Graham related, "was to buy some shares of DuPont and to sell seven times as many shares of General Motors short against it. . . . So DuPont was greatly undervalued by comparison with the market price of General Motors; in due course a goodly spread appeared in our favor, and I undid the operation at the projected profit." [Benjamin Graham, *The Memoirs of the Dean of Wall Street* (New York: McGraw Hill, 1996), 188]

233 Broadway in lower Manhattan, had died in 1919, but his successors had distinguished themselves in the depression. They had stopped buying any but essential merchandise after the break in wholesale prices in June 1920, while the customers, happily, had kept right on buying. Now 1921 sales were on track to surpass the total for 1920. While other chain stores had raised prices, Woolworth hewed to the letter of its five-and-dime appellation (15 cents was the top ticket west of the Mississippi). And how was this exemplar of deflation-era merchandising—about to close its year without bank debt and with no mispriced inventory—valued in the stock market on August 24, 1921? At a price of $105 a share, or 3.7 times imminent 1922 earnings and 3.3 times what would turn out to be 1923 earnings. The stock yielded 7.62 percent.

Ultralow-equity valuations naturally favored the "big constructive interests" who could avail themselves of them. But high real interest rates also advantaged the little American saver.

In the days before the governmental safety net, thrift was a life-saving virtue. The unemployed could fall back on friends, family members, charity—and their own savings. In 1920, the nation's mutual savings banks counted 9,445,327 depositors with aggregate deposits of $5,186,952,000. At an average of $549.16 per passbook, that was 40.9 percent of the $1,342 average national wage. In 1921, the population of depositors rose by 1.8 percent, the average deposit by 5.5 percent.[6]

Most of these deposits were rainy-day funds, a New York savings banker was quoted as saying in July 1921, "and it has been our experience that it must rain very hard to make a wide change in the totals. The average man or woman with a savings account considers it a sort of final line of defense, and we have records of extraordinary lengths to which depositors will go rather than dip into their accumulation."[7]

In New York, savings banks paid 4 percent on deposits, a handsome rate when the cost of living was falling. Four percent, however, was not so handsome as 5 percent or 6 percent, which is what high-grade bonds were paying in the summer of 1921—and paying in denominations small enough to entice the typical savings bank depositor. So it was that New York savers withdrew a net $21.1 million in the third quarter of that year. The rare outflow of deposits reflected, first, the poor job market and, second, better opportunities outside the walls of one's local mutual savings bank.[8]

For any without access to the forecasts of the big constructive interests, a tip from a mailman would have almost sufficed. In May 1922, postal receipts showed a year-over-year gain of 14.4 percent. In the final six months of 1922, a billion more stamps were issued than in the like period of 1921. In fiscal 1921, the Post Office had run a $60.8 million deficit. In the early weeks of 1923, it appeared as if that deficit were going to be erased.[9]

Likewise could an acquaintance in the railroading field have been a source of useful economic information. By the time accounts were cast at the end of 1922, railroads had moved more agricultural tonnage than in any year of their history. A coal strike led to an overall drop in tonnage compared to the year earlier. However, while 470,406 railroad cars had sat idle in 1921, the railroads were more than 105,000 cars short in 1922.

The fact is that in just about every branch of American business and finance—agriculture was the large and troublesome exception—things were humming. In 1921, there were just 17 days on which trading volume on the New York Stock Exchange topped one million shares; in 1922, there were 116. In 1922, the Dow Jones Industrial Average gained 21.5 percent and the Dow Jones Railroad Average 15.5 percent. Passenger-car production was up by 63 percent, to 1.83 million,[10] car registrations up by 16.2 percent, to 10.9 million.[11] There was a reciprocal decline in railroad passenger service of 6.6 percent.[12] As the tractor was overtaking the horse, so was the automobile displacing the passenger train.

The number of corporations reporting net income in excess of $100,000 jumped by 66.3 percent, to 8,864.[13] Daily newspaper circulation was up by 5 percent (to 29.8 million); strong, as well, were newspaper advertising lineage and advertising rates.[14]

There were unmistakable signs of prosperity in the patterns of American migration. In 1922, 309,556 people immigrated to the United States, which was down by 496,000 (62 percent) from 1921, the year of the restrictive Quota Act. More telling of the change in economic fortunes was the drop in emigration: 198,712 persons chose to leave the United States in 1922, 19.8 percent fewer than in 1921.[15]

Nominal wage rates continued to fall in 1922.* Average hourly rates in manufacturing industries dropped to 49 cents an hour from 52 cents an hour in 1921, a decline of 5.8 percent.[16] The stock market evidently intuited the fact that, in 1922, productivity leapt even as wage rates declined. In this year of recovery, overall manufacturing output matched the volume of 1920, while total employment was the lowest since 1915. The result was a 20 percent surge in output per person, the largest ever recorded up until that time.[17] In fact, nothing in the 20th century had come close. Business activity had slumped to one degree or another in 1904, 1908, 1911 and 1914. Increases in productivity in the years following those declensions were, respectively, 9 percent, 8 percent, 11 percent and 8 percent. The year 1922 stood alone.[18]

What accounts for the power of the 1922 rebound? Fast-paced replenishment of depleted inventories is one reason. Easier money—lower interest rates brought about by the influx of gold and the relaxation of Federal Reserve monetary policy—is a second. The very deflation of 1920–21 is a third. For those with money to spend, the dollar bought more of nearly everything, from cars to commodities to common stocks. "From practically all angles," judged the *Wall Street Journal* in a New Year's Day 1923 retrospective, "1922 can be recorded as the renaissance of prosperity."

The *Journal*'s reporter went on to assert that recovery was "inevitable," but succeeding generations have learned how conditional is the kind of resurgence that followed the 1920–21 downturn. Inventories were low, gold was plentiful and asset values were cheap. The price mechanism was allowed to function. These were the perhaps necessary but certainly not sufficient conditions for the 1922 recovery. Without confidence, even these bullish preconditions might have failed to ignite a boom.

Americans believed in themselves and in the future. (An American banker, freshly returned from Germany in November 1921, reported that the Germans believed in the present: As fast as they earned their fast-depreciating Marks, they spent them.)[19] Trusting in the secretary of the

---

*Not at the Harvester Company, which boosted wage rates by 20 percent in September 1922; this represented 45 percent of the reductions imposed in 1921. [Ozanne, *Century of Labor-Management Relations*, 138]

Treasury, they believed that the federal finances would be capably managed, the public debt paid down and the weight of taxes lifted. And they could see, in President Harding's rejection of a bill to distribute a soldiers' bonus in the fall of 1922, that the administration's financial program was more than words.

"Our heavy tax burdens reach, directly or indirectly, every element in our citizenship," the president's veto message said. "To add one-sixth of the total sum of our public debt for a distribution among less than 5,000,000 out of 110,000,000, whether inspired by grateful sentiment or political expediency, would undermine the confidence on which our credit is builded and establish the precedent of distributing public funds whenever the proposal and the numbers affected make it seem politically expedient to do so." The House overrode Harding's veto but the Senate voted to sustain it.[20]

The constructive interests, big and small, were in the money. Mellon's fiscal plans hinged on a favorable Senate outcome (just four votes was the margin of victory). Defeat would have meant new disturbances in the bond market and higher taxation or more inflation or—possibly—all of those scourges simultaneously. "There is now prospect of a continued and undisturbed orderly expansion of security values," the *Wall Street Journal*'s stock market writer ventured. On that count, the reporter was a prophet.[21]

ALL FOR STABILITY

No more for Harding than for Wilson did America stand up to cheer the achievement of a self-healing depression. There had been a great inflation and a great deflation. There had been high unemployment, commercial distress and an agricultural crisis. Many hundreds of small banks had failed, and the stock market had plunged. But there had been no general panic and no depletion of the public treasury. There had been no devaluation of the dollar. The depression, though painful, was not pointless. It had rebalanced costs and prices and exposed the investment errors of the boom. There had been no "liquidity trap," no "secular stagnation," as the 1930s presently brought. From peak to trough, a year and a half had elapsed. It was a relatively expeditious slump.

At the polls in 1922, Democrats made heavy inroads on the GOP, though the Republicans' setback was no worse than the incumbent party usually suffers in off-year elections, and in neither the House nor the Senate did the Democrats succeed in overturning the Republican majority. GOP losses were heaviest in the farm states, where there was no recovery to speak of, let alone to give thanks for.

Before long, the administration's economic achievements took a back seat to its ethical lapses. Harding died in San Francisco on August 2, 1923, 27 months after taking office. After his death, the secretary of the interior, Albert B. Fall, came under attack for bribe taking in the scandal that would presently take the name Teapot Dome. Harding had died beloved—and, it appeared, just in time.

Calvin Coolidge, the president's taciturn successor, made no substantial changes in the Harding policy agenda. Mellon was still at Treasury, Hoover at Commerce. It was still a business administration, still committed to low tax rates, though somewhat less than devoted to the free play of prices and wages (the Federal Reserve had something to do with that deficiency). In the three-way presidential race of 1924, John W. Davis, the Democrat, collected some 8.4 million popular votes and Robert M. LaFollette, the Progressive, 4.8 million. Coolidge won 15.3 million popular votes, 35 states and 382 electoral votes. The people had reelected normalcy.

Few who lost jobs, money or health in the 1920–21 downturn cherished the compensating gifts of their experiences. The merit, if any, that the slump acquired is owing to comparisons to what came after. Having no foreknowledge of the Great Depression and its aftermath, still less of the Great Recession and *its* aftermath, people didn't think to ask themselves why the depression was so relatively brief or the recovery so strong.

Nor, for the most part, did the economists of the Harding era stop to reflect on the blessings of flexible wages and prices, especially their flexibility to the down side. "It is a pity," regretted the September 1921 economic review of the National City Bank, "the agony must be so long drawn out, a pity the inevitable adjustments cannot be quickly made, with intelligent comprehension and a cooperative spirit."[1]

To shorten or forestall the cyclical agony, Irving Fisher and John Maynard Keynes, among others, talked up the virtues of stability. How much better, they proposed, if average prices neither rose nor fell but approximately remained the same. In 1923, Keynes urged the Bank of England to manage the pound with an eye to the trend of domestic prices. And if, in achieving the goal of stability, the Bank disturbed the sterling-to-dollar exchange rate, so be it; the exchange rate mattered a great deal less to the well-being of Britons who counted their wealth and debts in pounds, shillings and pence than did the prices they paid in British shops or the wages they earned in British jobs.

The violence of wartime and postwar price gyrations only sharpened Fisher's devotion to the cause he had taken up long before the war began. In the monetary world he envisioned, some prices would rise and others would fall—the law of supply and demand would determine which did what. Unwavering, though, would be the average level of prices—an enlightened Federal Reserve would somehow see to that. There was, for Fisher, no such thing as a "business cycle." What imparted the appearance of cyclicality to economic life was rather inflationary and deflationary movements in the price level. As the professor would express it later in the decade, "[N]early all inflation and deflation are man-made.... Why should we not therefore have a man-made stabilization?"[2]

In the theorists' footsteps trod Woodrow Wilson's avoidant vice president, Thomas R. Marshall, and a Democratic congressman from Maryland, T. Alan Goldsborough. Calling Marshall his muse, Goldsborough in 1922 introduced a bill to stabilize the price level by controlling the quantity of money and credit in circulation.

Fisher threw his considerable intellectual weight behind the proposal. "The present generation," the professor testified before the House Banking Committee in 1923, "is witnessing the most stupendous fluctuations in the purchasing power of money in the whole history of this long-suffering world. Never before have such fluctuations been so wide, so universal, so diverse or so long continued. For years to come the problem of the instability of money will continue to engage the attention of economists, businessmen and statesmen.... The need of our time is stabilization."[3]

Price stability was no part of the original mandate of the Federal Reserve, and the Federal Reserve Board resisted congressional attempts to incorporate a stabilization objective in the law during the 1920s.[4] "Now I don't like to talk about stabilizing gold, the purchasing power of money, or prices being stabilized by the Federal Reserve System, at all," Benjamin Strong confided to Carl Snyder, an economist and a colleague at the Federal Reserve Bank of New York, in 1923. "It is bound to lead to confusion, heartburn and headache. Look at sugar and wheat as examples—also wages and building costs. Our job is credit."[5]

Words were one thing, deeds another. Less and less did the Federal Reserve pattern its policies on the passive methods of central banking that the Bank of England had employed during the prewar era. More and more did the Americans pioneer in the active technique of open-market operations. Under classical doctrine, commercial banks took the initiative in monetary policy. It was their decision to borrow, or not, from the central bank. Under the new thinking, the Federal Reserve would originate action.

The contemplated action was the buying and selling of government securities. Purchases would tend to add dollars to the banking system, sales to remove them. Purchases would tend to depress interest rates, sales to raise them. Buying enough Treasury bills, the Federal Reserve might induce inflation. Selling enough, it might achieve the opposite. Buying and selling dexterously enough, a new kind of central bank—the Federal Reserve itself, in fact—might attempt to achieve stable prices, high wages and maximum production.

This dramatic restatement of mission the board presented to the country in a bland resolution in 1923. Said the text: "That the time, manner, character and volume of open-market investments purchased by the Federal Reserve banks be governed with primary regard to the accommodation of commerce and business and to the effect of such purchases or sales on the general credit situation."

The elliptical phrasing did not confuse the economist John R. Commons, an academic supporter of the Federal Reserve's new thinking. The Federal Reserve could talk about the "credit situation," he observed; what they really meant was the "price level." It was no easy mission on which the central bank was embarked, Commons acknowledged. The price level was a concept, not something one might see or touch. The cost-of-living index by which the Federal Reserve would measure the price level was a further abstraction. No wonder the authors of the new doctrine seemed to talk up their sleeves rather than come right out with it. What was really being proposed, Commons saw, "was to entrust a new and great semi-monopolistic agency with power to regulate that abstraction."[6]

"It is obvious," Keynes addressed an audience at the National Liberal Club in December 1923, "that an individualist society left to itself does not work well or even tolerably. . . . The more troublous the times, the worse does a laissez-faire system work." And what was the principal source of unemployment, profiteering and precarious expectations, a trio of circumstances that Keynes designated as the "evils of modern society"? Why, "the instability of the standard of value" was the main source. Then let the central bank regulate the supply of money and credit in relation to the volume of goods—"i.e., that the index number of prices will never move from a fixed point," Keynes replied to his own question. Mandarin rule was the new idea: governance by economists.[7]

Before the war, gold had for the most part moved freely, impersonally, disinterestedly and unpatriotically in response to changes in prices and interest rates. Its movement—whether by ship or rail, in physical form, or by undersea cable, in the virtual form of a coded message—tended to synchronize international trade and investment. "Stability," under the gold standard, meant an unshakable foreign exchange rate, expressed as a weight of gold.

Now this precept was out the window. In Genoa, in April 1922, 157 delegates from 34 nations met to discuss a range of world problems, from reparations and Bolshevism to the chaos of the unmoored currencies. On the monetary topic, they resolved to replace the prewar gold standard with a gold standard in name only. Its name was the gold exchange standard. Under the new regime, debtor nations—Britain now among them—would be allowed to build up IOUs in creditor countries, rather than promptly remitting gold to settle accounts; they could send securities or paper money instead. Absent from the meeting of the national minds was the only leading commercial power that retained a currency defined in gold at the pre-1914 value. The United States had declined to attend—a pity, remarked Britain's premier, Lloyd George, Genoa being the birthplace of Christopher Columbus.[8]

"Credit will be regulated not only with a view to maintaining the currencies at par with one another, but also with a view to preventing undue fluctuations in the purchasing power of gold," the conference's financial commission concluded at the end of its deliberations. In other words, the exchange rate would take a back seat to the price level. To which the commissioners added, "It is not contemplated, however, that the discretion of the central banks should be fettered by any definite rules framed for this purpose." Discretion without fetters pointed to a very different kind of gold standard than the true-blue, pre-1914 version.

Keynes, who procured press credentials and reported from Genoa for the *Manchester Guardian*, could see that gold had become a kind of monetary furniture. Piled in the basement vaults of the Federal Reserve Bank of New York, it continued to collateralize the dollar. The fact was that Benjamin Strong and his conferees in Washington, D.C., took their policy-making cues not from gold movements, as classical doctrine would have had them do. They rather looked to the domestic price level.

"For the past two years the United States has pretended to maintain a gold standard," Keynes wrote in his *Tract on Monetary Reform*, published in 1924. "In fact it has established a dollar standard; and instead of ensuring that the value of the dollar shall conform to that of gold, it makes provision, at great expense, that the value of gold shall conform to that of the dollar. This is the way by which a rich country is able to combine new wisdom with old prejudice. It can enjoy the latest scientific improvements, devised in the economic laboratory of Harvard, whilst leaving Congress to believe that no rash departure will be permitted from the hard money consecrated by the wisdom and experience of Dungi, Darius, Constantine, Lord Liverpool and Senator Aldrich."[9] Stability at home was the new all-in-all. After the creeping inflation of 1900–14, the galloping inflation of 1915–20 and the hurtling deflation of 1921, the prospect of peace and quiet had wide-ranging appeal.

In Britain, stability of wages and incomes came at the price of persistently high unemployment. In 1922—a year of developing labor shortages in the United States—the British jobless rate registered 16 percent and fell no lower than 8 percent during the rest of the decade. Unemployment in Britain had become a chronic problem, not a cyclical one.

It took a brilliant young French economist, Jacques Rueff, to diagnose the trouble. Pure and simple, observed Rueff, wages were out of synch with prices. While prices had fallen from their inflationary perch, wages remained elevated. In America, an unemployed worker had little choice but to accept the wages on offer. In Britain, the institution of unemployment insurance, in place since 1911, afforded the idle factory hand a viable option of not working. By 1923, the dole paid well enough to present stiff competition to low-paying employers.

Rueff formulated a simple means of forecasting the rate of unemployment. Divide the average wage by the average wholesale price level. As the ratio of wages to prices moves up and down, so does the jobless rate. "The astonishing thing is not that this relationship exists," wrote Rueff in his memoir, disavowing any claim to scholarly invention, "but that it should astonish anyone." His fans christened this clarifying insight "Rueff's Law."

Sir Josiah Stamp, banker, economist and industrialist, was the first to bring Rueff's insight to an English-speaking readership in a pair of articles in the *Times* of London in June 1931. Blame the dole for the persistence of British unemployment, Stamp asserted; more generally, blame the destruction of free and unfettered markets. Many were inclined to attribute the naggingly high unemployment problem to Britain's return to the gold standard at the old prewar rate. The exchange rate was not the cause, Stamp persuasively contended; economic sclerosis was.

"Instead of allowing economic forces to operate freely," Stamp concluded his first essay, on June 11,

> the tendency, since the War, has everywhere been in the opposite direction. The dole policy, the activities of the trade unions and the employers' associations, and the various hindrances to migration have all interfered with the freedom of the labor markets. At the same time the activities of the trusts, cartels, marketing schemes and the various restriction and valorization schemes have all retarded or suppressed the indispensable movement of prices. In a word, the whole economic organism has been drugged and paralysed. Hence the present deplorable situation.[10]

In the United States, the 1920s was a decade of fast-paced material progress. Investment and invention combined to generate strong and persistent gains in output per man hour. Between 1922 and 1927, the production of manufactured goods climbed by 4 percent a year, even as factory employment fell by 0.7 percent a year—and per capita earnings of factory employees increased by 2.4 percent a year.[11]

The price level hardly budged. Between 1922 and 1927, wholesale commodity prices fell by 0.1 percent a year. Over the same span, the cost of living rose by 0.7 percent a year. And because nominal wages rose by 2.8 percent a year, real wages rose by 2.1 percent a year. "Business and prices have both become more stable," asserted *Recent Economic Changes* in 1929. "There is evidence that our economic system is moving in this direction."

It was an artificial stability. In the late 19th century, prices had actually fallen in response to innovation. As it cost less to make things, so it cost less to buy them. There was no such technological dividend for the consumers of the 1920s.

The Federal Reserve seems not to have allowed it. Gold no longer constrained the policy-makers. Neither did the classical central-banking doctrine on which the Federal Reserve was founded. The post-1922 central bank was germinating enough money to create enough inflation to offset the tendency of prices to fall on account of sustained advances in manufacturing and agricultural efficiency.

The interest rates that the Fed imposed were evidently lower than the ones that might have been quoted if Woodrow Wilson had never signed the Federal Reserve Act into law. One could so conjecture by the torrid growth in lending and borrowing. Especially notable in the late phase of the boom was the more than doubling of broker's loans at New York City banks, to $6.7 billion from $3.1 billion, between 1926 and 1929.[12]

Certainly, interest rates were low enough to permit a surge in construction and capital investment. Between 1921 and 1929, steel production climbed at the annual rate of 21 percent. In no prior boom period, starting in the mid-1800s, had the production of either pig iron or steel expanded so fast or for so long. America's building boom left Keynes flabbergasted: "In the four years 1925–1928, the total value of new construction in the United States amounted to some $38,000,000,000. This was—if one can credit it—at the average rate of $800,000,000 a month for forty-eight months consecutively."[13]

Federal Reserve bank credit, now mixed with soaring stock prices and native American optimism, made a potent bullish elixir. Positively intoxicating was the central bank's policy in the wake of a secret monetary conclave on Long Island in July 1927. In attendance at the meeting were the governor of the Reichsbank, Hjalmar Schacht; the governor of the Bank of England, Montagu Norman; the deputy governor of the Bank of France, Charles Rist; and the governor of the Federal Reserve Bank of New York, Benjamin Strong.

The summit was Norman's idea; he was pushing Strong to coordinate a transatlantic relaxation of monetary policy to support the unsteady pound sterling. Schacht, who had seen quite enough inflation in Germany in the early 1920s, declined to participate. "Don't give me a low rate," the German banker reportedly protested. "Give me a true rate."[14] Neither did Rist, a classical gold-standard man, accept the invitation of the English-speaking world to join in a program of transatlantic credit expansion. So Norman and Strong shook hands on a policy of coordinated monetary stimulus.

Down went the discount rates of the Federal Reserve banks, to 3.5 percent from 4 percent. The Chicago Reserve Bank, protesting that credit was easy enough as it was, refused to comply until orders came down from the Federal Reserve Board in Washington to follow the lead of the other 11 banks.

Up went the Federal Reserve system's holdings of government securities. As the central bankers gathered on Long Island in July, the Federal's earning assets totaled $1,175 million. A year later, they footed to $1,531 million. By the close of 1928, they stood at $1,824 million, up by 55 percent in not quite a year and a half. Rist had heard Strong say that he proposed to administer "un petit coup de whisky for the stock exchange."[15] And so he did.

In 1914–20, the prices of agricultural and industrial commodities inflated. In 1922–29, the prices of investment assets inflated. By the reckoning of the economist Carl Snyder, a truly comprehensive price index, encompassing real estate, rents, stocks, bonds and wage rates as well as wholesale prices, rose at a compound annual rate of 2.7 percent from 1922 to 1929.[16]

Credit financed the levitation. As the central bank enlarged its balance sheet, so did America's commercial banks expand their balance sheets. Students of monetary data rubbed their eyes. The United States was seemingly awash in credit. In June 1914, $18.6 billion was on deposit at the nation's banks. Between 1921 and 1929, the *growth* in deposits topped $19 billion. It was a sign of the times that there was no corresponding expansion in the nation's bedrock monetary collateral. The ratio of member-bank deposits to Federal Reserve gold holdings stood at 7:1 in December 1921. By the month of the 1929 stock-market crash, that ratio had climbed to 11:1.*[17]

---

*Professor Bertil Ohlin of Stockholm University protested that American monetary policy had entirely disassociated itself from anything having to do with the orthodox gold standard. "The post-war gold standard is ... [a] kind of 'managed currency,' in which the control is exercised by the Federal Reserve

"[C]redit takes various directions," observed the British economist H.F. Fraser in 1933, "and the effects of inflation can only be measured best at those points in the business structure where the use of credit has been most active."[18] In the 1920s, those points included capital investment, real estate and common stocks. "Stability," according to a certain kind of index number, the Federal Reserve had achieved. Inflation had broken out in places where the stabilizationists weren't looking.

Board and the boards of the leading Federal Reserve Banks on the basis of considerations which have nothing to do with either gold cover or gold movements, but are dictated chiefly by the possibilities of keeping production going at full pressure." So Ohlin wrote in June 1927, the month before Strong decided to ease not chiefly for domestic reasons but rather to assist the Bank of England. [McManus et al., *Banking and the Business Cycle*, 198]

A TRIUMPH, IN ITS WAY

Over and done with in 18 months, the depression of 1920–21 was the beau ideal of a deflationary slump. This is not—so far—history's verdict. Nor is it yet, with a few notable and enlightened exceptions, the economists'. It is not even the judgment of many of the economists who have spent their careers studying the catastrophe of the Great Depression. I hope they may reconsider.

Harry Truman was a memoirist who did not reconsider. Is his telling, the Harding administration caused the depression to "put labor in its place," never mind that the economy had peaked under the Democrat Woodrow Wilson or that Andrew Mellon (contrary to Truman's recollection) helped to reduce interest rates, not to raise them.[1]

Not one tip of the hat did Truman make to the triumph of the invisible hand. As President Truman in 1946, the former disappointed haberdasher signed the Employment Act to settle responsibility on the federal government for price stability and high employment. The act created the Council of Economic Advisers to import the new "science" of macroeconomic management into the White House.

Leading writers of monetary history have given the Federal Reserve under W.P.G. Harding no higher marks than Truman accorded the administration of Warren G. Harding. "Whether judged by money, interest rates, or economic activity," judged Allan Meltzer, "policy failed in 1920–22." [2] Milton Friedman and Anna Schwartz, in their *Monetary History of the United States,* anticipated Meltzer.

Though policy may have failed, the depression, as we have seen, succeeded. There had been a war-induced, economy-crippling inflation. The central bankers chose to precipitate—or, at least, not to try to prevent— a synchronous, dislocating deflation. Wholesale prices fell by 20 percent within two years. Recovery ensued.

Came the 1929 Crash and the price level fell by an almost identical 20 percent over two years. No recovery ensued, though financial conditions were in some key respects less rugged than in 1920–21. Thus, in the Wilson-Harding depression, interest rates were higher and the burden of private debt was heavier than either was in 1929–31. [3] Why wasn't the 1920–21 affair just as terribly "great" as the one that enveloped Herbert Hoover?

John Skelton Williams died in 1926, at the age of 61, with both the national banking system and his personal reputation—banker, controversialist, railroad builder—intact. Benjamin Strong died in 1928, at the age of 55, a year before the new, post–gold-standard techniques of central banking were put to the test. He, too, died on a reputational high note.

It fell to Herbert Hoover and Andrew Mellon, each a veteran of the 1920–21 crisis, to apply the lessons of that affair to the events that followed the Crash. Presidents Wilson and Harding, each for his own reasons, had met the depression of 1920–21 with inaction. Harding's former secretary of commerce chose a whirlwind of intervention.

As he had fed the starving Belgians (and led Washington's efforts to relieve the suffering of the hundreds of thousands of victims of the great Mississippi flood of 1927), so Hoover moved now to stop a threatened business depression before it could start. "Words are not of any great importance in times of economic disturbance," the president declared in the wake of the 1929 Crash. "It is action that counts." [4]

Into the White House they trooped in late November: railroad men, industrialists, building and construction executives, public-utility chieftains, union presidents. They agreed that business was sound, that the Federal Reserve was on the job and that the country could survive Wall Street's ghastly error of judgment. Equally, under Hoover's leadership, they affirmed their commitment to voluntary relief through the offices of state and local government. The unifying thread of the meetings was a resolve to prevent the business cycle from taking its customary antediluvian course. Public-works spending, farm-price maintenance and wage support were rather the new, constructive responses to the weakening of aggregate demand.

Wage support was at the very top of the list, the president and his callers agreed. If wages must fall, they should fall not sooner but later. Profits and dividends—"business"—must bear the initial brunt of adjustment to plunging stock prices. The critical need was to protect the nation's buying power.

Henry Ford shone brightest among the business executives and union chiefs who strode through the executive-office doors on November 21. The lesser business lights nodded in agreement at Hoover's urging that management and labor strike a grand, depression-defying bargain. In exchange for no reduction in wages, the unions would seek no rise in wages.

After the meeting disbanded—Ford immediately made his escape in a waiting automobile—the industrialist's secretary distributed a two-page, typewritten policy statement. In it, Ford proposed his formula for recovery. He urged that prices be cut but wages be raised. "Nearly everything in this country is too high priced," said the Ford broadside. "The only thing that should be high priced in this country is the man who works. Wages must not come down, they must not even stay on their present level; they must go up." Whereupon Henry Ford announced that he was giving his employees a raise.[5] When news of the windfall reached them later that day, union chiefs at the White House event, William Green of the American Federation of Labor and John L. Lewis of the United Mine Workers, shook their heads. They could hardly believe it, they said, but they were certainly prepared to cheer it.

As for the industrialists not named Ford, at least there would be no going back to the bad old days of 1920–21. This they pledged to Hoover. Liquidation was the discredited idea, stabilization the constructive new thought. "In no previous instance of real or threatened depression, probably, have business leaders been so ready to bar wage reduction as a means to recovery," the *Wall Street Journal* commented.[6]

A wage rate was not just any price, according to emerging political doctrine, but a special and socially protected one. A phrase in Section 7 of the Clayton Antitrust Act of 1914 codified the idea: "[T]he labor of a human being is not a commodity or article of commerce."[7] To Hoover—as well as to many others in the 1920s—high wage rates were the foundation of American prosperity.

After the post-Crash flurry of White House conferences, the economist Wesley Mitchell addressed the Taylor Society at the Hotel Pennsylvania in New York. He told the Taylorites—proponents of scientific business management—that a living experiment in economic policy was unfolding on a national scale. "While a business cycle is passing over from the phase of expansion to the phase of contraction," said Mitchell, "the President of the United States is organizing the economic forces of the country to check the threatened decline at the start, if possible. A more significant experiment in the technique of balance could not be devised than the one which is being performed before our very eyes."[8]

As posterity knows, the experiment failed. Writing before posterity found out, Yale professor James Harvey Rogers predicted its failure. For one thing, prices and wages were less flexible than they used to be.*

For another thing, Rogers observed, price stabilization would paradoxically prove destabilizing. Whether or not it was a "commodity" or an "article," labor was a cost. A profit-seeking firm would meet a more than transitory drop in revenue by reducing costs. If it could not reduce wages, it might have to reduce head count. To avoid insolvency, it would certainly order layoffs or dismissals. While a fortunate few employees earned high wages, others would earn nothing.[9]

In January 1930, some 6,000 Virginia textile workers absorbed a 10 percent wage cut from the none-too-exalted 1928 average wage of $17.41 a week. In

---

*Subsequent economic research by the George Mason economist Bryan Caplan has confirmed this observation: "Despite some extraordinary shocks, the American economy swiftly recovered from the depression of 1920–21. In contrast, the recovery of the American and the world economies from the Great Depression was extremely slow. This would lead us strongly to suspect that wage flexibility during the depression of 1920–21 was markedly greater than during the Great Depression." [Caplan, "Wage Adjustment and Aggregate Supply in the Depression of 1920–21: Extending the Bernanke-Carey Model," Princeton University, Princeton, 14–15.]

February, Communist-led protests against rising joblessness turned violent in Cleveland, Philadelphia and Chicago; "Socialistic Prosperity in the Soviet Union—Poverty in the Capitalist Countries," said one of the handbills that the Chicago agitators thrust into the hands of curious passersby.

Still, the commodity-price decline was not so severe as in the 1920–21 collapse, and the street protests had not devolved into 1919–20-style bombings. Hunting for signs of hope, the Hoover administration could point to the exemplary conduct of members of a Cleveland electrical workers' union. In March, the tradesmen had agreed to forego the 10 percent wage increase to which they had every right. "Here," commented the *Wall Street Journal*, "is one more striking difference between present conditions and those following the 1920 debacle. Employers who then sought and obtained wage reductions were legion. They then had the sound argument of economic necessity on their side but they came face to face with the frightening determination of organized labor that its gains in the war period must be retained in toto."

How far the nation had come, the *Journal* marveled. Perhaps workers at the Wisconsin Steel unit of the International Harvester Company exclaimed along similar lines. Not until October 1931 did the company move to cut wages of its hourly employees, and then only by 10 percent (senior executives had been first on the chopping block; their salaries had been decimated in March). It was a far cry from the draconian reductions of the spring and summer of 1921.

Neither did the conduct of monetary policy resemble the pattern of 1920–21. From the heights of 6 percent in August 1929, the discount rate of the Federal Reserve Bank of New York plunged to 2 percent by the close of 1930. The reader will recall—Irving Fisher, in his criticism of monetary policy, certainly remembered—that the central bank had pushed this particular interest rate up, not down, in the formative stage of the 1920–21 depression. A 5 percent rate of interest might have appeared innocuous enough in 1921. It was a punishing rate in the light of plunging prices.[10]

One year after the Crash, the stewards of the Federal Reserve could look back with some satisfaction at the policies they had implemented. The Fed had infused the banks with cash by the purchase of $515 million of government securities and bankers' acceptances. True, the banks in their turn had reduced their borrowings from the Reserve banks by $854 million. If the banks had therefore, on balance, pulled in their horns, so be it; such was the usual response to a business cycle downturn. At least, one of the Fed governors reflected late in 1930, the Federal Reserve was not constrained by a loss of gold as it had been in 1920–21. "The Federal Reserve Banks are not now, as they were then, close to the limits of their lending power," said Charles S. Hamlin. "On the contrary, they have ample reserves and stand ready to finance a growing volume of business as soon as signs of recovery express themselves in an increasing demand for credit. That day cannot arrive too soon to please any of us."[11]

From their post-Crash low to their April recovery high, the Dow Jones industrials rallied by 50 percent. "It seems manifest," declared Fisher in May, "that thus far the difference between the present comparatively mild business recession and the severe depression of 1920–21 is like that between a thunder-shower and a tornado."[12]

Fisher had it backwards. The trouble with Hoover's policy is that it didn't conform more closely to Wilson's and Harding's nonpolicies. In particular, wage rates didn't follow prices lower, as they had during the slump that Wilson and Harding seemed to ignore. In May 1930, in a speech to the United States Chamber of Commerce, Hoover made bold to claim that, "for the first time in the history of great slumps, we have had no substantial reduction in wages." In a later totting up of data compiled by the Bureau of Labor Statistics, the American Federation of Labor found truth in that claim: Whereas 92 percent of reporting firms had reduced wages in 1921, only 7 percent did so in 1930.[13]

The landmark 100th issue of the *Survey of Current Business*, the monthly statistical bulletin of the U.S. Department of Commerce, had appeared in December 1929. The first edition of the *Survey*, produced under the guiding hand of then–Secretary of Commerce Hoover, was published in the depths of the postwar depression, in July 1921. There had been vast and gratifying improvement over the intervening eight years, the editors of the *Survey* now reflected. That first number of the monthly periodical—it was just 10 mimeographed pages—had carried only 200 statistical series; the 100th issue packed in more than 1,800.

"While it may be too early to say that the utilization of business data has entirely eliminated the business cycle," the hopeful editors speculated, "there is agreement to-day among business leaders everywhere that the wider use of facts will mitigate in a large degree many of the disastrous effects of the one-time recurrent business cycle."

The trouble lay not with the facts, which, indeed, the *Survey* produced in profusion. The missing link was rather a theory that would make the facts coherent. In the work of Lee E. Ohanian, professor of economics at UCLA, the facts have found a worthy 21st century theorist. In his 2009 monograph titled, "What—or Who—Started the Great Depression?" Ohanian forthrightly answered: "Hoover." Determined to shift the burden of economic suffering to capital from labor, the humanitarian unwittingly precipitated suffering enough for capital and labor. In 1920 and 1921, nominal wages fell as prices fell. There was no such adjustment in 1929, 1930 and 1931. "By late 1931," as Ohanian observed, "real manufacturing average hourly earnings had increased more than 10 percent as a consequence of the Hoover program and deflation. By September 1931, manufacturing hours worked had declined more than 40 percent, and the average workweek in manufacturing had declined by about 20 percent." [14]

There are no controlled experiments in economics. No one living through the Great Depression could be exactly sure how to apportion blame among domestic and foreign causes. Still less can posterity be certain. What we can observe, even at this great distance of years, is that the price mechanism worked more freely in 1920–21 than it was allowed to do in 1929–33. "[T]he end result of what was probably the greatest price-stabilization experiment in history proved to be, simply, the greatest and worst depression," concluded one of the wisest of the contemporary postmortems of the Depression, *Banking and the Business Cycle*, published in 1937.

The depression of 1920–21 was terrible in its own way. In comparison to what was to follow, it was also, in its own way, a triumph.

ACKNOWLEDGMENTS

Writing a book turns an author into a debtor. Senior most among my many creditors is the swell and eminent Alice Mayhew, vice president and editorial director of Simon & Schuster. I owe debts of gratitude, as well, to her assistants and colleagues at S&S. They include Stephen Bedford, Jonathan Cox, Leah Johanson and Stuart Roberts.

And what would a history be without historical facts? Katherine Crispi, Sam Isaac, John Millett and Laura Wacker contributed long and careful hours of searching in archives and newspaper records. I thank them as well as the staff of *Grant's*—especially Charley Grant, Evan Lorenz and David Peligal—who provided expert research, analysis and fact-checking.

Thanks go, too, to the helpful staff at the Albert and Shirley Small Special Collections Library at the University of Virginia, repository of John Skelton Williams's papers, as well as to Tab Lewis, archivist at the National Archives at College Park, Maryland, who graciously facilitated access to bank examiners' documents.

Professor Richard Sylla, the New York University economic historian; Paul Isaac and Seth Klarman, professional investors par excellence; and Patricia Kavanagh, M.D., read a draft of the manuscript and suggested welcome improvements. Ruth Elwell created the index.

Bob Castillo, my painstaking copy editor, saved me from the many errors that do not appear in these pages. I claim full credit for the ones that remain.

NOTES

PREFACE

1. Murray Rothbard, *America's Great Depression* (Kansas City: Sheed and Ward, Inc., 1963), 167.
2. Corporate profit data based on federal tax returns. Net income of all reporting corporations totaled $5,874 million in 1920, only $458 million in 1921. Committee on Recent Economic Changes of the President's Conference on Unemployment, *Recent Economic Changes in the United States*, vol. II (National Bureau of Economic Research, 1929), 854.
3. U.S. House of Representatives, Joint Commission of Agricultural Inquiry, "The Agricultural Crisis and Its Causes," part II (Washington, D.C.: Government Printing Office, October 1921) (67th Congress, 1st Session, report no. 408), 46.

1. THE GREAT INFLATION

1. Robert Higgs, *Crisis and Leviathan: Critical Episodes in the Growth of American Government* (New York: Oxford University Press, 1987), 84.
2. "Populist Party Platform of 1892," July 4, 1892, online by Gerhard Peters and John T. Woolley, *The American Presidency Project*. http://www.presidency.ucsb.edu/ws/?pid=29616.
3. Alphaeus Thomas Mason, ed., *Free Government in the Making* (New York: Oxford University Press, 1985), 649–50.
4. John D. Buenker, "Ratification of the Federal Income Tax Amendment," *Cato Journal* (Spring 1981), 1161.
5. John Milton Cooper, Jr., *Woodrow Wilson* (New York: Random House, Inc., 2009), 167.

6. Ibid.

7. Ibid., 165.

8. *New York Times,* May 7, 1913.

9. "History of Federal Individual Income Bottom and Top Bracket Rates," National Taxpayers Union, 2013, http://www.ntu.org/tax-basics/history-of-federal-individual-1.html.

10. *New York Times,* June 22, 1917.

11. Higgs, *Crisis and Leviathan,* 123.

12. Alexander D. Noyes, *The War Period of American Finance: 1908–1925* (New York and London: The Knickerbocker Press, 1926), 285.

13. Burl Noggle, *Into the Twenties: The United States from Armistice to Normalcy* (Urbana: University of Illinois Press, 1974), 68.

14. Allan H. Meltzer, *A History of the Federal Reserve,* vol. 1, *1913–1951* (Chicago: University of Chicago Press, 2003), 84.

15. Noyes, *War Period,* 287.

16. Adolph C. Miller speech to the American Association of the Baking Industry, September 24, 1919, 15; Noyes, *War Period,* 290.

17. Meltzer, *History of the Federal Reserve,* 91.

18. Wilson F. Payne, *Business Behavior 1919–1922: An Account of Post-war Inflation and Depression* (Chicago: University of Chicago Press, 1942), 208.

19. Noyes, *War Period,* 293–94.

20. Mark Sullivan, *Our Times: The United States 1900–1925,* vol. VI, *The Twenties* (New York: Charles Scribner's Sons, 1946), 163.

21. David Brody, *Labor in Crisis: The Steel Strike of 1919* (Philadelphia: J.B. Lippincott Company, 1965), 130.

22. Ibid., 129.

23. U.S. Department of Labor, Annual Report of the Secretary of Labor (Washington, D.C.: Government Printing Office, 1920), 113ff.

24. Gene Smith, *When the Cheering Stopped* (London: Hutchinson & Co., 1964), 62.

25. Beverly Gage, *The Day Wall Street Exploded: A Story of America in Its First Age of Terror* (Oxford: Oxford University Press, 2009), 118.

26. Ibid., 27.

27. Stanley Coben, *A. Mitchell Palmer: Politician* (New York: Columbia University Press, 1963), 206.

28. *New York Times,* August 7, 1919.

29. Alfred P. Sloan Jr., *My Years with General Motors* (New York: Doubleday, 1963), 29.

30. Lester V. Chandler, *Benjamin Strong: Central Banker* (Washington, D.C.: The Brookings Institution, 1958), 466.

31. Dwight D. Eisenhower, *At Ease: Stories I Tell to My Friends* (Garden City: Doubleday & Company, Inc., 1967), 159–66.

32. Sloan, *Years with GM,* 29.

33. David McCullough, *Truman* (New York: Simon & Schuster, 1992), 143ff.

34. Harold van B. Cleveland and Thomas F. Huertas, *Citibank: 1812–1970* (Cambridge: Harvard University Press, 1985), 102.

35. Ibid., 106.

36. James H. Shideler, *Farm Crisis 1919–1923* (Berkeley: University of California Press, 1957), 19.

37. Ibid., 38.

38. Ibid., 39.

2. COIN OF THE REALM

1. U.S. Department of Labor, Annual Report of the Secretary of Labor (Washington, D.C.: Government Printing Office, 1919).

2. Stanley Coben, *A. Mitchell Palmer: Politician* (New York: Columbia University Press, 1963), 160.

3. Marc Levinson, "Why Woodrow Wilson Wooed Shoppers and Snubbed Business," Bloomberg View, September 26, 2012.

4. U.S. House of Representatives, Joint Commission of Agricultural Inquiry, "The Agricultural Crisis and Its Causes" (Washington, D.C.: Government Printing Office, 1921), 58.

5. Coben, *A. Mitchell Palmer*, 163.

6. S. Mclean Hardy, "The Quantity of Money and Prices, 1860–1891," *Journal of Political Economy*, vol. 3, no. 2 (March 1895), 155–57.

7. *Historical Statistics of the United States: Colonial Times to 1970* (Washington, D.C.: U.S. Department of Commerce, 1975), 165.

8. Eleanor Lansing Dulles, *The French Franc 1914–1928: The Facts and Their Interpretation* (New York: The Macmillan Company, 1929), 123.

9. Arthur I. Bloomfield, *Monetary Policy under the International Gold Standard, 1880–1914* (New York: Federal Reserve Bank of New York, 1959), 9.

10. Commercial *Manchester Guardian* Reconstruction Supplement, April 20, 1922, quoted in Lewis Lehrman, *The True Gold Standard: A Monetary Reform Plan without Official Reserve Currencies* (United States, Lehrman Institute, 2012).

11. Sylvia Nasar, *Grand Pursuit: The Story of Economic Genius* (New York: Simon & Schuster, 2011), 53ff.

12. Irving Fisher, *Stabilizing the Dollar: A Plan to Stabilize the General Price Level without Fixing Individual Prices* (New York: The Macmillan Company, 1925), xxvii.

13. Roy W. Jastram, *The Golden Constant: The English and American Experience: 1560–2007* (Northampton: John Wiley & Sons, 1977).

14. Irving Fisher, "Standardizing the Dollar—Discussion," *American Economic Review*, vol. II, no. 1, Supplement (March 1912), 46.

15. Hartley Withers, *The Meaning of Money* (London: Smith, Elder & Co., 1909), 79.

16. U.S. Department of the Treasury, 1909 Annual report of the Office of the Comptroller of the Currency (Washington, D.C.: Government Printing Office, 1910), 30.

17. Carter Glass, "The Opposition to the Federal Reserve Bank Bill," *Proceedings of the Academy of Political Science in the City of New York*, vol. 4, no. 1 (October 1913), 18.

18. James Grant, *Money of the Mind: Borrowing and Lending in America from the Civil War to Michael Milken* (New York: Farrar Straus and Giroux, 1992), 142.

19. Ibid., 140.

3. MONEY AT WAR

1. Lester V. Chandler, *Benjamin Strong: Central Banker* (Washington, D.C.: The Brookings Institution, 1958), 48.

2. Ibid., 22–25.

3. Ibid., 39.

4. Ibid., 41.

5. H.G.S. Noble, *The New York Stock Exchange in the Crisis of 1914* (Garden City, N.Y.: The Country Life Press, 1915), 4–5.

6. John J. Arnold, "The American Gold Fund of 1914," *Journal of Political Economy*, vol. 23, no. 7 (July 1915), 697–98.

7. Alexander D. Noyes, *The War Period of American Finance: 1908–1925* (New York and London: The Knickerbocker Press, 1926), 61, 83.

8. Ibid., 56.

9. *New York Times,* August 1, 1914.

10. Noble, *New York Stock Exchange*, 5.

11. Ibid., 14.

12. *New York Times*, August 1, 1914; Noble, *New York Stock Exchange*, 12.

13. Noyes, *War Period*, 68.

14. Robert J. Shillady, "Planning Public Expenditures to Compensate for Decreased Private Employment during Business Depressions," speech to the National Conference of Charities and Correction, Indianapolis, May 16, 1916, 5.

15. Noyes, *War Period*, 70–71.

16. Ibid.

17. Lawrence E. Clark, *Central Banking under the Federal Reserve System* (New York: The MacMillan Company, 1935), 74ff.

18. Ibid., 76.

19. Chandler, *Strong*, 65.

20. Liaquat Ahamed, *Lords of Finance: The Bankers Who Broke the World* (New York: The Penguin Press, 2009), 69–70.

21. *Wall Street Journal*, August 14, 1914.

22. Noyes, *War Period*, 73.

23. Ibid., 71–72.

24. *Wall Street Journal*, August 17, 1914.

25. *Wall Street Journal*, August 14, 1914.

26. Arnold, "American Gold Fund," 696.

27. Benjamin M. Anderson, *Economics and the Public Welfare: A Financial and Economic History of the United States, 1914–46* (Indianapolis: Liberty Press, 1979), 35.

28. Chandler, *Strong*, 59, 63.

29. *New York Times*, September 26, 1914.

30. Anderson, *Economics and Public Welfare*, 35.
31. Ibid., 37.
32. *Historical Statistics of the United States: Colonial Times to 1970* (Washington, D.C.: U.S. Department of Commerce, 1975), 226, 126; Noyes, *War Period*, 96.
33. Noyes, *War Period*, 94.
34. Ibid., 114.
35. Ibid., 96.
36. Robert Sobel, *The Big Board: A History of the New York Stock Market* (New York: The Free Press, 1965), 213.
37. *Historical Statistics of the United States*, 226.
38. Allan H. Meltzer, *A History of the Federal Reserve*, vol. 1, *1913–1951* (Chicago: University of Chicago Press, 2003), 76.
39. Chandler, *Strong*, 87.
40. Ibid., 81.
41. Ibid., 30.
42. *New York Times*, April 13, 1921.
43. Chandler, *Strong*, 95.
44. Meltzer, *History of the Federal Reserve*, 84.
45. Andrew Austin and Mindy Levit, "The Debt Limit: History and Recent Increases," *Congressional Research Service*, October 15, 2013, 2–3.
46. Chandler, *Strong*, 100.
47. Ibid., 101.
48. Ibid., 105.
49. Ibid., 107.
50. Ibid., 108.
51. Ibid., 116.
52. Ibid., 104.
53. Ibid., 111.
54. James Grant, *Money of the Mind: Borrowing and Lending in America from the Civil War to Michael Milken* (New York: Farrar Straus and Giroux, 1992), 146.
55. Meltzer, *History of the Federal Reserve*, 84.
56. *Wall Street Journal*, September 28, 1918.
57. Meltzer, *History of the Federal Reserve*, 87.
58. Chandler, *Strong*, 113.

4. LAISSEZ-FAIRE BY ACCIDENT

1. John M. Blum, *Joe Tumulty and the Wilson Era* (Cambridge: The Riverside Press, 1951), 150–51.
2. John Milton Cooper, Jr., *Woodrow Wilson* (New York: Random House, Inc., 2009), 404.
3. James Grant, *Bernard Baruch: The Adventures of a Wall Street Legend* (New York: Simon & Schuster, 1983), 151.
4. *New York Times*, August 22, 1917.

5. *Wall Street Journal*, August 24, 1917.

6. *New York Times*, January 9, 1918.

7. *New York Times*, January 16, 1918.

8. *New York Times*, January 20, 1918; Robert H. Ferrell, *Presidential Leadership: From Woodrow Wilson to Harry S. Truman* (Columbia: University of Missouri Press, 2006), 21; Cooper, *Wilson*, 406.

9. Cooper, *Wilson*, 447.

10. Blum, *Tumulty*, 195.

11. Ibid., 306–9.

12. Ibid., 198.

13. Cooper, *Wilson*, 508.

14. Blum, *Tumulty*, 204–5.

15. Cooper, *Wilson*, 511–12.

16. Ibid., 510.

17. *Wall Street Journal*, August 27, 1919.

18. Gene Smith, *When the Cheering Stopped* (London: Hutchinson & Co., 1964), 60.

19. Ibid., 89.

20. Ibid., 93.

21. Ibid., 96.

22. Ibid., 100.

23. *Wall Street Journal*, October 4, 1919.

24. Henry Pringle, *The Life and Times of William Howard Taft* (New York: Farrar & Rinehart, Inc., 1939), 927.

25. Smith, *Cheering Stopped*, 98.

26. Ibid., 103.

27. Ibid., 99.

28. Ibid., 125.

29. Ibid., 125.

30. Ibid., 110.

31. Ibid., 120.

32. Ibid., 124–25.

33. Cooper, *Wilson*, 562.

5. A DEPRESSION IN FACT

1. Robert K. Murray, *The Harding Era: Warren G. Harding and His Administration* (Newtown, CT: American Political Biography Press, 1969), 267–68.

2. Christina Romer, "World War I and the Postwar Depression: A Reinterpretation Based on Alterative Estimates of GDP," *Journal of Monetary Economics*, vol. 22, no. 1, 93.

3. Oskar Morgenstern, *On the Accuracy of Economic Observations* (Princeton: Princeton University Press, 1963), 256–57.

4. *Recent Economic Changes in the United States*, vol. II (National Bureau of Economic Research, 1929), 853.

5. *Recent Economic Changes*, 852.
6. T.F. McManus, R.W. Nelson, and C.A. Phillips, *Banking and the Business Cycle: A Study of the Great Depression in the United States* (New York: The Macmillan Company, 1937), 1.
7. Burl Noggle, *Into the Twenties: The United States from Armistice to Normalcy* (Urbana: University of Illinois Press, 2003), 165.
8. "A Byte Out of History: Terror on Wall Street," Federal Bureau of Investigation Web site, 2013.
9. U.S. House of Representatives, Joint Commission of Agricultural Inquiry, "The Agricultural Crisis and Its Causes" (Washington, D.C.: Government Printing Office, 1921), 14.
10. *Recent Economic Changes*, 854.
11. Ibid., 856.
12. Wilson F. Payne, *Business Behavior 1919–1922: An Account of Post-war Inflation and Depression* (Chicago: University of Chicago Press, 1942), 174.
13. Ibid., 195; Lester V. Chandler, *Benjamin Strong: Central Banker* (Washington, D.C.: The Brookings Institute, 1958), 240.
14. Lawrence R. Gustin, *Billy Durant: Creator of General Motors* (Grand Rapids: William B. Eerdmans Publishing Company, 1973), 205.
15. Ibid., 199.
16. Payne, *Business Behavior*, 175.
17. *Recent Economic Changes*, 339.
18. Payne, *Business Behavior*, 174–75.
19. Alfred P. Sloan Jr., *My Years with General Motors* (New York: Doubleday, 1963), 30.
20. Ibid., 31.
21. Payne, *Business Behavior*, 178.
22. Chandler, *Strong*, 486.
23. Gustin, *Durant*, 218.
24. Chandler, *Strong*, 491.
25. U.S. Department of Agriculture, 1919 Report of the Secretary of Agriculture (Washington, D.C.: Government Printing Office, 1920), 17.
26. United States Department of Agriculture, 1921 Report of the Secretary of Agriculture (Washington, D.C.: Government Printing Office, 1922), 2, 7.
27. 1919 Report of the Secretary of Agriculture, 2.
28. Ibid., 23–24.
29. James H. Shideler, *Farm Crisis 1919–1923* (Berkeley: University of California Press, 1957), 40.
30. Ibid., 41.
31. Ibid., 40.
32. Ibid., 44.
33. Ibid., 45.
34. 1921 Report of the Secretary of Agriculture, 12.
35. Shideler, *Farm Crisis*, 55.

36. Ibid., 56.
37. Ibid., 65.
38. *New York Times*, January 7, 1921; Shideler, *Farm Crisis*, 49.
39. U.S. House of Representatives, Joint Commission of Agricultural Inquiry, "The Agricultural Crisis and Its Causes" (Washington, D.C.: Government Printing Office, 1921), 11.
40. Robert H. Ferrell, *Harry S. Truman: A Life* (Columbia: University of Missouri Press, 1994), 87.

6. CITY BANK ON THE CARPET

1. John Skelton Williams, "Task Titanic: Strength Supreme; Faith Invincible," speech to the Maine Bankers Association, Bangor, Maine, June 26, 1920, 1–6.
2. *Wall Street Journal*, January 24, 1920.
3. *Wall Street Journal*, January 30, 1920.
4. Alexander D. Noyes, *The War Period of American Finance: 1908–1925* (New York and London: The Knickerbocker Press, 1926), 331.
5. U.S. Department of the Treasury, Annual Report of the Comptroller of the Currency (Washington, D.C.: Government Printing Office, 1920), 4.
6. *New York Times*, April 18, 1920.
7. Noyes, *War Period*, 336.
8. Office of the Comptroller of the Currency, Examiner's Report on the Condition of the National City Bank (February 13, 1920), OCC 1920, E-1ff.
9. Harold van B. Cleveland and Thomas F. Huertas, *Citibank: 1812–1970* (Cambridge: Harvard University Press, 1985), 106.
10. Office of the Comptroller of the Currency, Examiner's Report on the Condition of the National City Bank, January 4, 1921 (College Park, MD: National Archives and Records Administration), 67.
11. Ibid., 343.
12. Allan H. Meltzer, *A History of the Federal Reserve*, vol. 1, *1913–1951* (Chicago: University of Chicago Press, 2003), 74.
13. *New York Times*, January 3, 1908.
14. U.S. Department of the Treasury, Annual Report of the Comptroller of the Currency (Washington, D.C.: Government Printing Office, 1914, 92–95.
15. OCC Transcript, 3.
16. *Bankers Magazine*, vol. 68, 651.
17. OCC Transcript, 17–21.
18. Ibid., 23.
19. Ibid., 23–25.
20. Ibid., 346.
21. Ibid., 347.
22. Ibid., 356.
23. Ibid., 357.
24. Ibid., 224.

7. EGGING ON DEFLATION

1. Lester V. Chandler, *Benjamin Strong: Central Banker* (Washington, D.C.: The Brookings Institution, 1958), 122–24.
2. W.P.G. Harding, *The Formative Period of the Federal Reserve System (During the World Crisis)* (Boston: Houghton Mifflin Company, 1925), 137.
3. Ibid., 161.
4. Allan H. Meltzer, *A History of the Federal Reserve*, vol. 1, *1913–1951* (Chicago: University of Chicago Press, 2003), 104; Milton Friedman and Anna Jacobson Schwartz, *A Monetary History of the United States: 1867–1960* (Princeton: Princeton University Press, 1963), 230.
5. Alexander D. Noyes, *The War Period of American Finance: 1908–1925* (New York and London: The Knickerbocker Press, 1926), 335.
6. *New York Times*, May 19, 1920.
7. Sidney Homer and Richard Sylla, *A History of Interest Rates* (New Brunswick, NJ: Rutgers University Press, 1991), 347.
8. Harding, *Formative Period*, 172.
9. Ibid., 176.
10. Ibid., 177–78.
11. Williams to Aldrich, August 3, 1920, John Skelton Williams Papers, University of Virginia.
12. Williams to Harding, May 25, 1920, John Skelton Williams Papers.
13. *Wall Street Journal*, June 2, 1920.

8. A DEBACLE "WITHOUT PARALLEL"

1. *New York Times*, September 1, 1920.
2. U.S. House of Representatives, Joint Commission of Agricultural Inquiry, "The Agricultural Crisis and Its Causes," part I (Washington, D.C.: Government Printing Office, 1921), 58.
3. Report and Recommendations of a Committee of the President's Conference on Unemployment, *Business Cycles and Unemployment* (New York: McGraw-Hill Company, 1923), 26.
4. Report of the Joint Commission of Agricultural Inquiry, part I, 107ff.
5. Wilson F. Payne, *Business Behavior 1919–1922: An Account of Post-war Inflation and Depression* (Chicago: University of Chicago Press, 1942), 89.
6. Report of the Joint Commission of Agricultural Inquiry, part II, 46.
7. Morris to Harding, January 9, 1922; John Skelton Williams Papers, University of Virginia.
8. *New York Times*, October 21, 1920.
9. *New York Times*, October 18, 1920.
10. *New York Times*, October 19, 1920.
11. *New York Times*, October 21, 1920.
12. *Wall Street Journal*, November 24, 1920.
13. *New York Times*, October 23, 1920.

14. *New York Times*, November 28, 1920.
15. *New York Times*, December 27, 1920.
16. Williams to Harding, December 28, 1920, John Skelton Williams Papers.
17. Ibid.
18. Ibid.
19. Ibid.
20. "Regarding Indebtedness of Chairman Wiggin to the Chase National Bank and to the Chase Securities Corporation," December 28, 1920, John Skelton Williams Papers.

9. THE COMPTROLLER ON THE OFFENSIVE

1. Harding to Williams, January 13, 1921, John Skelton Williams Papers, University of Virginia.
2. Ibid.
3. Richard McCulley, *Banks and Politics During the Progressive Era: The Origins of the Federal Reserve System* (New York: Garland Publishing, 1992), 145.
4. *New York Times*, January 18, 1921.
5. *New York Times*, January 30, 1921.
6. Williams to Harding, February 28, 1921, John Skelton Williams Papers.
7. Ibid.
8. W.P.G. Harding, *The Formative Period of the Federal Reserve System (During the World Crisis)* (Boston: Houghton Mifflin Company, 1925), 204.
9. Ibid.
10. Ibid., 211.
11. U.S. Department of the Treasury, Annual Report of the Comptroller of the Currency (Washington, D.C.: Government Printing Office, 1920), 6.
12. Ibid., 2.
13. Ibid., 11.

10. A KIND WORD FOR MISFORTUNE

1. "Van Lear Black," Wikipedia, 2013; *New York Times*, December 21, 1920.
2. *New York Times*, March 13, 1921.
3. *Business Cycles and Unemployment* (New York: McGraw-Hill Company, 1923), 100–102.
4. Ibid., 102.
5. Ibid., 107.
6. *New York Times*, August 8, 1921.
7. *New York Times*, September 4, 1921.
8. Jay N. Darling, "Removing the Ingrowing Toenail," September 13, 1920, John Skelton Williams Papers, University of Virginia.
9. Gustav Cassel, *Money and Foreign Exchange after 1914* (London: Constable & Co. Ltd., 1922), 207.
10. Ibid., 225.

11. Ibid., 226.
12. John Maynard Keynes, *A Tract on Monetary Reform* (London: Macmillan & Co., 1924), 144.
13. Quoted in Cassel, *Money and Foreign Exchange*, 221.
14. Keynes, *Tract on Monetary Reform*, 149.
15. Williams to Harding, February 26, 1921, John Skelton Williams Papers.
16. Harding to Williams, March 2, 1921, John Skelton Williams Papers.
17. *Wall Street Journal*, August 4, 1921.
18. Lester V. Chandler, *Benjamin Strong: Central Banker* (Washington, D.C.: The Brookings Institution, 1958), 180.
19. *New York Times*, August 4, 1921.
20. Chandler, *Strong*, 179.
21. *Wall Street Journal*, August 9, 1921.

11. NOT THE GOVERNMENT'S AFFAIR

1. *Business Cycles and Unemployment: Report and Recommendations of a Committee of the President's Conference on Unemployment, Including an Investigation Made Under the Auspices of the National Bureau of Economic Research* (New York: McGraw-Hill, 1923), 22–26.
2. Robert K. Murray, *The Harding Era: Warren G. Harding and His Administration* (Newtown, CT: American Political Biography Press, 1969), 32.
3. "Eugene V. Debs," Wikipedia, 2013.
4. Wesley M. Bagby, *The Road to Normalcy: The Presidential Campaign and Election of 1920* (Baltimore: The Johns Hopkins Press, 1962), 128.
5. Ibid., 132–33.
6. *New York Times*, August 11, 1920.
7. *Business Cycles and Unemployment*, 26.
8. Mark Sullivan, *Our Times: The United States 1900–1925*, vol. VI, *The Twenties* (New York: Charles Scribner's Sons, 1946), 129.
9. Murray, *Harding*, 22.
10. Ibid., 171.
11. Ibid., 62.
12. Bagby, *Road to Normalcy*, 144.
13. Marion Elizabeth Rodgers, ed., *The Impossible H.L. Mencken: A Selection of His Best Newspaper Stories* (New York: Anchor Books Doubleday, 1991), 255–56.
14. Murray, *Harding*, 185.
15. John Milton Cooper, Jr., *Woodrow Wilson* (New York: Random House, 2009), 570.
16. Bagby, *Road to Normalcy*, 125.
17. Murray, *Harding*, 46.
18. Ibid., 52.
19. Ibid., 70.
20. Ibid.

21. Ibid., 52.
22. Sullivan, *Our Times*, 130.
23. Bagby, *Road to Normalcy*, 144.
24. Ibid., 142.
25. Ibid., 145.
26. Murray, *Harding*, 66.
27. Sullivan, *Our Times*, 137.

12. CUT FROM CLEVELAND'S CLOTH

1. *Wall Street Journal*, January 26, 1921.
2. David Cannadine, *Mellon: An American Life* (New York: Alfred A. Knopf, 2006), 274, 278.
3. Robert K. Murray, *The Harding Era: Warren G. Harding and His Administration* (Newtown, CT: American Political Biography Press, 1969), 172.
4. Roy G. Blakey, "The Revenue Act of '21," *American Economic Review*, vol. 12, no. 1 (March 1922), 77.
5. Murray, *Harding*, 175.
6. Mark Sullivan, *Our Times: The United States 1900–1925*, vol. VI, *The Twenties* (New York: Charles Scribner's Sons, 1946), 209.
7. Ibid., 194.
8. W.P.G. Harding, *The Formative Period of the Federal Reserve System (During the World Crisis)* (Boston: Houghton Mifflin Company, 1925), 277.
9. Sullivan, *Our Times*, 210.
10. James Grant, *Mr. Speaker!: The Life and Times of Thomas B. Reed, the Man Who Broke the Filibuster* (New York: Simon & Schuster, 2011), 255.
11. *New York Times*, September 4, 1920.
12. *New York Times*, July 7, 1921.
13. *New York Times*, July 13, 1921.
14. *New York Times*, August 19, 1921.
15. *New York Times*, July 14, 1921.

13. A KIND OF RECOVERY PROGRAM

1. Andrew W. Mellon, *Taxation: The People's Business* (New York: The Macmillan Company, 1924), 25.
2. Lester V. Chandler, *Benjamin Strong: Central Banker* (Washington, D.C.: The Brookings Institution, 1958), 174.
3. Elmus R. Wicker, *Federal Reserve Monetary Policy 1917–1933* (New York: Random House, 1966), 55.
4. *Wall Street Journal*, April 15, 1921.
5. *New York Times*, May 6, 1921.
6. Chandler, *Strong*, 175.
7. *New York Times*, June 9, 1921.

8. Roy G. Blakey, "The Revenue Act of '21," *American Economic Review*, vol. 12, no. 1 (March 1922), 82.

9. Mark Sullivan, *Our Times: The United States 1900–1925*, vol. VI, *The Twenties* (New York: Charles Scribner's Sons, 1946), 224.

10. *New York Times*, August 8, 1921.

11. Blakey, "Revenue Act," 81, 86, 89.

14. WAGES CHASE PRICES

1. *Wall Street Journal*, December 30, 1921.

2. *Wall Street Journal*, November 1, 1919.

3. *Wall Street Journal*, November 4, 1919.

4. *Wall Street Journal*, September 17, 1920.

5. *Wall Street Journal*, November 4, 1920.

6. *Wall Street Journal*, January 4, 1921.

7. *Economist*, January 1, 1921.

8. *Economist*, December 25, 1920.

9. *Wall Street Journal*, July 29, 1920.

10. T.F. McManus, R.W. Nelson, and C.A. Phillips, *Banking and the Business Cycle: A Study of the Great Depression in the United States* (New York: The Macmillan Company, 1937), 236.

11. *Wall Street Journal*, December 18, 1920.

12. *New York Times*, December 14, 1920.

13. *Wall Street Journal*, December 21, 1920.

14. *New York Times*, February 3, 1921.

15. *New York Times*, March 11, 1921.

16. Robert Ozanne, *A Century of Labor-Management Relations at McCormick and International Harvester* (Madison: University of Wisconsin Press, 1967), 133–35.

17. *New York Times*, March 10, 1921.

18. *New York Times*, March 24, 1921.

15. SHREWD JUDGE GARY

1. *Wall Street Journal*, March 22, 1922.

2. Wilson F. Payne, *Business Behavior 1919–1922: An Account of Post-war Inflation and Depression* (Chicago: University of Chicago Press, 1942), 133.

3. *New York Times*, November 4, 1919.

4. Payne, *Business Behavior*, 141, 145.

5. *New York Times*, February 26, 1921.

6. *Wall Street Journal*, April 2, 1921.

7. *New York Times*, March 2, 1921.

8. *New York Times*, March 3, 1921.

9. *Wall Street Journal*, April 2, 1921.

10. *New York Times*, March 30, 1921.

11. *Wall Street Journal,* May 11, 1921.
12. *Wall Street Journal,* July 27, 1921.
13. *New York Times,* April 20, 1921.
14. *Wall Street Journal,* April 13, 1921.
15. *Wall Street Journal,* February 25, 1922.
16. *Wall Street Journal,* August 25, 1921.

16. "A HIGHER SENSE OF SERVICE"

1. U.S. Department of the Treasury, Annual Report of the Secretary of the Treasury on the State of the Finances (Washington, D.C.: Government Printing Office, 1920), 4.
2. *Freeman,* January 19, 1921.
3. Mark Sullivan, *Our Times: The United States 1900–1925,* vol. VI, *The Twenties* (New York: Charles Scribner's Sons, 1946), 182.
4. *New York Times,* December 7, 1920.
5. Gerald D. Nash, "Herbert Hoover and the Origins of the Reconstruction Finance Corporation, *Mississippi Valley Historical Review,* vol. 46, no. 3 (December 1959), 460.
6. Carolyn Grin, "The Unemployment Conference of 1921: An Experiment in National Cooperative Planning," *Mid-America: An Historical Review,* vol. 55 (April 1973), 86.
7. U.S. Department of Commerce, "Commerce Reports," vol. 3 (Washington, D.C.: Government Printing Office, 1921), 274.
8. *New York Times,* September 9, 1921.
9. *New York Times,* September 23, 1921.
10. *New York Times,* September 24, 1921.
11. National Industrial Conference Board, "The Unemployment Problem" (research report no. 43, November 1921), p. 10.
12. *Wall Street Journal,* September 26, 1921.
13. *New York Times,* August 17, 1921.
14. *New York Times,* September 14, 1921.
15. *New York Times,* September 2, 1921.
16. *New York Times,* September 10, 1921.
17. Grin, "Unemployment Conference," 86.
18. *New York Times,* September 27, 1921.
19. *Wall Street Journal,* September 22, 1921.
20. Grin, "Unemployment Conference," 85.
21. Ibid., 102.
22. *New York Times,* October 14, 1921.
23. Grin, "Unemployment Conference," 94.
24. Otto T. Mallery, "The Long-Range Planning of Public Works," in *Business Cycles and Unemployment* (Washington, D.C.: National Bureau of Economic Research, 1923), 241.

25. Grin, "Unemployment Conference," 107.

26. *New York Times*, October 14, 1921.

27. *New York Times*, October 14, 1921.

28. *New York Times*, October 16, 1921.

29. Robert Skidelsky, *John Maynard Keynes*, vol. 2, *The Economist as Saviour, 1920–1937* (New York: The Penguin Press, 1992), 133.

17. GOLD POURS INTO AMERICA

1. Williams to Mellon, July 2, 1921, John Skelton Williams Papers, University of Virginia.

2. *Wall Street Journal*, June 14, 1921.

3. *Wall Street Journal*, August 24, 1921.

4. U.S. Department of the Treasury, Annual Report of the Secretary of the Treasury on the State of the Finances (Washington, D.C.: Government Printing Office, 1921), 31.

5. *Wall Street Journal*, April 15, 1921.

6. *New York Times*, May 5, 1921.

7. Sidney Homer and Richard Sylla, *A History of Interest Rates* (New Brunswick: Rutgers University Press, 1991), 350.

8. *Wall Street Journal*, May 9, 1921; *New York Times*, May 10, 1921.

9. *Wall Street Journal*, May 11, 1921.

10. *Wall Street Journal*, May 11, 1921.

11. *Wall Street Journal*, August 1, 1921.

12. Chester Arthur Phillips, *Bank Credit: A Study of the Principles and Factors Underlying Advances Made by Banks to Borrowers* (New York: The MacMillan Company, 1920), 108.

13. *Historical Statistics of the United States: Colonial Times to 1970* (Washington, D.C.: U.S. Department of Commerce, 1975), 536.

14. *Wall Street Journal*, May 19, 1921.

15. *New York Times*, January 6, 1921.

16. *New York Times*, July 20, 1921.

17. W.P.G. Harding, *The Formative Period of the Federal Reserve System (During the World Crisis)* (Boston: Houghton Mifflin Company, 1925), 224.

18. "BACK TO BARBARISM?"

1. *Wall Street Journal*, March 8, 1922.

2. *Recent Economic Changes in the United States*, vol. II (National Bureau of Economic Research, 1929), 478.

3. George Henry Soule, *Prosperity Decade: From War to Depression, 1917–1929* (Armonk, N.Y.: M.E. Sharpe, 1989), 108.

4. *Recent Economic Changes*, 854.

5. Ibid., 60.

6. Ibid., 524.

7. *Wall Street Journal*, March 10, 1922.

8. *Wall Street Journal*, March 11, 1922.

9. *Wall Street Journal*, April 2, 1923.

10. *Wall Street Journal*, February 4, 1922.

11. Herbert Hoover, "Herbert Hoover on the Domestic Commercial Situation," speech to the National Association of Real Estate Boards, Chicago, July 15, 1921.

12. *New York Times*, January 1, 1923.

13. James H. Shideler, *Farm Crisis 1919–1923* (Berkeley: University of California Press, 1957), 189.

14. *New York Times*, January 1, 1923.

15. Shideler, *Farm Crisis*, 193.

16. Ibid., 194.

17. Ibid., 201.

18. Alexander D. Noyes, *The War Period of American Finance: 1908–1925* (New York and London: The Knickerbocker Press, 1926), 407–8.

19. *Recent Economic Changes*, 558–59.

20. Ibid., 585, 587; *Grant's Interest Rate Observer*, April 8, 2005.

19. AMERICA ON THE BARGAIN COUNTER

1. *Wall Street Journal*, April 13, 1922.

2. *Wall Street Journal*, April 13, 1922.

3. *New York Times*, March 26, 1922.

4. *Wall Street Journal*, April 22, 1922.

5. *Wall Street Journal*, November 17, 1922.

6. U.S. Department of the Treasury, Annual Report of the Comptroller of the Currency (Washington, D.C.: Government Printing Office, 1922), 131.

7. *New York Times*, July 3, 1921.

8. *Wall Street Journal*, November 29, 1921.

9. *New York Times*, January 28, 1923.

10. *Recent Economic Changes in the United States*, vol. II (National Bureau of Economic Research, 1929), 60.

11. Ibid., 59.

12. Ibid., 269.

13. Ibid., 180.

14. Ibid. 403–4.

15. Ibid., 427.

16. Ibid., 432.

17. Ibid., 855.

18. Ibid., 456.

19. *Wall Street Journal*, November 10, 1921.

20. Mark Sullivan, *Our Times: The United States 1900–1925*, vol. VI, *The Twenties* (New York: Charles Scribner's Sons, 1946), 211.

21. *Wall Street Journal*, September 21, 1922.

20. ALL FOR STABILITY

1. *New York Times*, September 1, 1921.
2. William J. Barber, *From New Era to New Deal: Herbert Hoover, the Economists, and American Economic Policy, 1921–1933* (Cambridge: Cambridge University Press, 1985), 25.
3. *New York Times*, December 19, 1922.
4. Allan H. Meltzer, *A History of the Federal Reserve*, vol. 1, *1913–1951* (Chicago: University of Chicago Press, 2003), 182.
5. Lester V. Chandler, *Benjamin Strong: Central Banker* (Washington, D.C.: The Brookings Institution, 1958), 202.
6. John R. Commons, "The Stabilization of Prices and Business," *The American Economic Review*, vol. 15, no. 1 (March 1925), 43–44.
7. Robert Skidelsky, *John Maynard Keynes*, vol. 2, *The Economist as Saviour, 1920–1937* (New York: The Penguin Press, 1992), 152.
8. *New York Times*, April 11, 1922.
9. Keynes, *Tract on Monetary Reform*, 198 and ff.
10. The *Times*, London, June 11, 1931.
11. *Recent Economic Changes in the United States*, vol. II (National Bureau of Economic Research, 1929), 607.
12. Benjamin M. Anderson, *Economics and the Public Welfare: A Financial and Economic History of the United States* (Indianapolis: Liberty Press, 1979), 200.
13. T.F. McManus, R. W. Nelson, and C.A. Phillips, *Banking and the Business Cycle: A Study of the Great Depression in the United States* (New York: The MacMillan Company, 1937), 124–25.
14. Anderson, *Economics and the Public Welfare*, 189.
15. Priscilla Roberts, "Benjamin Strong, the Federal Reserve, and the Limits to Interwar American Nationalism," *Economic Quarterly*, vol. 86/2 (Spring 2000), 80.
16. McManus et al., *Banking and the Business Cycle*, 191.
17. Ibid., 82–84.
18. Ibid., 190.

EPILOGUE: A TRIUMPH, IN ITS WAY

1. Harry Truman, *Memoirs, Vol. 1: Year of Decisions* (Garden City, N.Y.: Doubleday & Co.), 134.
2. Allan H. Meltzer, *A History of the Federal Reserve*, vol. 1, *1913–1951* (Chicago: University of Chicago Press, 2003), 120.
3. Harold L. Cole and Lee E. Ohanian, "Re-examining the Contributions of Monetary and Banking Shocks to the U.S. Great Depression," *NBER Macroeconomics Annual 2000*, vol. 15, 186–88.
4. William Starr Myers and Walter H. Newton, *The Hoover Administration: A Documented Narrative* (New York: Charles Scribner's Sons, 1936), 25.
5. *New York Times*, November 22, 1929.

6. *Wall Street Journal*, November 27, 1929.
7. T. F. McManus, R. W. Nelson, and C. A. Phillips, *Banking and the Business Cycle: A Study of the Great Depression in the United States* (New York: The MacMillan Company, 1937), 190.
8. *New York Times*, December 5, 1929.
9. James Harvey Rogers, *America Weighs Her Gold* (New Haven: Yale University Press, 1931), 177–79.
10. Meltzer, *History of the Federal Reserve*, 117–18.
11. Ibid., 323.
12. Walter A. Friedman, *Fortune Tellers: The Story of America's First Economic Forecasters* (Princeton: Princeton University Press, 2014), 200.
13. William H. Barber, *From New Era to New Deal: Herbert Hoover, the Economists, and American Economic Policy, 1921–1933* (Cambridge: Cambridge University Press, 1985), 84–85.
14. Lee E. Ohanian, "What—or Who—Started the Great Depression?" *Journal of Economic Theory*, no. 144, 2311.

A SELECT BIBLIOGRAPHY

John Skelton Williams, the color and condiment of this story, has no biography, though his papers are on deposit at the University of Virginia. There is no such biographical deficit for other major characters in the book. Bland, indeed, was the public face of Andrew W. Mellon, but rich is David Cannadine's biography of Harding's (and Coolidge's and Hoover's) secretary of the Treasury: *Mellon: An American Life*. Lawrence R. Gustin's *Billy Durant: Creator of General Motors* is a fine telling of the career of the flamboyant entrepreneur; in *My Years with General Motors*, Alfred Sloan relates his version of the automaker's progress and missteps.

Benjamin Strong: Central Banker, by Lester V. Chandler, is the story of the governor of the Federal Reserve Bank of New York (and, practically, during much of the 1920s, of the Federal Reserve System in toto) who never went to college; try to imagine such a thing now that the gold standard has given way to the Ph.D. standard. Benjamin Graham, the storied value investor, came of age during the 1920–21 depression; *Benjamin Graham: The Memoirs of the Dean of Wall Street* is his highly readable posthumously published autobiography.

For President Wilson, I have chiefly relied on Gene Smith's masterly *When the Cheering Stopped: The Last Years of Woodrow Wilson*, and on John Milton Cooper's *Woodrow Wilson: A Biography*. Wilson led the nation into war, instituted the federal income tax, and presided over the opening months of the 1920–21 depression; historians appraise him a successful president (No. 9 on the 2009 C-Span Historians Presidential Leadership Survey). Warren G. Harding, the subject of Robert K. Murray's excellent *The Harding Era*, summoned a world disarmament conference, set in motion tax and spending reductions, and presided over the recovery from the 1920–21 depression; historians appraise him a failed president (No. 38 in the C-Span rankings). I would suggest that the historians reconsider.

One may criticize Herbert Hoover's economic policies, as I have done in this book, while admiring the 31st president's qualities as a businessman, philanthropist, and—yes, in partnership with his wife, Lou Henry—amateur scholar. Hoover wrote his *Memoirs* in three volumes, the first of which, *Years of Adventure*, deals in part with early-20th-century finances. "The overriding characteristic of all mining booms is the *nth* degree of optimism," the author observed about an element of investor psychology that hasn't changed in a hundred years and may well never change.

The myth that Hoover turned a garden-variety cyclical downturn into the Great Depression by bullheadedly clinging to the shibboleths of the free market is neatly disposed of by Harris Gaylord Warren in *Herbert Hoover and the Great Depression*; by Benjamin Anderson in *Economics and the Public Welfare*; and—with particular gusto—by Murray Rothbard in *America's Great Depression*. Warren and Rothbard cite chapter and verse on Hoover's ill-fated determination to prop up wages in a time of falling prices; by eviscerating corporate profit margins, the wage-maintenance scheme all but guaranteed mass unemployment. Anderson, whose lively chronicle unjustly wears one of the dullest titles a publisher ever affixed to the spine of a book, properly characterizes the hyperactive and unavailing Hoover interventions as the "First New Deal." Rothbard, an exponent of pure laissez-faire, attacks the notion that the price level can or should be "stabilized" through monetary policy. That such a thing as the price level can even be properly measured is a question that Oskar Morgenstern answered in the negative more than a half century ago in his *On the Accuracy of Economic Observations*. Morgenstern's subject matter may strike some as prosaic. It evidently did not so seem to the author, who, in places, wrote in what appears to be a kind of controlled rage.

The three scholars responsible for one of the best postmortems of the 1929–33 Depression—they are C. A. Phillips, T. F. McManus, and R. W. Nelson—unjustly languish in bibliographic obscurity. Their *Banking and the Business Cycle*, published in 1937, anticipates Rothbard in laying blame for the slump on the misbegotten doctrine of price stabilization. In an age of material progress, Phillips et al. propose, prices at the checkout counter ought to dwindle, not inflate. To create new credit in order to reverse that wholesome tendency is more likely to promote instability than its opposite, they showed. Arguing just as ardently for the opposite point of view was Irving Fisher, in *Stabilizing the Dollar: A Plan to Stabilize the General Price Level without Fixing Individual Prices* (1925). Milton Friedman and Anna Schwartz, coauthors of *Monetary History of the United States: 1867–1960*, and Alan Meltzer, author of the two-volume *History of the Federal Reserve*, have chronicled American central banking in the Fisherian tradition.

What was it like to do business in America in the early 1920s? A scholarly monograph, *Business Behavior, 1919–1922: An Account of Post-war Inflation and Depression*, by Wilson F. Payne, cites chapter and verse. James H. Shideler, in *Farm Crisis: 1919–1923*, does much the same for agriculture. What was it like to live in America in the era of Wilson and Harding and Prohibition and Teapot Dome? The sixth volume of Mark Sullivan's *Our Times: The United States, 1900–1925* vividly conveys a sense of the age. Especially perceptive is the author on the changes wrought in the economic and political life of the country by the expansion of federal power attendant on World War I. There emerged, as Sullivan wrote, "an exceptional market for intermediaries and fixers, many legitimate and some sinister, who, by methods in some cases regular and in other cases furtive, could get the government to grant some privilege that an honest citizen desired and had a right to, or some immunity that a corrupt person had no right to but ardently wished." Here was the political backdrop to the Harding scandals.

Viewed from the post-Crash vantage point, the decade of the 1920s may look like a financial accident just waiting to happen. It did not seem so in 1928, when the Hoover-inspired, two-part, thousand-page tome, *Recent Economic Changes*, went to the printers. Published in 1929, the volumes constitute possibly the richest trove of economic data and commentary bearing on America in the 1920s. "Never before has the human race made such progress in solving the problem of production," marveled Dexter S.

Kimball, a Cornell engineering professor who contributed the chapter headed "Industry."

The 21st-century reader may scratch his or her head over the institution of the gold standard and the controversy that surrounded it, and, indeed, continues to surround it up until this day. Lewis E. Lehrman's *Money, Gold, and History*, a persuasive brief for the restoration of gold convertibility, may help to lift the veil of mystery. Arthur I. Bloomfield's *Monetary Policy under the International Gold Standard* and Kenneth W. Dam's *The Rules of the Game: Reform and Evolution in the International Monetary System* are accessible descriptions on how the classical, or pre–World War I gold standard actually functioned. Its essential characteristic was simplicity, a point that the economist T. E. Gregory wistfully remarked upon in his *The Gold Standard and Its Future* (1925): "The whole difficulty in understanding modern currency systems arises from the fact that we have departed from the sweet simplicity of earlier days." Just how much more complex things could at length become might have left Gregory flabbergasted.

INDEX

ABOUT THE AUTHOR

JAMES GRANT is the editor of *Grant's Interest Rate Observer*, a twice-monthly journal of the financial markets, which he founded in 1983. He is the author of numerous books on finance and financial history as well as biographies of John Adams and Thomas B. Reed. A father of four grown children, he lives in Brooklyn with his wife, Patricia Kavanagh, M.D.